UNDER THE TABLE
& How to Get Up

UNDER THE TABLE
& How to Get Up

Jewish Pathways Of Spiritual Growth

by Avraham Greenbaum

TSOHAR PUBLISHING
Jerusalem / New York

ISBN 0930213-41-6

First Edition

For further information:

Avraham Greenbaum
POB 50037
Jerusalem 91 500 Israel

United States
POB 587
Monsey, NY 10952-0587

Cover Design: Ben Gasner

In loving memory of

Barney Aronson

by

Stephen Aronson

Contents

Sanctuary of the King, royal City:
Rise up, come out of this upside-down confusion!
You've sat in the valley of tears long enough.
Now He will shower you with compassion.

Shake off the dust and arise!
Put on your clothes of splendor, My People,
Through David, the son of Yishai, from Bethlehem.
Come close to my soul — redeem it!

Wake up! Stir yourself —
For your light has come. Rise up and shine!
Awaken, awaken, sing a song!
God's glory is revealed upon you!

(from *Lecha Dodi* in the Shabbat Eve Service)

Introduction

This book is offered as an introduction to the Jewish spiritual pathway for contemporary English-speaking Jews.

Many people today find it hard to understand how the ideas discussed in the classic texts of Torah spirituality — Mussar and Chassidut — relate to themselves and their lives. They do not see clearly how to put these ideas into practice in modern times. This book is an attempt to explain some of these ideas in contemporary terms and to offer suggestions as to how to apply them in day-to-day life.

It is a book for the committed Jew who would like to follow the Torah pathway in order to achieve personal growth and spiritual connection. It is also for those who are uncommitted, who are puzzled by the variety they see in different areas of the Jewish world, and who wonder how to find spirituality through Judaism. Finally, it is for those who have experienced spirituality in some form in a non-Jewish context and who ask where meditation, diet, breathing, exercise, and other growth activities come into Torah life.

The motif of the book is the amusing, yet deeply profound, parable of the Prince who thought he was a Turkey, by the outstanding Chassidic luminary, Rebbe Nachman of Breslov (1772-1810). Though first told some two hundred years ago, the story is as relevant as ever. We may not think we are turkeys, but in one way or another we are all "under the table." In our essence, we are sons and daughters of the King of the Universe, but the upside-down world around us makes it easy to forget this fact. How can we overcome the challenges facing us, whether from within ourselves or the surrounding environment, in order to rise to our spiritual destiny?

Sources for many of the suggestions offered in this book are to be found in the writings of Rebbe Nachman himself. However this is emphatically not so in all cases. This book should in no way be seen as an attempt to offer an "official" formulation of the spiritual pathway of Rebbe Nachman and his followers, the Breslov Chassidim. In particular, the practical guidance offered on the subjects of relaxation, diet, breathing and exercise is, for the most part, not based on Rebbe Nachman's teachings but on other sources, as indicated in the text and in the appendix on Sources and Further Reading. The view put forward here as to the place of such practices in the Jewish spiritual pathway is the personal view of the author.

The detailed interpretations of the imagery found in the story of the Turkey-Prince are my own. I have taken my licence from Rebbe Nachman himself, who encouraged students of his teachings to use them as a basis to develop *chidushey Torah* — original Torah ideas. (See *Likutey Moharan* II:105.) However, Rebbe Nachman made one stipulation: "You may expound the Torah and innovate in any area you wish, on condition that you do not use your interpretations to innovate or change any law" (*Rabbi Nachman's Wisdom #267*). I hope and pray that everything in this book is in full accord with both the letter of the *Shulchan Aruch* and with the spirit of Rebbe Nachman's teachings.

Undoubtedly, the story of the Turkey-Prince contains far greater wisdom than I have begun to bring out in this work. The interpretations offered here are certainly not the only ones possible, nor are they definitive. I hope that people with different interpretations or who feel that more emphasis should be given to other dimensions of the story will develop and publish their ideas.

The Wise Man who cured the Prince asked nothing for himself. All he wanted was to show the Prince how to be *him*self. With the help of HaShem, may each one of us find the simple path of truth that will lead us to our selves, to our souls and our Source. Let us walk on it, step by step, securely and joyously, and welcome Mashiach soon in our lifetimes. Amen.

I thank HaShem for all His countless blessings to me every day and every moment, and in particular for inspiring me with the idea for this book, and for creating everything needed to make it possible to bring it to fruition.

I want to express my deep appreciation to the many relatives and friends who have helped me in so many different ways, and in particular to Trevor Bell, Dr. Yehuoshua Leib Fine, Gershon Ginsburg, David Gross, Jay Gottleib, Reuven Halevi, Shmuel Lazar, Meir Maimoni, Asher Morvay, Chaim Rohatiner, Isaac Shamah, Larry Spiro and Micha Taubman. I am grateful to Mervyn Waldman for his advice on the material in Chapters 4 and 5 on relaxation, nutrition, breathing and exercise.

Special thanks to the good and noble-hearted friend whose munificent support made it possible to write the greater part of this book. True to character, you insisted on remaining anonymous. To my friend and colleague, Chaim Kramer: you have never asked for thanks, but at every step you have proven yourself a *chaver* second to none. To my dear parents: no words can adequately express my feelings, and my gratitude to you for your unfaltering support and encouragement. Finally, *acharon acharon chaviv*, my most precious wife, *Yaffa at ra'yati*: to you I dedicate this book.

Avraham Greenbaum
Jerusalem, Lag Ba-Omer 5751

The Story of the Turkey-Prince

The Story of the Turkey-Prince

Once the king's son went mad. He thought he was a turkey. He felt compelled to sit under the table without any clothes on, pulling at bits of bread and bones like a turkey. None of the doctors could do anything to help him or cure him, and they gave up in despair. The king was very sad...

Until a Wise Man came and said, "I can cure him."

What did the Wise Man do? He took off all *his* clothes, and sat down naked under the table next to the king's son, and also pulled at crumbs and bones.

The Prince asked him, "Who are you and what are you doing here?"

"And what are *you* doing here?" he replied.

"I am a turkey," said the Prince.

"Well I'm also a turkey," said the Wise Man.

The two of them sat there together like this for some time, until they were used to one another.

Then the Wise Man gave a sign, and they threw them shirts. The Wise Man-Turkey said to the king's son, "Do you think a turkey can't wear a shirt? You can wear a shirt and still be a turkey." The two of them put on shirts.

After a while he gave another sign and they threw them some trousers. Again the Wise Man said, "Do you think if you wear trousers you can't be a turkey?" They put on the trousers.

One by one they put on the rest of their clothes in the same way.

Afterwards, the Wise Man gave a sign and they put down human food from the table. The Wise Man said to the Prince, "Do you think if you eat good food you can't be a turkey any more? You can eat this food and still be a turkey." They ate.

Then he said to him, "Do you think a turkey has to sit *under* the table? You can be a turkey and sit up at the table."

This was how the Wise Man dealt with the Prince, until in the end he cured him completely.

(Rebbe Nachman of Breslov)

*

Turkey (Hebrew *Tarnegol Hodu* — "the Indian Cock"; Yiddish *Indick*; Latin *Meleagris gallopavo*): type of large land-bird of the family Meleagrididae, originating in the New World, whence the Spanish introduced it to Europe in the early 16th century. The English called it turkey-cock after the guinea fowl of the Islamic (or "Turkish") lands. The domesticated turkey is valued as a table-fowl.

Basically dark in color, with iridescent bronze and green plumage, and a naked, warty, red head turning blue or white with excitement. The male, called gobbler or tom, may be 130 cm. long and weigh 10 kilograms; hens generally weigh half as much as the males. Eats seeds, insects, an occasional frog or lizard, etc.

When excited, the male spreads his tail like a fan, droops his wings, shaking the quills audibly, retracts his head and struts around uttering rapid gobbling sounds. He assembles a harem, which, after mating, he abandons.

The hens lay 8-15 brownish spotted eggs in a hollow in the ground, and the young hatch in 28 days. Turkey life-expectancy: around 5 years.

Under the Table
& How to Get Up

1

Turkey!

Once the king's son went mad. He thought he was a turkey...

Have you ever wished you could live up to your highest ideals, only to look at your shortcomings and failures and conclude that you'll probably never succeed?

The moral of the tale of the Turkey-Prince is that you *can* succeed, and the story shows you how.

We all have two sides to us, the Prince (or Princess) and the Turkey. The Prince is the higher self, or soul — the child of God, which we all are. The Prince is the potential self, the person we *can* be if we learn the right way to nurture ourselves and grow. There are practically no limits to the levels of development within our grasp. Every soul is unique, and each one of us has the power to realize our potential in our own unique way.

The Turkey is the lower self, the side that is averse to sacrifice, hard work and effort, preferring easy solutions and instant pleasures. God gives everyone a Turkey self, not because He wants us to follow its demands, but in order to challenge us. The Turkey side makes it harder to be the Prince or Princess we should be — and the reward for succeeding is therefore greater.

The Turkey's main strength is its stubbornness. Day after day it pushes its way into our minds and hearts. How often do we know exactly what we ought or ought not to do, only to find ourselves driven into acting in the most self-defeating and destructive ways! Each time we follow the Turkey it becomes all the more entrenched, while the Prince grows discouraged and goes further and further underground. The resulting depression only makes us give in to the Turkey even more.

There are all manner of "doctors" offering advice about what we should do with our lives. There are innumerable books on self-help and self-improvement. How many programs have all of us started, then abandoned less than half-way along? The real question is: even when you know what you ought to do to take yourself in hand, how do you get yourself to actually *do* it? How do you carry it through to the end? This is what the Wise Man in the story comes to teach us.

The story of the Turkey-Prince may be amusing, but the madness it depicts is no laughing matter. The Rabbis characterize the madman as someone who loses everything he is given (*Chagigah* 4a). The madness of the Turkey-Prince is that he is losing the most precious gift he has: his soul. The soul is life, eternal life. This kind of madness is sheer self-destruction.

After death comes the reckoning. What did we spend our life running after? Crumbs and bones? What are we going to be left with? Will we let ourselves get away with being less than we could be? This life is our one chance for self-realization. What are we going to do with it?

"On the day of reckoning," said the famous Chassid, Reb Zusya, "when they ask me, 'Why weren't you like Abraham, Isaac and Jacob?' I won't be afraid. But when they ask me, 'Why weren't you like *Zusya*?' — that's when I'll be afraid."

2

Under the Table

The Prince felt compelled to sit under the table without any clothes on, pulling at bits of bread and bones like a turkey.

"Woe to the children who are in exile from their Father's table."

Berachot 3a

The Prince is sitting there naked under the table. His clothes are strewn all around. If he doesn't put them on, he won't be able to sit up at the table together with his father. But the Prince doesn't move. As far as he knows, he isn't a Prince at all. He's a Turkey. He doesn't even recognize those fine, stiff clothes. As far as he is concerned they have nothing to do with him. Of what interest could they be to a Turkey — they're not edible! The crumbs and bones are much more interesting.

A humorous story? Strange? Tragic? Absurd? What does it mean? Why a Turkey? Why naked? What are the crumbs and bones? And why under the table of all places?

Order vs. Meaninglessness

There is more to sitting up at the table than the physical act of eating. There is a whole culture: the way the table is set, the order of serving the courses, the manners and conversation. Eating at the table is symbolic of *order*. Especially at court, when the king banquets ceremonially with his intimates, officers and distinguished guests, "everything says 'Glory!' " (Psalms 29:9) — the august banquet hall with its brilliant chandeliers, emblazoned chairs and sumptuously spread tables; the courtiers clothed in their appropriate robes and badges, each seated in his proper place in strict order of precedence; etiquette, decorum, and a flurry of palace servants.

At the very center of everything sits the king, with the royal table before him. And there is the Prince, crouched down underneath it, pulling at the crumbs and bones.

The Prince sees nothing of the order and splendor around him. All he sees is a world without order, a Turkey world! Down where he is, nothing looks the way it is supposed to from a normal vantage point. The rich, heavy fabric of the royal tablecloth, draped down on all sides, is in fact blocking out most of the light from the hall, throwing everything underneath into shadow and gloom. Peering out at the world beyond the tablecloth, all the Prince can see is the lower part of everything — all legs and no faces.

From his present vantage point, nothing except the crumbs and bones has any meaning at all. But, being convinced that he is a Turkey, the Prince assumes that what he sees is just the way a Turkey world *should* look. Why should he think for a moment that the bizarre shapes around him are in fact only the lowest parts of something far grander, a world he is looking at from the worst possible vantage point?

Given the apparently random way his crumbs and bones drop down, what would make him think that anyone in his lonely world cares about him? How could he know that his father, the king, is beside himself with worry, hanging on his every move for even the faintest sign of improvement? Yet the king has surely given all the butlers special instructions to surreptitiously slip down a steady supply of nutritious lumps so that the poor boy shouldn't starve. After all, the royal guests are normally more polite than to drop half their food on the floor.

But as far as the Prince is concerned, he's a Turkey in a Turkey world, and there *is* no king and no court. Nobody cares about anyone, nothing is under anyone's control. There is no government, providence or order. Everything is chance. Down here is all there is. Nothing else has any meaning. This is the entire universe.

The little world under the table is really inside the king's palace. The boards of the table that constitute its sky, the carved table legs holding them up, the tablecloth marking its boundaries, the courtiers' feet that close in all around, the floor on which everything is standing, and even the scraps of food the Prince is living off — all are integral parts of the royal court. Yet to the Prince it doesn't seem like the inside of a great palace at all. In his eyes, the world around him is a separate, independent realm. It is outside, a Turkey world.

The Paradox of Creation

Inside seems like outside. Yet outside is really inside. The situation of the Turkey-Prince under the table is a metaphor for our situation in This World — the world we live in for our hundred and twenty years, the world we can see, feel, hear, smell and taste all around us, with the entire array of mineral, vegetable, animal and human forms it contains: the skies, the planets, the stars and heavenly bodies, and outer space stretching to who knows where.

From our perspective, the material, sensible world may seem like an independent, self-existing realm. It is impossible to see indisputable evidence of a higher power controlling or influencing events. The universe appears to run according to its own rules — the laws of nature, probability, etc. We ourselves may be aware that our behavior is to a large extent determined by circumstances beyond our control: our physical nature, our upbringing and environment etc. At the same time, over wide areas, we have the freedom to act as we wish. When we want to lift up a hand, we just do. We feel like independent, autonomous beings.

Yet in telling us that, "In the beginning God created..." (Genesis 1:1) the Torah is teaching us that this world is not independent and self-existing. The material world we experience through our five senses is far from being the sum total of what exists. In reality it is a created world, the lowest of an entire system of interconnected worlds-upon-worlds, which together make up the creation. They are the kingdom of God. He created them all.

In Hebrew, the totality of the creation is called *yesh*. The word *yesh* signifies something that exists in itself. The first Hebrew word of the Torah — translated as "In the beginning" — is *Bereishit*. If the Hebrew consonants of the word *BeREiSHiYT* are rearranged, they spell out the phrase *BaRATa YeSH* — "You created *yesh*." Even what appears to exist independently is in fact the creation of God.

BeREiSHiYT BaRA — "In the beginning [He] created." The first word of the Torah, *BeREiSHiYT*, contains the three consonants making up the second word, *BaRA*. Even before *BaRA* appears as an independent concept, it is implicit in the concept of *BeREiSHiYT*. *BaRA* has the connotation of "outside" (in the Aramaic language, a close relative of Hebrew, *BaRA* means "outside"). *BaRA* — the seemingly independent, outside creation, is in fact contained within *BeREiSHiYT*.

If the consonants of *BeREiSHiYT* are rearranged differently, they make up the words *ROSH BaYiT*. *RoSH* is a head. *BaYiT* is a house. *RoSH BaYiT* is the Head of the House. What seems like *BaRA*, independent existence, is in fact inside *BeREiSHiYT* — inside a "house". And the "house" has a Head: God. God is the Head of the House, Creator of all the worlds. The worlds may seem separate from God, but in reality they are all inside the palace. Everything is in the palace of the King. Everything is under His rule.

The paradox of creation is that nothing exists without God, yet God willed into being a realm that appears to exist independently. Why?

A World of Choice

Our Sages explain that God is intrinsically good. The essence of goodness is to do good to others. Accordingly, God's purpose in the creation was to bring forth creatures who would be the recipients of His goodness.

Since God Himself is the only true good, His purpose would only be accomplished through bestowing His own perfect goodness upon His creatures. He therefore arranged the creation in a way that would give created beings the opportunity to attach themselves to God Himself, the ultimate good, as fully as possible. Although created beings are unable to attain God's own perfection, they can share in it through attachment to Him on every level of their being. The creature that was created to be the receiver of this goodness is man.

God could have granted man His goodness as an outright gift. However, in order to have complete enjoyment of the good, the recipient must be its master. In other words, he must have worked to earn perfection for himself, rather than receiving it as a complimentary gift. The creation of man therefore entailed the creation of a system whereby man could earn his connection with God of his own free will and through his own efforts.

This was accomplished by constructing a realm that contains abundant opportunities to pursue Godly perfection, side by side with other opportunities that detract from that pursuit. Man is placed in this realm for a specific period of time to work. By struggling to embrace Godliness and striving toward perfection, while avoiding everything that might lure him away from them, man earns his closeness to God through his own efforts. He can then enjoy the pleasure of God's goodness in an ensuing period of reward.

Godliness is intrinsically good. Anything which pulls one away from Godliness is evil, and therefore undesirable. However, if this were perfectly evident to man during his period of work and effort, there would be no challenge. It would be obvious that Godliness is the only goal worth pursuing. In order to provide the challenge, it was necessary that God's true goodness should be somewhat concealed from man during this period of work, while evil should possess an attraction of its own, making it a plausible choice. God is all-powerful, and therefore able to create evil and even make it appear attractive.

Thus God brought This World into being—a world offering us abundant possibilities either to draw ourselves into a closer connection with God, or to embrace evil and become separate from Him. We are given complete freedom of choice. Although in fact God is everywhere, this world is designed in such a way as to conceal Godliness. On the surface, the attractions of evil may seem as great as those of good. Our mission in this world is to uncover the Godly possibilities that are present by learning to distinguish between true good and evil: we must reject the evil and embrace the good, so as to incorporate Godliness into our very souls. The labor itself gives us a taste of God, and then, after our allotted time in this world, we go on to enjoy the fruits of our efforts in the World to Come.

In the parable of the Turkey-Prince, This World is represented by the shadowy realm in which the Prince is sitting, down there under the table. Although his little world is an integral part of the court, to the Prince it *seems* completely independent and separate. This is because his view of the court is almost completely blocked by the tablecloth. Even the legs and feet and other shapes that *are* visible from his unusual perspective are so bizarre-looking as to be incomprehensible. In the same way, the entire creation is God's kingdom. This World is an integral part of it, and Godliness is everywhere. But here in This World our view is distorted. This is because in order to bring it into being, God concealed Himself with veil after veil, screening off the light so as to create the conditions of man's test.

The Prince's clothes are strewn all around. If he would only put them on, he could be part of the court and enjoy all the privileges and pleasures that are his due. In the same way, This World is full of opportunities to lift ourselves into a closer connection with God — if we would only recognize and embrace them. But just as the Turkey-Prince finds the crumbs and bones far more relevant and satisfying, so we are apt to be much more interested and involved in the great multitude of highly attractive alternatives all around us.

The Torah

Godliness is called light — but what kind of light is it? When we come into this world and open our eyes, it seems bright enough. We find color, activity and excitement all around us. What is this world? What is this life? What does it mean?

As presented to us through secular education and the mass media, this world is a chance agglomeration of matter in the middle of nowhere, bustling with billions of people of all races, cultures and creeds, organized in a spectacular array of social, political and economic structures. The first priority for most of the world is to earn a basic living, and then to enjoy themselves in any number of different ways before they die and turn to dust. Many go for the simple physical pleasures: food, drink, sex and material comfort. Others prefer more refined delights: wealth, power, status, knowledge, literature, music, art, sports, and many, many others.

Especially in the most developed parts of the world, there is a dazzling multitude of opportunities in every direction: media and information sources of every kind, any number of belief systems and ideologies, career avenues in every field, entertainment and leisure-time activities to suit all tastes, shops and services of every description, catering to every conceivable need or whim. What should one go for?

Most of the world would say "Happiness." "The main thing is to enjoy!" This may well be true, but what *is* genuine happiness? Even little children soon learn how short-lived most kinds of happiness are: they turn out to have been illusions. Many of the struggles of later life are bound up with trying to find something that will hopefully turn out to be more enduring. But how enduring? Most of the world evidently believes that this life is all there is. In that case, the road to happiness would seem to be to pack in as much enjoyment as possible before illness, debility, death and oblivion strike.

Godly light means insight, wisdom and understanding that penetrate beneath and beyond the surface appearances of this world to the ultimate truth. Delicious-looking berries may actually be poisonous. Without deeper knowledge, surface appearances will tell us nothing about the long-term effects of eating them. The same applies to all the different options that confront us in this world. With a bit of research and intelligence, we can often ascertain the possible short- and long-term effects of our choices on our well-being in *this* life. But what about their effect on our eternal souls?

God's light shines to us through the Torah. The Torah reveals the wisdom of God, and is thus the key to the entire order of creation, which was itself brought about through that wisdom. The Hebrew word *Torah* is a noun from the verb *hora*, which means to teach or guide. The Torah derives from God's true vantage point *beyond* this world — "above the table," as it were. It was sent down into our world to guide us as to its true meaning and its place in the total order, and to teach us how to steer a pathway for ourselves through its multitude of options in order to fulfill our destiny.

The Torah code thus teaches us how to evaluate the various phenomena we encounter in terms of how they relate to our eternal mission, showing us how to respond in virtually every conceivable situation in life. The path of the Torah consists of numerous *mitzvot* — "commandments." (*Mitzvot* is the plural form of the Hebrew word *mitzvah*, from the root *tzivah*, meaning to give an order.) The various mitzvot apply to every sphere of human activity — from eating, drinking, dressing, making a living and building a house to relationships with parents, children, spouse, work associates, members of the wider community, the environment, space and time. The mitzvot apply on every level of behavior — thought, emotion, speech and action.

Each mitzvah is a detailed pathway of practical action relating to a particular facet of life in this world and leading to its own unique form of connection with God. The word mitzvah is thus also related to the Hebrew root *tzavat*, which means "connect." One might think that since God is everywhere, it should be possible to find God through embracing anything and everything. However, this is not so. God created our world as an arena of challenge. Side by side with Godly opportunities are pathways and options that can take us away from God. Our task is twofold: to search for and embrace the Godliness in ourselves and the world around us, and to reject anything that may pull us away from it.

Accordingly, there are two kinds of mitzvot: the positive mitzvot, teaching us what to do in order to connect with God, and the negative mitzvot, the Torah prohibitions, teaching us what *not* to do, so that we may avoid becoming entangled in the evil of the world and alienated from God. Altogether the Torah consists of two hundred and forty-eight positive mitzvot and three hundred and sixty-five prohibitions, making a total of six hundred and thirteen.

Faith

The light of the Torah is itself covered with many veils in this world. Often, its wisdom is cast in the form of opaque stories and proverbs, replete with mysterious symbols. At times its teachings are very recondite, seeming to bear little relationship to the everyday world as we know it.

While some of the mitzvot appear to be understandable in terms of earthly commonsense — love your neighbor, pursue justice, and the like — others are completely incomprehensible. For instance, it seems to make no difference whatsoever to physical health whether the food people eat is kosher or not. Why is it permissible to shift heavy furniture about inside the house on Shabbat but forbidden to flick on an electric-switch? Not the least of the veils which hide the light of the Torah are the many doubts and questions people have about it. Is it valid? Is it relevant? Is it true? Can it be proved?

Under the table, the Prince cannot see that the world around him is anything but a Turkey world. From his lowly vantage-point he can see nothing of the royal court except a partial, distorted aspect which is all but senseless. Now suppose someone from the court came down to the Prince and tried to explain to him the real significance of all the shoes and legs around him, and how inferior his crumbs and bones are to the delicacies being served at the table. Would the Prince believe him? What could the courtier say to him, except: "Put your clothes on, get up, and come and see for yourself."

There is no way to come to know the truth of the Torah except through first accepting and practicing it on trust. The Torah is the key to the entire order of creation, but this order is so overwhelmingly grand that from our lowly vantage-point in this darkened world, we can barely catch the merest glimpse of it. Given that this world was made to be misleading, we cannot find irrefutable proof of the higher order from the way things appear here. On the contrary, the various belief-systems claiming that there is no higher order, and that man is merely a complex animal, may at times appear highly plausible. As long as we are in this world, our grasp of the order of creation cannot be through clear knowledge of the truth. Our connection with the truth can only be established through *Emunah* — faith.

Emunah means more than mere intellectual belief that God exists. It is first and foremost an admission of our own limitations within a universe confronting us with mysteries that we simply cannot fathom. Emunah is founded on our deepest intuitive sense that there is something grand and wondrous about life. Emunah is an acceptance of the superior wisdom of the Torah without asking for proofs. It is an affirmation of God and a willingness to reach out to Him on every level of our being: in our thoughts, feelings, words and actions.

Those seated at the table see the king in all his radiance, they converse with him and participate in the life of the court and the kingdom. Sitting at the royal table is symbolic of intimate connection with God. The ultimate connection with God comes in the time of reward in the World to Come. But Emunah turns the Torah path into one of ever-deepening connection and partnership with God even in This World. With Emunah, even This World becomes the royal table.

Turkey Consciousness

The life of a Turkey has many attractions. Turkeys do what they want when they want. Minimal work. Instant gratification. They eat whatever they like: crumbs, bones... never mind the odd beetle or lizard. If they get fat, so much the better. The male Turkey has an entire harem of wives to enjoy for just as long as he desires and then abandon, leaving him with no worries or responsibilities whatsoever. He gallivants around to his heart's content, sporting his gorgeous feathers. And if ever things get a little dull, he can always fan his tail — and yap yap squaaawk to the rest of the world.

Actually, they're just fattening him up to eat him. But so what! He has his five years of fun, and just hopes he won't feel it when the end comes and they slit his throat, feather him, pull out his guts, salt him, roast him, slice him, chew, swallow and digest him. No tombstone to cover his bones, nor the faintest memory of his vain little life. But who cares? If tomorrow we die, then today we should eat, drink and be merry!

To be honest, even the glamor of the five fat years is more of a dream than a reality for regular, run-of-the-mill turkeys — i.e. the majority. Scratching in the soil all day is hard work, extremely repetitive, and, as often as not, unproductive. The hungry intervals between one worm and the next are gray, uncertain, and tinged with despair. Is it any wonder turkeys are so irritable? It could also explain their compulsive search for love. With only the slaughterer's knife to look forward to, what else offers some sense of meaning and comfort in the bleak, lonely interval between egghood and roasting?

If you're a Turkey, there may not be much you can do about it. But if you're really a Prince, or a Princess, it's mad to go through life thinking and acting like a Turkey. The Turkey-Prince is a graphic symbol of the loss of Emunah and its replacement with a devastating counter-ideology: materialism.

Those suffering from the Prince's malady are simply taken in by the way this world appears. To them, appearance *is* reality. The logic seems so compelling. "All we can see and feel is the material world. Therefore that's all that exists. In certain respects the human body resembles that of the ape. Therefore man must be an animal. Animals follow their instincts. So should we. If you feel it, do it!"

For the Prince under the table, it is not only the lack of light that makes it hard for him to understand the true nature of his world. If he could remember who he was and where he came from, he would not be deceived by the strange appearance of things down under the table. His knowledge of the truth would enable him to compensate for his present strange perspective. However, the Prince has lost this knowledge. He thinks he is a Turkey, he has a Turkey mind and outlook, and that is why he is convinced that the world down there must be a separate, independent, Turkey realm.

Similarly, the power of This World to confuse us does not only derive from its physical nature. The material attractions of the world are indeed a veil throwing the spiritual opportunities it offers into deep shadow. The temptations of the crumbs and bones of life can be so overwhelming that some people spend most, if not all, of their days racing after them, without even a pause to reflect on their higher purpose. Nevertheless, these material distractions would be powerless to entice us if we retained clear spiritual vision. It would be perfectly clear how pale they are compared to the supreme joy of attachment to God.

However, our spiritual vision is itself dimmed in this world. The real essence of man is not, as most of the world is inclined to think, his physical body, but his soul. The soul is the Prince: it comes from the highest realms — the "court of the King" — and is ultimately destined to rise and return to its proper place, enjoying the true goodness of closeness to God. If we came into this world with all our higher soul-powers intact, we would always recall the spiritual worlds from which the soul originates. Seeing this world in its true perspective, we would understand its material dimension for what it is — a limitation that has to be mastered and transcended in order to acquire the spiritual goodness that is our destiny.

What creates the test of the soul is that "the Prince thinks he is a Turkey." The Prince in us is the authentic soul, but when we come into this world, our higher, spiritual consciousness is mostly lost to us. In order to function and go about our everyday business, a lower form of consciousness comes to the fore — this-worldly, material, Turkey consciousness. This is what tends to blot out our awareness of the lowly nature of this world and our true purpose in it.

The Soul in This World

> *"The soul of man is a lamp of God searching all the chambers of the womb."*
>
> Proverbs 20:27

What is the soul? The intrinsic nature of the soul in its disembodied state is beyond our comprehension as long as we are in this world. The soul originates beyond this world, whereas we are currently in it and have this-worldly minds and patterns of understanding. Since the soul's powers are dimmed upon its entry into this world, we cannot learn about its intrinsic nature from the way it appears to us here. While the soul is often spoken of as being "eternal," "pure spirit," etc. it is impossible for us to have more than the vaguest notion of what these terms really mean.

"The soul of man is a lamp of God searching all the chambers of the womb." As we have seen, Godliness is metaphorically called light. The soul is called a "lamp" because it is a small spark of God's light, "a part of God above" (Job 31:2). In its intrinsic essence, the soul is a part of God: it is ultimately rooted in God's perfect unity. Yet it is God's will to give the soul a separate, independent existence in order to test it and enable it to return to Him and be merged in His unity on an even higher level. This is the ultimate destiny of the soul. Just as a candle leaps up to merge with a great fire, so the soul yearns to return to its Source.

This darkened world into which the soul is sent for its test is a "womb," a place of development and growth in preparation for the eventual "birth" of the soul into the higher spiritual realm to which it ascends after the death of the body. In order to provide the necessary conditions for the challenge, this world had to be created as a very different environment from the eternal spiritual realm. Since this world is physical and temporary, the soul can only enter it in a temporary physical body, with its own needs and desires. This is what creates the conditions for the challenge of the soul.

The soul needs the body as a vehicle through which to operate in and upon the finite, physical world in order to accomplish its spiritual work. The body is superbly fashioned to carry out an endless array of activities. Using the body as a medium, the soul is able to form structures in the physical world that reveal the Godliness concealed beneath the surface. (Thus, many of the practical mitzvot involve the use of physical objects, such as the parchment and leather of the Torah scroll, Tefilin and Mezuzah, or vegetation, as in the case of the Lulav and Etrog, etc. to manifest God's sovereignty over the world.) These activities bring Godliness into the soul itself, benefitting it when it eventually leaves this world and returns to the higher spiritual realms. In order to achieve its spiritual mission in this world, the soul should master the body, using it for Godly purposes.

However, the body is of this world and has various material needs of its own just to be able to survive. It is possible to satisfy all the body's real needs in a pure and holy manner, and the purpose of the soul is in fact to do this as a means of manifesting God's sovereignty. Yet even satisfying our most basic physical needs — food, clothing, shelter, procreation, etc. — involves many complex, time-consuming activities and relationships that can easily distract us from our spiritual objectives.

To further intensify the challenge to the soul, the body is the source of an array of material drives and desires that go beyond what is necessary for survival. These not only hamper the soul in fulfilling its mission; they may even divert it completely.

Which foods and in what quantities are necessary for sound nutrition? When does the desire to eat become excessive? How much do we need to sleep and how much do we like to be lazy? To what extent is work a quest for a decent livelihood and genuine security, and when does it turn into an obsessive race after phantoms? How much sexual desire is natural and desirable, and when does it become a mind-consuming, life-destroying passion? To what extent should a person stand his ground, and at what point does pursuit of one's own interests and legitimate self-defense turn into hunger for power and aggression? And so on, and so on.

In every area of material life, the borderline between what is necessary and what is excessive is vague. The nature of the body is to be drawn further and further beyond the limit. The material temptations in the surrounding environment, and our inner urges to go after them, darken the "womb" — this world — cluttering its intricate chambers with every kind of pitfall, obstacle, and blind ally. The task of the soul — the "candle of God" — is to shine Godly light and wisdom into these chambers in order to distinguish between what is good, necessary and beneficial, and what is excessive, damaging and evil.

The Nefesh

Our Sages teach that the soul consists of three main parts: the *neshamah*, the *ru'ach* and the *nefesh*. Of these, the neshamah is the most exalted: it is the ultimate source of all our soul-powers as they appear in this world, but the neshamah itself is not directly manifested in this world at all. It remains bound up with God on a plane of pure spirit. It is the nefesh that comes into this world, residing in and animating the body. The nefesh is connected to the neshamah via the ru'ach, which is a kind of spiritual "channel" through which Godly vitality — potential — flows from the neshamah down into the nefesh.

Each one of us is a separate, independent, thinking, sentient being. We are not objects but *subjects*, experiencing and responding to the world around us and a rich inner domain of thoughts, feelings, emotions, instincts, impulses, wants and desires. The subject experiencing all these stimuli and acting in response — I, the ego — is the nefesh.

The nefesh manifests itself to us as a plurality of all the different mental and physical faculties we are given for our sojourn in this world, from the most spiritual and other-worldly to the most material and this-worldly. It is the nefesh that gives us our sense of existence as independent beings with various levels of consciousness and our awareness of ourselves, our bodies and our environment. The nefesh is the source of our faculties of language, reason, feeling, memory, imagination and creativity, and our ability to conceive goals, formulate plans and execute them. It is also through the nefesh that our bodily needs and wants enter our consciousness in the form of instincts and desires.

The nefesh is not a fixed entity feeding us specific, pre-programmed impulses and responses. Our faculties are not fully developed at birth and do not remain static throughout our lives. Perhaps it would be better to characterize the nefesh as potential — potential that we may actualize to a greater or lesser extent and in a variety of different directions as we go through life. The specific way in which we actualize ourselves depends on many different factors, including the physical body and innate powers with which we are endowed, the material, family, social and cultural environments in which we are raised and live, the various influences we are exposed to, our life experiences, and all the different choices we make throughout our lives.

Therefore our most important faculty is the ability to conceive goals and pursue them with appropriate action. This is the way we actualize our potential. The world around us presents all kinds of options, possibilities, suggestions and imperatives — to which we respond in our own individual way, developing our own goals and ambitions, from the most simple and immediate to the most grandiose and far-reaching. Much of the life of the mind is made up of a succession of thoughts, pictures, projects, plans, hopes and dreams of things we might like to achieve, ranging from the possible and practicable to the wildly fantastic.

Every goal begins as an idea that may be either clear or vague. To realize a particular goal, the idea behind it has to be developed and acted upon. The moving force that brings about the transition from potential to actual is *will*. Through willpower, we take command of the necessary faculties of reason, emotion, physical execution, etc. in order to pursue what we want. What is our goal, and how motivated are we to achieve it? How much do we want what we want? Do we want it enough to actually do it? Will is the very essence of the nefesh.

The Battle of Wills

If we were completely single-minded, achievements would come easily, without inner struggle. But we aren't. One wants to be fit and healthy, but one likes to eat all the wrong foods.

One wants to study, but one is tired and wants to rest, or read the papers or a novel. One would like to save money for something important, but can't resist an attractive bargain here, a little luxury there. One wants to be kind and charitable, but ends up angry and selfish. And so on.

The challenge facing us in this world emanates from our lack of single-mindedness. The more we develop the spiritual side of the nefesh, the more we receive from the neshamah, enabling us to rise to increasingly higher levels of Godliness. But every step of the way we are tempted by material distractions. Sometimes the things we want conflict with one another, and we find ourselves pulled in different directions.

Although we may experience all these contradictory wants and desires as coming from inside ourselves — all of them may seem equally "ours" — it is important to understand that they stem from two fundamentally opposing poles of the nefesh. Despite the fact that most people normally think of themselves as being one entity — I — the nefesh is in fact dual in nature. The nefesh is the interface of the two opposing planes of our being.

Through the nefesh the higher soul strives to pursue spiritual opportunities in the world around us by practicing the mitzvot. The neshamah seeks to take command of the various faculties of the nefesh — intellectual, emotional and physical — in order to accomplish its mission. On the other hand, the material attractions of the surrounding world arouse the lower self, which strives to commandeer these same faculties in the pursuit and gratification of *its* desires.

Thus there are two separate sources of will in the one nefesh: a source drawn to spiritual goals and aspirations, deriving from the neshamah, and a source craving material satisfaction and pleasure, rooted in the body. In Torah literature, each of these poles is sometimes referred to as a nefesh or soul in itself — respectively, the Godly Soul and the Animal Soul. More often they are called the *Yetzer HaTov* and the *Yetzer HaRa* — the Good and Evil Inclination. In our story they are symbolized by the royal Prince and the bloated Turkey self that has taken him over.

The word *Yetzer* is from the Hebrew root *yatzar*, meaning to form or construct. The formation in question is that of the actualized self — the person one becomes through the actions one chooses. Formation begins with conception, thought and motivation. The Yetzer is the source of thoughts, feelings and impulses oriented in a particular direction. The Yetzer HaTov is the source of those oriented toward Good in the absolute sense of the term, that which is truly Godly and in accord with our ultimate purpose. The Yetzer HaRa is the source of all our urges for the things that draw us away from our ultimate purpose, from the crudest physical lusts to the most sophisticated social and cultural delights.

Although at root the two Yetzers are opposites, as long as the soul is attached to the body these two poles of the nefesh are wedded together in a seamless unity. They both talk inside us as "I." We may experience the flow of consciousness as a single, continuous tapestry, but in fact all our thoughts, feelings, impulses and responses derive from one or other of these separate sides of the nefesh as they develop in the course of our lives. They are the well-springs of the self and the source of our multiplicity of conflicting thoughts, feelings, impulses and aspirations — all of them "ours." The Godly and Animal Souls both talk within us in our own inner voices, dialoguing, arguing, struggling... "I think this..." "but I feel that." "I ought to do this..." "but I want to do that..." etc.

The two Yetzers are our potential selves, the higher and the lower. Which self we actually become depends upon how we respond to the different promptings of the Yetzers. An idea, feeling or impulse comes into mind: do we dwell on it, let it develop and take hold of us, until we act on it? Or do we ignore it, let it pass, dismiss it or even forcibly suppress it? Every decision we make has an effect on the balance between the two Yetzers and the future course of the struggle between them. And the person we become is a composite of all the choices we make throughout our lives.

Clothing of the Soul

The Prince's clothes are strewn all around, but the Prince is not in the least interested. As far as he knows, he is a Turkey — what do clothes have to do with him? To understand the symbolism of the Prince's clothes, let us turn to another parable, also about clothes, this time by Rebbe Nachman's foremost disciple, Rabbi Nathan:

A king informs his loved ones that he wishes to give them the most amazing precious gifts on such and such a date. Since they obviously won't be able to come to his banquet and receive their gifts if they are not presentable, he gives them advance notice. This will give them plenty of opportunity to prepare themselves. They must clothe themselves in lovely garments, perfume themselves with delicate fragrances, and adorn themselves with beautiful ornaments. Then they will be fit to enter the royal palace, mingle with the king's ministers and servants, and receive his gifts.

In his great compassion, the king first provides them with all the different things they will need to prepare their clothes and ornaments and perfumes. He sends emissaries to teach them how to prepare each item. And he tells them to be sure to take full advantage of the advance notice in order to get themselves ready. Above all, the king warns them to keep away from anything that might possibly make them dirty.

If they do slip up by mistake, he tells them how they can clean themselves. He provides special fountains which have the power to cleanse and purify even those who have become extremely dirty. When everyone is ready, they will be able to come and receive the free gifts the king has prepared for them (*Likutey Halachot, Choshen Mishpat, Hilchot Matanot* 4).

The hero of *our* parable is sitting under the table without any clothes on whatsoever, revelling in the crumbs and bones. He has done the very opposite of what the king in Rabbi Nathan's parable (who is, of course, the same King as in the tale of the Turkey-Prince) has asked. Far from carefully guarding his royal clothes, the Prince has stripped them all off.

The royal banquet in Rabbi Nathan's parable, at which the king's beloved subjects will receive the wonderful gifts, represents the World to Come. This is where the souls attain the ultimate good — closeness to God. The king's invitation is the Torah, which teaches us the true meaning of our life in This World, and how to achieve our ultimate destiny. Naturally, you cannot just show up at the banquet. You have to prepare in advance. The king's emissaries are the saints and sages who have taught the Torah in each generation. They explain how we should act in the time we have in This World — how to prepare our "clothes." The clothes symbolize the mitzvot of the Torah: these are the garments worn by the soul in the World to Come.

Before we discuss in what sense the mitzvot are "clothes," let us first consider our physical clothes. Man is the only creature in the world who makes himself clothes. One of the functions of clothing is obviously to give the body protection against possible harm from the physical environment, whether because of fluctuations in temperature, objects which could injure the skin, dirt and other health hazards, and so on.

In a certain sense, our physical clothes also give us protection *against* the body. Wearing clothes is one of the most important marks of our dignity as humans. We are more than mere physical beings, far more. We have the power to control and channel our material instincts. By covering up the body, which no animal does, we affirm the primacy of the soul. Indeed the first parts of the body we cover are those where our strongest physical desires are centered. On a simple level, the Prince's taking *off* his clothes is a stark symbol of the animalistic obsession with sensual pleasure in contemporary culture.

Communication

Wearing clothes is a sign that we are more than just physical creatures. Indeed, clothes do not simply cover the body. They express a message of their own about the inner essence of the people wearing them. Not only do we wear different kinds of clothes for different purposes — work, dirty work, leisure, sports, parties, warfare, maternity, etc. We also wear clothes to *communicate*. Kings, sheikhs, chieftains, priests, policemen, business executives, bohemians and many others all have their own special costumes. Ordinary people use clothing styles in all kinds of subtle ways to make statements about who they are, or aspire to be. Clothes are a language of their own.

Not only are our clothes vehicles of expression in the literal sense. We also speak of "clothing" our thoughts and feelings in words, symbols, artefacts etc. Even to communicate to our own selves, we have to clothe our ideas in language. Sometimes an idea begins to form in our minds, but it remains inchoate and unformed until we develop our thoughts, even if only in our own private language. Certainly when we wish to communicate our thoughts and feelings to others, we are obliged to find the right garb in which to express them.

A brilliant visionary may grasp concepts that are beyond the understanding of most other people, but in order to bring his perceptions to their level, he has to find ways of "clothing" them in simple stories, parables and the like so that they *can* be understood. These are analogues, each detail of which corresponds to and expresses some facet of the original idea. Sometimes people *act out* what they want to say, because "actions speak louder than words." The action is a garment for the thought.

One of the most powerful forms of communication is ritual. A ritual is an ordered sequence of prescribed actions encoding a message that would have a totally different effect if it were merely expressed in words. In a ritual, the message is not simply handed over from one party to another. Instead of being passive receivers of information, the participants act out the steps of the ritual for themselves, and through this they inwardly *experience* the intended message far more vividly.

God uses "clothes" of many different kinds to communicate with us. In Himself, God is infinitely great. It is impossible for any finite creature to experience God directly, for "no man can see Me and live" (Exodus 33:20). Yet God's whole purpose in the creation is to reveal something of Himself to us. God's revelation to His creatures is called "light," not in the sense of physical light, but metaphorically, to express, in terms familiar to us, something that would otherwise be completely incomprehensible. Physical light is the most subtle of all material phenomena, and therefore an appropriate symbol for Godly revelation.

We are unable to gaze at the sun without being blinded. However, if we take a piece of colored glass and hold it in front of our eyes, the glass blots out most of the light, allowing only certain wavelengths to pass through. In the full intensity of the white light of the sun it was impossible for our eyes to see this color, but now we can enjoy it in comfort. Different colors of glass will enable us to see other components of the white light of the sun.

It is impossible for any creature to perceive the Infinite Light of God. In order to make it possible for us to experience something of this light, the Sages tell us that God "veiled" it with cover after cover in order to reduce its intensity. The physical universe itself is a "garment" cloaking the higher levels of the Divine order and enabling them to shine through in a muted form.

"You have garbed Yourself with majesty and splendor, cloaking [Yourself] in light as with a garment, stretching out the heavens like a curtain" (Psalms 104:1-2). We look up at the heavens, the stars and celestial bodies and wonder at the marvels of this world — mineral, vegetable, animal and human. Every detail we see in the world around us was created as an analogue of some higher level of Godliness that is not in itself accessible to our minds.

The Torah itself is a garb for God's Wisdom. It consists of books, chapters, paragraphs, sentences, words and letters, stories and concepts that are accessible to our understanding. It may be impossible for us to grasp the divine *chesed*, *gevurah*, and *tiferet* (kindness, power, and beauty) in their intrinsic essence, but even a child can relate to the Torah stories about Abraham, Isaac and Jacob, who are the embodiment of these qualities. The more the student matures and delves into the depths of the Torah the more he will begin to perceive its inner meaning.

A small child may have a vivid picture of hundreds of thousands of Israelites marching out of Egypt, and see Moses climbing up Mount Sinai and returning with two tablets of stone. The mature adult may grasp the Exodus as the release of the spirit from bondage to the material world, and see Mount Sinai not only as a physical but also a spiritual mountain, a mountain climbed through prayer, self-purification, meditation and contemplation. These in turn open the spiritual seeker to a message so important that it must be inscribed upon the tablets of his memory and consciousness.

Badges of the King

At court, it is not only the King who wears clothes of splendor but also the courtiers. The different ranks and officers have their own special robes and costumes expressing their individual status and power. Their court clothes are signs of royal favor. Through them the courtiers are associated with the King's splendor and majesty and have a share in them. They must wear their designated apparel to enjoy admission to the court and participate in affairs of state.

The mitzvot of the Torah are the "clothes" God has given us in order to enable us to connect with Him and experience His majesty. Each of the different mitzvot is a separate "garment" encoding and expressing a facet of Divine Wisdom. By practicing the mitzvot, we become more than passive recipients of the Divine message. We put on the garments ourselves. Like the participants in a ritual, we can then experience and internalize the message in the fullest possible way.

God is infinite, and totally beyond our grasp, but the mitzvot are finite, man-sized "garments" with which we can experience Godliness even in this world. The mitzvot are prescribed sequences of thoughts, feelings, words and actions relating to the things of this world. The various mitzvot apply to every sphere of human activity. Each one leads to its own particular form of connection with God.

The mitzvot provide "clothing" for the Godly Soul. The Princely higher self with which each of us is endowed is potential. It is up to us to make it actual. Thoughts, emotions, words and actions of any kind are the "clothing" through which we express and actualize the inner self. Different kinds of thoughts, words and actions will nurture the personality in different ways. As we have seen, the mitzvot are detailed patterns of divinely prescribed thoughts, words, feelings and actions oriented toward God and connecting us with Him. By carrying out the mitzvot and "putting on" these "garments", the Godly Soul is able to express and actualize itself.

For example: the whole creation is an overwhelming act of Divine charity. God had no need of the world for Himself. He created it for the benefit of His creatures. The sun and the stars shine down into the world, the winds blow and the rains fall... all out of charity: no one asks us to pay! To help us grasp the Divine quality of charity, the Torah teaches that we too should give charity, thereby clothing ourselves in a "coat of charity" (Isaiah 61:10).

Anyone can perform this Divine act with one of the most mundane items in our lives — money. By taking from our own money and giving it to someone in need, we come to understand what it means to do something purely for the benefit of another. Thus we become inculcated with the quality of altruism. Prior to physically handing over the money, we may have had a charitable inclination — rooted in the Godly Soul — but still only in potential. By performing the mitzvah, we actualize it. The mitzvah changes us. Charity is now a part of us. Through the act of charity we participate in the charity and love through which God creates the world. At this moment, like God, we are the giver. We experience the Divine quality of charity internally. This is how we bring Godliness into ourselves.

Another example: Shabbat. God makes the world, yet God is beyond the world. We too make our world: day after day, six days of the week, we labor to feed, clothe and shelter ourselves, etc. Then, on the seventh day we rest: we stop and take ourselves beyond the world. We too experience transcendence. The detailed laws of Shabbat ensure our complete detachment and rest from the world of work, making it possible for a spirit of transcendence to descend from God and "clothe" us in the "extra soul" of Shabbat, experienced in the joyous energy and enhanced spiritual insight of the day.

The body is made up of different limbs having their own distinctive clothes: hats for the head, scarves for the neck, gloves for the hands, etc. The soul also has limbs: a "head" (the intellect), a "heart" (feelings and emotions), a "mouth" (the faculty of speech), "arms" and "legs" (the ability to act in the world in different ways) etc. All the limbs of the soul have their own distinctive mitzvot. The two hundred and forty-eight positive mitzvot of the Torah clothe the two hundred and forty-eight "limbs" of the soul, which in turn correspond to the same number of limbs of the body.

Each of the different mitzvot brings out and develops different facets of the Godly Soul in particular ways. The mitzvot we observe each day (such as reciting Sh'ma and putting on Tefilin) or periodically (e.g. Shabbat and the festivals) provide rhythms for life through changes in the times, keeping our minds constantly focused on God's presence. The observances which depend on particular circumstances (such as circumcision when a baby boy is born, fixing mezuzot on the doorposts of our houses, paying employees on time, and many, many others) put a Divine stamp on our conduct when the relevant circumstances arise.

The various mitzvot bound up with the satisfaction of our basic material needs — food (Kashrut, blessings, etc.), clothing (Tzitzit, Sha'atnez — the prohibition of wool mixed with linen, modesty, etc.), shelter (Mezuzah, Ma'akeh — the obligation to make a parapet for a roof, etc.) transform what would otherwise be animal functions into spiritual activities. By restraining the material ego, the Godly Soul is able to shine. The many different mitzvot governing relations between people — parents and children, husbands and wives, friends and neighbors, borrowers and lenders, buyers and sellers, business partners, etc. — inculcate respect and responsibility for others.

Most important are the mitzvot which apply constantly, such as faith, love and fear of God, and the love of one's fellow. These mitzvot profoundly shape not only the way we go about our lives, but our innermost being. "And you shall go in His ways" (Deuteronomy 28:9) — just as God is loving, gracious, long-suffering and full of mercy, so we should clothe ourselves with these qualities and make ourselves true sons and daughters of the King. Through Torah study, we steep our minds and hearts in the Divine Wisdom, refining and elevating our intellect and emotions. Through prayer and meditation, we attach ourselves to the Divine Presence, opening ourselves to undreamed of levels of awareness, connection and illumination.

The full array of the six hundred and thirteen mitzvot provides scope for the complete development of all aspects of the personality, from the most other-worldly to the most mundane. Everyone has his own unique potential. Whether in the home, at work or at leisure, in friendship, marriage, parenting, education, business, administration, counselling, health-care, art, crafts, sport or any other sphere, there is a way of developing one's skills and elevating one's activities for the sake of God, deepening one's connection and spreading Godly revelation in the world. The more fully one steeps oneself in the life of the mitzvot, the more one's unique Godly Soul becomes actualized.

Because the Divine Wisdom is infinite, the mitzvot are far more than limited prescriptions for standardized, repetitive action. One may recite the same prayers every day, observe Shabbat every week, and perform the other mitzvot regularly, but the profound, indeed endless, inner dimensions they contain make it possible to fulfill them on deeper and deeper levels as one grows in understanding and experience.

The mitzvot are expressed in the language of this world and involve the way we relate to familiar objects and situations. But the message they encode goes way beyond this world, reaching to the most exalted spiritual worlds and to God. The message we internalize through practice of the mitzvot may go far beyond our conscious understanding. Certainly the entire system of the mitzvot was designed to be fulfilled by us in this world, within the parameters of our physical existence. They vitally affect this world, and the quality of our lives and experience in it. Still, their main purpose goes beyond this world — to prepare the Godly Soul for the World to Come. By performing the mitzvot in this world, we are donning the garments worn by the soul at the King's banquet in the World to Come.

But the Prince in our story has taken *off* his clothes. Instead of sitting at the King's table, he is on the floor pulling at the crumbs and bones. What is the significance of the crumbs and bones?

Crumbs and Bones

The crumbs and bones have dropped down from the plates of the diners at the table, who discarded them as they ate their food. The crumbs and bones are the waste of the meal. They symbolize what our Sages call the *Sitra Achra.* This Aramaic term literally means the "other side." It refers to the unholy side of the Creation — the secondary and inessential, the refuse, that which is rejected.

The primary purpose of the Creation was to bestow the gift of Godliness on man, but as we have seen, this could only be accomplished by putting him through a trial. This entailed the setting up of test conditions, in which man would be exposed to unGodliness and evil as well as Godliness and good, so as to be able to choose good of his own free will. God has no desire for evil in itself. Falsehood, corruption, wickedness, divisiveness, destruction and everything else that is evil are the very opposites of Godliness, whose stamp is truth, purity, goodness, harmony and life. God created evil for a limited purpose only, after which it is discarded and falls away.

The relationship of evil to good is compared to that between the shell of a nut and its kernel. The shell covers the fruit for as long as required for its growth and development, but the shell has no intrinsic worth of its own. It's the fruit hidden beneath it that we really want. In order to get to it, we have to break open the shell, then remove and discard it. This is what God wants man to do with evil: peel it off and throw it away, in order to enjoy the good. Thus the realm of evil is also referred to as the realm of the *kelipot*, the shells or husks. Just as there are many different levels and aspects of holiness, so there are many different levels and kinds of kelipot, each one covering and concealing a particular aspect of Godliness to a given extent.

A simple example of a kelipah would be a lie. Tom dislikes Dick and resents the fact that Harry is friendly with him. Tom artfully tells Harry a lie about Dick — a lie sufficiently plausible that Harry believes it. The lie has no real basis in truth at all, but from now on, whenever Harry sees or thinks about Dick, the lie is in his mind. It affects his entire perception of Dick. It colors the way he interprets everything Dick does. The lie has no substance whatsoever, but it conceals the truth and brings a train of fantasy in its wake — fantasy that may change the whole course of Harry's relationship with Dick and his behavior towards him.

The kelipot are distortions, fantasies and lies that cast shadows over the Godly possibilities in the world and within ourselves, drawing people along avenues that lead away from God. In the world around us we are surrounded by kelipot on all sides. The Rabbinic description of the great city as the "den" of the kelipot could be applied to our urbanized, technological world as a whole. Whether you go out into the street, or bring the world into your home, turning on the TV or radio or glancing at the newspapers and magazines, there is the ubiquitous, frenetic race for money and pleasure, there are the flashing lights and arrows, the blaring, glaring slogans, the fresh, beckoning smiles, the suggestive images, the explicit indecency, the lavish promises: "Come here... buy this... do this... and you'll be *happy!!!*" Where in the midst of all this do you find a single sign or advertisement to do a mitzvah for the sake of Heaven?

"Everything is permitted" is one of the most insistent messages transmitted over wide areas of the educational system, in the mass media, by many of the most highly respected contemporary intellectuals, thinkers and writers, in psychology, literature, art, music, and in popular entertainment and culture. Traditional wisdom and values are the butt of every kind of skepticism and irreverence, while the utmost veneration is accorded to any pseudo-scientific, philosophical, ideological or cultish idea or theory that negates — whether implicitly or explicitly — Torah truth, the Divine origin of the Creation, and man's spiritual nature.

For the Animal Soul, all this is food, glorious food! Not only are the tempting aromas, the youthful faces and figures, the fancy clothes, and all the rest of the "false charm and vain beauty" of the world so attractive; we are also amply provided with the most excellent rationalizations for going after them.

Truth and Madness

"Woe to those who call evil good, and good evil" (Isaiah 5:20). The most important soul-power that helps us find our way through this shadowy world is that of judgment: the ability to stand back from the world and our very selves, to penetrate beneath surface appearances, and *evaluate* what we see in the light of truth. Even when our strongest instincts are aroused, we have the power to restrain ourselves and stop to consider whether following temptation is really in our own true best interests. The soul is thus the "lamp of God, searching all the chambers of the womb." The Torah is God's light, and the soul has the power to direct this light so as to illumine the most intricate recesses of the world around us and our inner world, to sift and discriminate between truth and falsehood, genuine and purported good, and choose the right path to our destiny.

If the Godly Soul shines with the light of truth, the kelipot fight against it with a weapon of deadly potency: deception. The kelipot posture as the truth. Nevertheless, all the false images and messages would be powerless to sway us but for the flaw that comes into the nefesh because of the wedding of the soul to the body. The result is that the clear spiritual vision of the Godly Soul becomes dimmed in this world, opening us to the artful persuasions of the Animal Soul. The whole power of the Animal Soul derives from its ability to blur the line between what is really good for us and what is not.

The satisfactions of spiritual life are not always felt immediately. Pursuing spiritual goals requires discipline over long periods of time. The "crumbs and bones" of this world offer far more immediate gratification. Instant, easy success and pleasure is the bribe held out by the Animal Soul to "blind the eyes of the wise" (Deuteronomy 16:19) — distorting our judgment and inducing us to turn aside from our true purpose.

The Hebrew term for turning aside is *SoTeh*. This is related to the word for a madman, which is *ShoTeh*. Our Sages taught that "a person only transgresses because a spirit of madness gets into him" (*Sotah* 3a). The madness is that of the Animal Soul, the Turkey in us. It is literally mad to turn aside from the path of the mitzvot, because this is the only way we can come to lasting good and happiness. Turning aside from the path of Torah is ultimately against our own best interests, regardless of any apparent short-term benefits.

The three hundred and sixty-five prohibitions of the Torah teach us how to avoid the kelipot that exist in the different spheres of creation, so as to be able to keep our eyes focused on the truth and find our way to God. The Torah's prohibitions apply to every area of human activity — from what we eat, drink and wear, how we work the land, do business, relate with family, associates, friends and enemies, etc., to ritual life and the way we worship God. The function of the prohibitions of the Torah is to provide the guidelines we need in a deceptive world, so as to avoid straying beyond the bounds of holiness in any direction.

For example, foods of many kinds contain "Divine sparks" that can give us energy to study Torah, pray, fulfill the mitzvot and connect with God. On the other hand, the creation also contains certain foods that will only generate impure thoughts and feelings in the people who eat them, leading them to unholy actions. Their minds and hearts simply become foreclosed to Godly awareness. Regardless of the physical nutritional properties of these foods, the spiritual energies they contain are inherently *bound up* with God-concealing kelipot. The Hebrew term for "bound up" is *assur* (usually translated as "forbidden.") The Torah teaches us which foods are "bound up" in this way and must therefore be avoided — such as the various impure species of animals, animal blood, meat cooked with milk, etc.

All the different things prohibited by the Torah are likewise bound up with kelipot of various kinds, each in a particular way, as laid down by the wisdom of the Creator. Any kind of involvement with something forbidden by the Torah necessarily unleashes impure energies which deepen the concealment of God. This applies not only to the the most serious prohibitions — those the majority of people know to be sinful, such as idolatry, murder and adultery, etc. — but even to those many people hardly consider sinful at all — a little angry outburst, a momentary swell of pride, a word or two of gossip, an innocent lie, an untoward glance, a cynical smirk, and many others.

We have seen that the two hundred and forty-eight positive mitzvot of the Torah are the "clothes" worn by the Godly Soul. Through "putting on the clothes" — practicing the mitzvot — it is possible to express and actualize the Godly Soul in this world, thus preparing ourselves for the "banquet" — reunion with God — in the World to Come. In his parable about the banquet, Rabbi Nathan also tells us that when the king issued his invitation to his beloved subjects, he warned them not to let themselves become soiled in any way. The king's warning symbolizes God's prohibitions in the Torah. Their purpose is to keep us clean of the "dirt" — the kelipot.

"The Prince felt *compelled...*"

Transgressions bring kelipot into the inner world of the self. The Hebrew word for transgression is *aveirah*, literally "moving over." To the exact extent that a person transgresses on any level, whether in thought, feeling, speech or action, he is moving himself and his life-energy over from the side of the holy and investing it in the "other side," the realm of the kelipot. This gives the kelipot power over him.

Every mitzvah a person does — whether great or small — contributes to the actualization of the Godly Soul, becoming part of the fabric of the personality and influencing his states of consciousness, thoughts, feelings and subsequent actions. Conversely, every move one makes into the area of the kelipot also leaves its mark on the personality. The Godly Soul becomes stained in proportion to the transgression, while the Animal Soul becomes strengthened, driving the Godly Soul into further retreat.

The kelipot of the inner self range from the merest day dreams and fantasies that pass across the mind to the most deeply-entrenched structures of belief, outlook and personality. Different kinds of kelipot may obscure the spiritual awareness of the individual in different ways. The nagging thought or impulse that attacks us repeatedly, no matter how much we fight against it, is a kelipah that we may recognize for what it is. On the other hand, the bouts of nervous tension, fear, anxiety, negativity, depression and despair that people often experience for no readily apparent reason may be far less recognizable to them as kelipot. Among the most powerful kelipot of all are the compulsive passions and crazy involvements that drive so many people, consuming ever greater parts of their lives — such as addiction to alcohol, cigarettes, drugs, food, sex, shopping, television or anything else.

The kelipot of the personality do not necessarily cause conscious pain or anguish. People may be under the sway of the most powerful destructive passions, or allow their entire lives to be governed by profound misconceptions about themselves, other people, and the world in general, yet go on for years without seeming to be overly troubled. The tragedy is that their potential for genuine spiritual growth and fulfillment simply remains stunted.

"He thought he was a Turkey"

The Turkey-Prince is the extreme archetype of the kelipah-dominated personality. He is under a complete misconception about who he is, the meaning of the world, and what his purpose is in life. The illusion is total: he is convinced he just *is* a Turkey in a Turkey world. As far as he is concerned, this is the rock-bottom truth. What possible reason could there be for trying to be something else?

In his blissful unawareness of the depth of his own tragedy, the Turkey-Prince is symbolic of the millions of people who are convinced that this world is nothing but a chance agglomeration of dust, that man is merely an animal, and life is a matter of making a living, doing whatever else one has to do, and spending the rest of the time as pleasantly as possible before passing into oblivion. Such people may even find spiritual values laudable and charming: love your neighbor, give a bit of charity from time to time, etc. But praying? studying? keeping mitzvot? growth? You must be kidding!

If life does indeed have a higher purpose, we may well wonder why so many people are so far from attaining it. If the mission of the soul in this world is to peel away the kelipot and choose Godliness, what chance do all those people have who have been sunk in Turkeyhood from birth, having had a secular upbringing and education, and having been totally immersed in the dominant materialistic culture? Granted: they, their parents, and their parents' parents may have been wide open to the onslaught of the kelipot as a result of having contravened the prohibitions of the Torah. But did they do so willfully? Is it just that they should suffer? Did they ever know of the Torah code or understand its importance?

Rebbe Nachman himself does not explain *why* the Turkey-Prince went crazy, or ask whether it was *fair*. These are topics that could be discussed at great length. Not only would we need to go more deeply into Chassidut and Kabbalah, psychology and sociology; we would have to consider the entire course of human history, and why the world is so far from the Torah. Yet all this would be beside the main point. Now that the Prince has gone out of his mind, *how is he to be cured?*

The situation may seem very bad, yet Rebbe Nachman always encourages us to look at the positive side of things. What could possibly be positive about the Prince's fall into madness?

What is positive is that falling down... is the first step towards getting up. This is one of the most important principles of spiritual life. Before someone can advance spiritually, he must first experience a fall. It's like a high-jumper taking a few steps back first in order to get a good run up. When things go too smoothly, people tend to become complacent. But when something goes wrong and they "fall down," it forces them to wake up and apply more effort. To find God, we have to search. There are many different ways we can fall, but they all force us to start searching harder. Being aware of this can help us take full advantage of our failures in life.

The story of the Turkey-Prince is a challenge to each one of us. How have *we* fallen? Where are we in *our* lives? Are we where we *could* be? What are the illusions and obsessions that hold *us* back from being the people we could be?

The key to transforming any fall into an advance is through honesty and truth. "No matter who you are," says Rebbe Nachman, "you can always get new life and strength through being truthful. The truth is God's own light — and there is no darkness in the world that is too dark for God. There is no impurity or unholiness in the world without exits for escape. It is just that people don't see them because of the intense darkness all around them. Through the truth, however, God Himself will shine to them and help them see the openings of hope that exist even in their lowest depths. This is the way to escape the darkness and go into the light and constantly come closer to God" (*Tsohar* p.3).

The underlying truth of the creation is God Himself. However, this truth is beyond our reach: in Himself, God is totally unknowable. One's own personal situation, small, private, even prison-like, may seem like a barrier holding one back from God. Yet this specific situation was created by God down to the very last detail as part of His ultimate purpose, which is to reveal the truth on all levels. So when we honestly search for the truth of our actual situation — when we grasp that things are exactly the way God has planned them — the barrier itself turns into a pathway to God, because we realize that our situation was created in order to lead us to God. The situation itself is really our route to God, as long as we look at it with an eye to the truth.

The first lesson of the story of the Turkey-Prince is to be truthful about the problem and call it by the right name: madness. To live in the creation of the King, yet to be unaware of the King and our closeness to Him, is mad. The truth is that "You are the children of HaShem your God" (Deuteronomy 14:1). To leave aside our precious garments and run after the crumbs and bones of the world is to abandon the most valuable gift we have been given: eternal life. Most tragic of all is to believe that we are so enslaved to our own weaknesses that we will never be able to change.

The Turkey cannot change. The Turkey is a Turkey — that's the way God made it. But the *Prince* can change — he can get back to being himself. And so can every one of us. No matter how strong the Turkey in us is, no matter how much we may have allowed it to grow, the Turkey is ultimately nothing but an imposter. The Turkey talks inside as "I," but the authentic "I" is the Prince or Princess inside every one of us. As children of the King, we have all the power of the Infinite God, the Source of our being, to call upon.

Even if all this only makes us sigh, that is also good. "When a person is very low down and sees that he is on the bottom level and very far from God, this in itself should encourage him. This is God's way of drawing him near, because he now *realizes* that he is far from God. Before, he was so far away that he was not even aware of it. Now that he *knows* he is far away, this in itself is a sign of growing closeness. This should give him fresh life and hope and help him come back to God" (*Likutey Moharan* II:68).

"If you will learn to understand yourself," says Rebbe Nachman, "you can rid yourself of all your irrational fears and desires. You must only realize that something else within you is responsible for them. Understand this and you can overcome everything. You have free will. You can easily train your mind to avoid the thing inside you that is responsible for your irrational fears and desires" (*Rabbi Nachman's Wisdom* #83).

The Turkey is not the authentic self, but an imposter. The Prince is the authentic self. No matter how far he goes into exile, even under the table, he is always the Prince. Understanding this is the first step to emancipating ourselves from our weaknesses and coming to our true fulfillment. In the words of Rebbe Nachman: "Don't be like a big elephant or a camel that will let a little mouse pull it around by the nose — and all because of a crazy mistake, that they don't know their own power" (*Shir Na'im*).

Know your own power!!!

The Story of the Tainted Grain

There is a surviving fragment of another story of Rebbe Nachman, also on the theme of madness — only this time a madness that had not yet struck. It was just about to. A king once told his prime minister, who was also his good friend, "I see in the stars that everyone who eats from this year's grain harvest is going to go mad. What do you think we should do?" The prime minister suggested they should put aside a stock of good grain so they would not have to eat from the tainted grain.

"But it will be impossible to set aside enough good grain for everyone," the king objected. "And if we put away a stock for just the two of us, we'll be the only ones who will be sane. Everyone else will be mad, and they'll look at us and think we are the mad ones. No. We too will have to eat from this year's grain. But we'll both put a sign on our heads. I'll look at your forehead, and you'll look at mine, and when we see the sign, at least we'll remember we've gone mad" (*Rabbi Nachman's Stories* p.481).

Mad can mean many things, from fairly foolish to utterly deranged. Anyone who has seen the suffering caused by clinical insanity knows what a serious matter it can be. People who are genuinely unbalanced may be unable to function appropriately in normal situations. But it does not follow that everyone who can function normally is sane. The story of the tainted grain suggests that even whole societies can go mad. When that happens, the norms themselves are crazy.

Looking at the world today, we are very likely to agree. Vast numbers of people seem to think the whole purpose of life is purely to gratify the material ego. The rich and comfortable dream up ever more lavish and sophisticated ways of spending money, while millions go hungry and waste away. Despairing of ever achieving what they want by lawful means, alienated youngsters turn into hardened gangsters and terrorists, parading lofty slogans as they strike at innocent civilians. Meanwhile the nations of the world eye each other jealously, lecture one another about peace, and pour money and manpower into armies and weaponry.

Most of us are way beyond being shocked. If we even pay attention to the newest outrages and absurdities, we just shrug, mutter "Crazy!" and carry on with our own business. In a way, we even welcome a peppering of madness in the world around us. Looking at how overboard most of the others are may help us feel that we ourselves are basically fairly sane. Oh, we're the first to admit we may be a bit mad at times. But do we really believe that our own pet follies may be more than a joke? Yet if they're preventing us from being our real selves, aren't we hurting ourselves?

In the story of the grain, the king did not take madness lightly. He understood its devastating power to deceive, and he knew this could be catastrophic. If the crazed people of his country were to decide that he and his prime minister were the mad ones, they would very likely kill them. The wise star-gazer surely did not relish the idea of willfully submitting to madness. But death would be too high a price to pay even for staying sane during the year of the tainted crops. It would be better to join the rest of the country in their madness and hope things would change after the following harvest.

What alternative was there? Even if the king and the prime minister were to keep a stock of good grain, was there any guarantee they would be able to retain their sanity when everyone else went mad? Evidently the king had enough humility to know that even the strongest people are not necessarily immune to madness. We are fools if we think that when we look at others and find them mad, it means we ourselves are sane.

The king had the courage to face up to his own frailty. At times we may not be able to help being mad, since we are only human. But the king and his prime minister would put signs on their heads so that they would constantly be reminded they were mad. That was the honest truth, and the wise king knew that truth is worth more than anything. The lesson of the story of the tainted grain is that it's better to *know* you are mad than to be mad but think you are sane. If we deceive ourselves in our madness and tell ourselves we are sane, we can lose everything. But understanding that there's a problem is the first step toward finding the solution. Truth is the gateway to redemption.

3

The Wise Man and His Cure

None of the doctors could do anything to help him or cure him, and they gave up in despair. The king was very sad. Until a Wise Man came and said, "I can cure him."

The world has no lack of "doctors." Philosophers, therapists, gurus, syndicated columnists, workshop-instructors, the authors of self-help manuals, and many, many others, all have plenty of advice for us, free or otherwise, as to what we should do about our problems. What is the path to happiness?

Any "solution" that does not help us recover our connection with God through the Torah and mitzvot can never bring genuine healing and joy. "The Holy One created the *Yetzer HaRa*, the Evil Urge, and He created the Torah as a spice to temper it" (*Bava Batra* 16b). Only through Torah can there be any cure for the Jewish soul.

The Torah is the cure, but the question is: how can we bring ourselves to *practice* the Torah the way we should?

The literature of Mussar and Chassidut is rich in guidance about *Teshuvah*, the path of "return" to God. But the pathway itself can be daunting. The ideals of *Ahavah*, love, and *Yir'ah*, awe of God, are so exalted that we may well wonder how people like ourselves can ever hope to approach them. When we read of the great damage caused by minor transgressions, we may take a single, sweeping look at ourselves and our past lives, and fall into despair. How can we ever rectify the damage we have done, most of all to ourselves? How can we ever cleanse ourselves, let alone turn ourselves into the noble saints Mussar tells us to become?

Despair is the worst kelipah of all. It is like a black hole that swallows every positive thought or feeling, locking people into prisons of negativity and self-rejection, and driving them to recklessness and self-destruction.

"The king was very sad." God grieves over our despair, not our failures. This world was set up to make it easy to fall down. All around us are distractions and temptations; inside us is a "madman" — the Yetzer HaRa — ready to jump out at every turn. Is it any wonder if we keep falling down? But "the Holy One does not come against His creatures angrily and critically" (*Avodah Zarah* 3a). When the Rabbis said that "Teshuvah is great — it preceded the creation of the World" (*Midrash Rabbah* 1:5), they meant that the possibility of climbing out of sin and failure was built into the very plan of creation. Besides the pitfalls in this world, God, in His boundless compassion, also created everything we need to get back up. If we despair, we are pulling a black cloak over God's very goodness itself.

Does God really grieve? The purpose of the creation was for our benefit, not His — that we should lift ourselves up and actualize our spiritual potential of our own free will, in order to earn a share of God's goodness. If we fail, what does God lose? Is God "sad" the way a human being might be? Surely on God's supreme level — "in His place..." — all is "...splendor and delight" (I Chronicles 16:27).

Actually God cherishes each one of us more than we can know, more than the most loving parent cherishes a little child. It is our despair that keeps us from God. Despair is a denial that God loves us, preventing us from embarking on the path that is the greatest expression of His love: Teshuvah. Then God's ultimate purpose in the creation — the revelation of His compassion and kindness — is thwarted. Yes, God grieves over this, but in a way that is beyond human understanding. "In secrecy, My Soul weeps" (Jeremiah 13:17).

In his parable about the king who invited his subjects to a banquet (above pp. 23-4), Rabbi Nathan tells us how the king warned his subjects to keep away from anything that might possibly make them dirty. But he also told them what they could do if they slipped up by mistake: he provided the most wonderful fountains which had the power to cleanse and purify even those who had got themselves extremely dirty.

The fountains are the clear, sweet waters of the Torah of Teshuvah — the Torah of compassion that guides us even if we have strayed from the mitzvot and fallen into the worst kelipot. How can we get up? How can we clean off the dirt? How can we get back to our true selves? Where can we find these sweet, soul-reviving waters?

*

"The king was very sad." Imagine the father in his innermost private chamber, broken and distraught, crying the cry of the heart. "Please God, please help!"

And what will the parent not give to have back the lost child? "I'll give anything, pay anything, just heal my precious child!"

When everything seems black and you feel completely helpless, call out to God in your own words. Whisper. Cry out in your heart, even without words. Ask God to help you and give you what you need.

And give charity. Take even a small coin and put it aside to give to someone in need at the first opportunity. In teaching us to give charity to the poor, the Torah has an unusual turn of phrase. “Open open your hand...” (Deuteronomy 15:8). The Hebrew root meaning “open” appears twice in succession in the same verse. When we open our hand, it causes something else to open as well. The act of charity opens a channel of love into the creation, causing the gate that has been closed to us to open up, providing us with an exit from our darkness. (See *Likutey Moharan* II:4,2.)

*

The sweet, cleansing waters are the teachings of the true Wise Men, the outstanding Torah guides — human beings who actually embody the wisdom of the Torah in their lives. Through their teachings, and by their personal example, they show us how we can embody it in *our* lives.

The true Wise Men’s ability to connect with us comes from the fact that despite all their spiritual achievements, they are not angels but real human beings, just like us. They too have had to face the challenges of the human condition, only they succeeded in mastering themselves. They know exactly what we face and can therefore show us the best way to overcome our challenges.

“This can be understood by thinking of an amusement maze of the kind found in the stately homes of the aristocracy. Tall hedges are planted to make up a series of walls, between which run a medley of complicated, seemingly identical paths. The object of the game is to reach a tower standing in the middle. Some of the paths lead directly to the tower, but others are deceptive and take you away from it. However when you are actually walking on any given path, it is impossible to determine if it is the right or the wrong one. All the paths look the same. The only way you can know is if you have already found your way through the maze successfully and reached the tower.

"Someone standing on the tower is in a position to see all the pathways and knows which are right and which are wrong. He can tell the people down in the maze exactly which way they should go. Those who are willing to believe him will get to the right destination. But someone who refuses to believe him and insists on following his own eyes will undoubtedly stay lost and never get to the tower" (*Mesilat Yesharim* Ch. 3).

Who is the Wise Man? Through the entire story of the Turkey-Prince, Rebbe Nachman does not characterize him at all. He simply tells us what he *did*. We may be curious to know more about the Wise Man — and certainly we need to be able to identify him, so as to know to whom we should go to learn the compassionate Torah of Teshuvah. However, the private personality of the Wise Man is of little significance to us. What is important is what he is coming to teach us. This we learn from examining what he actually *does* — the practical steps he takes to cure the Prince.

Many lessons can be gleaned from his every word and move. Some of these lessons we will explore in the chapters to come. Right now, let us consider some of the more general features of the Wise Man's approach.

Humility

In a sense, the Wise Man doesn't have a personality. He seems to show up out of nowhere. He puts aside his own clothes of splendor, sacrificing his dignity in order to lower himself to the very place where the Prince is. Even when the Prince asks him who he is, he side-steps the question.

The Wise Man is the model of self-effacement. The foundation of his wisdom is humility. "Wisdom comes out of *AYiN*, nothingness" (Job 28:12). Obviously this does not mean that wisdom comes from sitting around idly doing nothing. It comes to teach us that in order to open ourselves to genuine wisdom, we have to quieten the lower self that is constantly pushing itself forward, saying "*ANiY*" — "I... me... my...." We have to turn *ANiY* into *AYiN* — nothingness.

People have all kinds of ideas and theories of their own, but real wisdom begins with the admission that we ourselves ultimately know nothing. We can never be certain whether or not we are right in what we think. God alone knows the truth. God alone knows what is really good for us. It follows that God's Wisdom — the Torah — is the only certain guide in life. To solve our Turkey problems, the first thing we need is the humility to admit that we have to turn to the Torah and its teachers for help and guidance.

Life is so rich in opportunities of every kind, especially for spiritual growth and deepening our connection with God. However, much of the time we simply do not see these opportunities because our existing involvements and preconceptions stand in the way. Rather than always trying to force reality to fit into a rigid framework of existing views and opinions, learn to avoid hasty conclusions about people and circumstances and listen for the messages life is trying to give *you*.

Faith

The Wise Man comes along and boldly announces: "I can cure the Prince." What makes him so confident? All the other doctors had tried and failed. How can he be so optimistic?

The Wise Man's optimism is an off-shoot of his humility. When he says "I can cure him," he does not mean this in the egotistical sense of "through *my* strength and the power of *my* hands" (Deuteronomy 8:17). The Wise Man knows that no matter what he himself may do, everything depends upon God. When the Wise Man says "I," it is as one who is always seeking to efface his own ego and give himself and all his faculties to God's service. Any power he possesses is the power of the Torah, which is God's supreme wisdom. The Wise Man has complete faith in God and the Torah. This is what gives him his confidence.

Indeed, God is completely dependable. God wants good. And God has the power to do anything. God wants the Prince — the soul — cured, and God has a way to make even what seems impossible possible. "Even when things seem to be at their worst, there is a way that the situation can turn around to one's full advantage" (Rebbe Nachman).

We too must believe that no matter what condition we may have fallen to, God's real desire is that we should reach our complete fulfillment. We must have faith that God has the power to bring us to it even *with* our many flaws and weaknesses, even if until now we may have failed time after time. We must have faith in the power of the Torah, and trust that by following its pathways we will come to true goodness and happiness.

Finding the Good

How many doctors and psychiatrists look over at their patients from their high places and chillingly invite them to "tell me about your problems." Not so the Wise Man. In his humility, he takes himself right down to where the Prince is, there under the table. The Wise Man will only be able to cure the Prince when he can evoke a response from his buried inner self. To do this, the Wise Man must first get to the truth of the Prince's situation. The Wise Man does not spin lofty theories about it. He projects himself directly into it, empathizing with the Prince in every way he can. The Wise Man removes his own "clothes" — his preconceptions and prejudgments — sits down next to the Prince, and starts getting to know him.

The honest search for truth is the key to redemption. It is no good living with illusions about ourselves. In order to achieve anything in life, we have to be realistic. One of the most important things we can learn from the Wise Man is *how* to be truthful.

If the Wise Man had looked at nothing but the pathetic external appearance of the naked Prince, squealing like a Turkey and grobbing around in the dirt, he might well have thrown *his* hands up in despair, just like the other doctors. But because of his faith in God's omnipresent goodness, he refuses to be discouraged by surface appearances, and determinedly searches for the good in the Prince. The Wise Man *knows* that beneath his Turkey exterior, the Prince's royal essence is unchanged, albeit hidden. All that is needed is to awaken it, gently but surely.

We need this same faith when we look at ourselves. We may see much that we do not like, but we must also search for the underlying good within us. We must be honest with ourselves about ourselves, but the truth does not have to hurt. Humility does not mean you have to eye yourself scathingly, condemning yourself and everything you do as worthless. True humility is to acknowledge your real worth and know that it is God's gift to you. God created everything, and God is good. Therefore good is to be found everywhere and in every person. No one is ever so far gone as to be beyond redemption.

Similarly, when thinking about the various problems you face, remember that they must have good in them somewhere. God has the power to turn everything around to your advantage. While it is foolish to minimize genuine difficulties, you should try to search for the positive factors as well. If things go against you, or your efforts seem to be frustrated, don't be discouraged. If what you want is God's will, failure is only a preparation for success: take it as a sign that you should make greater efforts. And if, after all your efforts, you still do not succeed, have faith that whatever God wants will ultimately be for the best.

Patience

The Wise Man's faith in God gives him one of the most important qualities he needs to cure the Prince: patience. Since he is sure God is good and constantly helping, the Wise Man does not insist on having things exactly the way he might want them to be. He is content to accept things the way God wants them to be.

Right now the Prince is thinking and acting like a Turkey. Okay. That's the way it is. Moaning about the situation, or wishing it were different, won't help. The question is: what practical steps can be taken to bring the situation nearer to the way we would like it to be. What you can change, change. What you cannot, live with as best you can, until such time as you *can* do something about it.

People often feel that if they cannot achieve everything they want, it is not worth trying to achieve anything. This is a mistake. Things do not have to be "all or nothing." The Wise Man is prepared to live with imperfection even while striving to make progress. Things can be "both... and..." "You can wear a shirt and still be a Turkey." "You can wear trousers and still be a Turkey." "You can eat good food and still be a Turkey."

Rebbe Nachman does not waste a single word in telling this story, so it is noteworthy that he repeats this idea *three times*. It is one of the most important lessons of the whole story.

When you want to change yourself in any way, be realistic about what you are capable of right now and what is presently beyond you. Be patient with yourself and go steadily. You may be very ambitious, but it is impossible to transform yourself all in one step. If you undertake a heavier load than you can manage, you may end up accomplishing nothing. If you try to change too many things in your life at once, you may not be able to cope with all the changes, and risk ending up worse off than when you started. To make genuine progress, be content to take modest, steady steps, one after the other. This is the way to make solid gains and build up your strength.

As you try to change, you are likely to see aspects of "the old you" surfacing repeatedly. Don't let this discourage you. Carry on with your work in the areas you have decided to concentrate on for the time being. Rather than allow yourself to be depressed because some of what you want to shed still clings to you, take delight in the new, better you that is emerging.

Simplicity

All the other doctors had failed. Perhaps some of them had been willing to compromise and settle for less than a complete recovery for the Prince. Even so, none of them had been able to do anything for him. The Wise Man, on the other hand, wanted nothing less than perfection. He was determined to cure the Prince completely. Despite his patience and willingness to accept slow, gradual improvement, the Wise Man was the most ambitious of all. How did he succeed?

Essentially, through simplicity. Simplicity is another facet of humility. One admits one's limitations, and instead of attempting things that are too difficult, one only ever tries to take simple steps. Said Rebbe Nachman: "The greatest art of all is to be simple" (*Likutey Moharan* II:44). The point is brought out in another of his stories.

"There was a certain king who sent his son to distant places to study. Eventually the son returned to the king's palace, fully versed in all the arts and sciences. One day the king gave his son instructions to take a particular stone which was as big as a millstone and carry it up to the top floor of the palace. Needless to say, the stone was so big and heavy, the prince couldn't shift it in the slightest. He was very depressed.

"Eventually the king said to his son, 'Did you really imagine I would tell you to do the impossible? Would I tell you to try to carry this stone up just as it is? Even with all your learning, how could you do it? What you should do is take a hammer and smash the stone into little pieces. This way you will be able to bring them up one by one and so get the whole stone up to the top floor' " (*Tzaddik* #441).

Breaking the Whole into Small Parts

Sometimes our personalities are like a heavy stone. We are asked to lift up our hearts and bring Godly awareness into every aspect of our being. "Know this day and take to your heart that HaShem is the only God in heaven above and on the earth below" (Deuteronomy 4:39). But the heart is a "heart of stone" (Ezekiel 36:26). The only way to lift up the heart is by taking a hammer, as it were, and breaking our major goals, ambitions and projects into small, practicable tasks.

The Wise Man wanted to cure the Turkey-Prince completely. His ultimate goal was perfection. But when he contemplated his goal he said to himself, "That's impossible to achieve all at once. It involves so much, it's overwhelming. I am unable to do hard, complicated things. I can only do simple, easy things. I have to break the long-term goal into small, manageable steps."

The Wise Man analyzes the ultimate goal into its component sub- and sub-sub-goals, and works out an order of priorities. What will it mean for the Prince to be cured? He must behave normally, sitting up at the table. To sit up at the table will involve eating the royal food and wearing his royal clothes.

The first goal, then, is to get the Prince to put his clothes on. But that's still too complicated. You'll never get him to put on all his clothes in one go. This sub-goal must also be divided into its component parts. The Prince has to put on his shirt, his trousers, his socks, his shoes... The Wise Man breaks everything down into simple, manageable, steps, which he then proceeds to take one by one. "He put on a shirt."

True, you must be patient and wait when necessary. But when the time is ripe you have to *act*. People often sit doing nothing because the task they face seems so forbidding. Simplify larger goals into a series of small, easy steps. What is the next step? Go ahead and take it.

Time

To cure the Prince, the Wise Man stopped everything else he may have been doing and made the necessary *time*. Not that he *wasted* time. When the moment came for him to act — to put on the shirt and the trousers, or eat the royal food — he went in like an arrow and did what he had to do. But one of the most important parts of the whole cure was to get to know the Prince intimately and establish a good working relationship with him. This could only be achieved by sitting with him patiently for lengthy periods without being in any hurry to get up.

No matter what you want to accomplish in life — whether a specific task or the ultimate goal of finding fulfillment and happiness — you must give it time. Not only the time required to take whatever practical steps may be necessary. Even more important is the time you invest working out *which* steps to take and *how* you are going to achieve what you want.

People have all kinds of ideas about things they would *like* to achieve, ranging from simple, everyday goals to grandiose, far-reaching ambitions. Many of our ideas are completely unrealistic — and we may know it. They are fantasies which will never materialize: they never leave the realm of thought. Others may be practicable. Potentially they could be realized. We may even want to realize them very much, or think we do. Yet for some reason we never succeed. They never become actual. Sometimes it doesn't matter. Ideas are free! They can be fun! But what if the goals are important?

Success means making the transition from potential to actual. The goal starts off as an idea. It may be clear or vague. To make it actual, the idea has to be developed and acted on. What is the key to success?

Many of the things we do in our lives are quite routine: we don't need to think too much about them. Other things require a more conscious effort. This is especially the case if we want to change something — whether in ourselves or in the outside world — or create something new. The more ambitious the goal, the more likely it will require a conscious effort.

Just wanting to succeed is not enough. Wishing for something will not bring it about. What is the difference between wishing and willing? There is no magic about willpower. Some people manage to get things done. It is not that they have some mysterious power of wanting which automatically makes their goals come about. They work. But hard work alone is not sufficient. In order for our efforts to succeed, they have to be properly attuned to the goal we are aiming for. We have to be clear what our goal really is. Time, energy and other resources are all limited. To achieve one goal may necessitate giving up others. We may have to moderate some of our desires and ambitions. Having decided on the goal, we then have to take account of all the relevant circumstances, and work out exactly what we will have to do, step by step, in order to accomplish it. All this requires careful thought and planning. And this takes *time*. Taking the time to do this will only *save* you time in the long run.

Time is precious. We all know that. Time is life. We all have to die, and our time in this life is limited. We want to make the most of it. In fact, we may want to get so much out of it that we feel we are too busy to be able to stop for a moment to think about how we're using our time. The result? How often do we get ourselves into situations which cause us the most colossal wastes of time, leaving us frustrated and disappointed? Sometimes a real crisis develops, finally forcing us to try to work things out. Only by then it could be too late. Nobody knows how long he will be healthy or when he will die.Why wait? Time is more precious than money. Time is love. All the good ideas in the world will not help you unless you take the time to put them into practice. Giving yourself time — to work out your goals, analyze what's holding you back, decide how to overcome the obstacles and achieve what you want — is the greatest love you can show yourself.

The Wise One Within Us

In the story, the Wise Man and the Turkey-Prince are two separate characters. However it is also possible to see them as symbolic of two separate facets of ourselves. We may be Princes or Princesses with our own Turkey problems, but we also have a Wise One within ourselves — a level of our being from where we are able to observe ourselves calmly and clearly, without self-deception, to know what is really right for us to do, and to take ourselves in hand and do it.

To reach our true fulfillment, we need to strengthen this Wise One within us. We do this by studying the teachings of the outstanding Torah guides at every opportunity, and asking seriously how they apply to us and how we can put them into practice.

"With intelligence," said Rebbe Nachman, "you can stand up to all human weaknesses... Everyone has the potential of wisdom. All that is necessary is to actualize it... You may have succumbed to desire and sinned in many ways. You may have damaged your intellect, making it confused and weak, but you still have some intelligence, and with this alone you can overcome all human weaknesses. One grain of intelligence can overcome the world and all its temptations" (*Rabbi Nachman's Wisdom* #51).

4

The Art of Sitting

The Wise Man took off all *his* clothes, and sat down under the table...

"The only reason why people are far from God and don't come closer to Him is because they don't have yishuv ha-da'at, *calm and clarity, and they don't sit and think. The main thing is to try to sit calmly and think carefully where all the bodily desires, psychological cravings and material involvements of this world ultimately lead to, and then one will certainly come back to God."*

Likutey Moharan II:10

The Wise Man went under the table, and the very first thing he did — his first lesson — was just to sit there. You might have thought he would have been anxious to get started and take the first steps in his plan to cure the Prince. In fact, sitting *was* the first step.

Indeed, if you think about the story as a whole, you notice that most of the time the Wise Man took to cure the Prince was spent just sitting with him (interspersed with pulling at crumbs and bones, yelping like a turkey, chatting etc.) The action — putting on the shirts and trousers, and eating the royal food — accounted for only a small part of the total time needed for the cure.

If you want to think clearly, you have to be able to sit. To find lasting happiness, you must take time to think. You need to sit down and calmly work out exactly how you want to live.

You have to think about who you are and what you want, and what your real goals should be. Then you have to examine the various things you are actually doing in your life, and ask whether they are leading you toward your goals or in fact keeping you back from them. You have to work out practical programs for attaining your goals and ambitions. It takes time to think about all this. This is not something you can do in one session. You should invest in regular, undisturbed, private sessions with yourself in order to do it properly. This could be the single most important thing you do in order to fulfill yourself in life and find HaShem.

"It is a gift," says Rebbe Nachman, "if one is able to sit calmly for a time each day to survey one's life and work through any feelings of regret, etc. Not everyone manages to attain a state of calm contemplation for a time each day: the days pass and are gone, and one is too busy to sit down and settle one's mind even once in one's entire life.

"You must make a determined effort to set aside special times to reflect carefully on everything you are involved with in your life. Examine yourself and your behavior, and ask yourself if the various things you are doing are in fact in your own best long-term interests.

"It is because people do not give themselves time to settle themselves that they go through life mindlessly. Even when one attains some clarity and insight, they tend to be very short-lived, passing quickly. Even the little clarity and insight one does have are not strong and incisive. This is the reason why people don't understand the madness of this material world. If one had clear, strong insight, one would understand that everything is madness and vanity" (*Rabbi Nachman's Wisdom* #47).

Yishuv Ha-Da'at

To think calmly, you must be able to sit calmly. But try it! Find somewhere private, have a watch or a clock handy to check the time, and sit yourself down in a chair for twenty minutes. Now see what happens.

How did it go? Were you able to think? Did you have a clear idea how you wanted to spend the twenty minutes? Or did you sit there not knowing what you were supposed to be doing? Did you get bored and restless? Did you want to get up and do something? Did you want to turn on the radio, play some music, read something, eat a snack, make a phone call, get back to work...?

Thought is in the mind and heart. To be able to think clearly, you must not be distracted. The reason for going somewhere private is obviously to minimize outside distractions. But even when you find somewhere that you can be alone, the most lively and active source of distractions in your life comes with you: your body. The body expresses itself in its own language: feeling uncomfortable, shifting, trying to get comfortable, becoming restless, etc. In addition, the body also talks loud and clear in the mind and the heart, competing with our efforts to think, understand, and follow our chains of thought and feeling through to the end. Bang in the middle: "I'm hungry!" "I'm sleepy!" "I have to run an errand... make a call..." etc. etc. etc.

In fact the body and its faithful ambassador, the Animal Soul, are so active and powerful in most people's lives that we may not be able to discipline ourselves to make the time to sit down and think *at all*. We tend to plan things only partially (if we even plan), and jump into action on impulse. Often we are divided over what we really want: the Prince wants one thing, the Turkey something else. Instead of pursuing our goals single-mindedly, we allow ourselves to be distracted and side-tracked. Even the slightest obstacles often throw us off course — be they obstacles from the outside world or those from within ourselves. We then become discouraged by these set-backs and failures. Either we're so busy and tense that we don't have *time* to think things out, or so disheartened and depressed, we don't *want* to think about anything.

In order to cure the mad Turkey-Prince, the Wise Man started with sitting, because the ability to sit calmly is one of the most important prerequisites of clear-headedness. To be able to think clearly and work things out, the body has to be comfortable and quiet. The Hebrew term for a calm, settled state of mind, *yishuv ha-da'at*, is thus bound up with the concept of sitting. *Da'at*, often translated as knowledge, refers to awareness or consciousness, whether intellectual, emotional, meditative, intuitive or some combination. The word *yishuv* is a noun from the Hebrew root *yashav*, meaning to sit, rest or dwell.

The verb *yashav* also has a transitive form, *le-yashev*, which means to *cause* someone or something to sit or dwell. (A good English equivalent would be the word "settle," which can be used both intransitively — "one settles in a place" — and transitively — "to settle someone somewhere.") *Le-yashev et ha-da'at* thus means to settle the mind — to prepare the mind to receive *da'at*. A *yishuv* is a settlement, and *yishuv ha-da'at* means the settlement of consciousness — the settled frame of mind.

The first preparation for this is to physically sit comfortably. The Rabbis bring out the connection between calm clarity of mind and sitting in their comment on the opening phrases of the Book of Esther: "And it was in the days of Achashverosh...when King Achashverosh was *sitting* on his royal throne... in the third year of his reign..." (Esther 1:1-3). "Why are we told that he was *sitting*?" ask the Rabbis. "It signifies that his *mind was now settled*" (*Megilah* 21a).

Sitting in this sense not only signifies the physical act of seating the body quietly. It suggests the whole principle of taking a break from the active business of day to-day living in order to think and work things out. The Hebrew word for sitting, *shevet*, is thus connected with the idea of *Shabbat*, when we pause and sit back from our workaday activities in order to cultivate the spirit.

Bilbul Ha-Da'at

The opposite of *yishuv ha-da'at* is *bilbul ha-da'at*. *Bilbul* means confusion, turbulence and disorder: the state of *bilbul ha-da'at*, is one in which it is impossible to focus clearly on a single idea or follow through a train of thought. The mind darts around uncontrollably from one distraction to another. Compulsive thoughts, inner urges, impulses, fears and worries compete for attention with an endless succession of outside distractions. Or one may feel so weighed down with heaviness, sluggishness, depression and the like that one's entire consciousness seems somehow clouded.

Bilbul ha-da'at is the mental equivalent of bodily tension. In a state of bodily tension, muscles are contracted in excess of the needs of the action in hand. You may be trying to do one thing, while consciously or unconsciously your body is also busy with something else — something that puts it at odds with you. Similarly, in a state of *bilbul ha-da'at* you may be trying to direct your mind one way, only to find yourself repeatedly straying along other pathways of thought, feeling and desire. The Godly Soul is reaching out in one direction, but the Animal Soul keeps on interfering.

Not all tension is bad. Just as any bodily activity requires contraction of the appropriate muscles, similarly, effective mental activity requires *at*-tention and full involvement of the relevant faculties. Bad tension is tension in excess of, or contrary to, what is needed.

Quiet Sitting

How can we free ourselves from the unnecessary tension and constriction that prevent us from thinking clearly and acting decisively in pursuit of our goals?

It is important to understand that bodily tensions and mental turbulence are often deeply rooted in one or more of a whole variety of physical, emotional, spiritual and environmental factors. The tensions generated by contemporary life and work conditions, and the various problems we encounter every day, often combine to reinforce whole ranges of powerful inner barriers that have been built up from earliest childhood and through the course of our upbringing, education and later experiences. In the long run, the only way to attain deep and lasting release is through an extended process of self-understanding and self-transformation.

Nevertheless, there is a simple, practical procedure that can help break the vicious cycle of tension and constriction, making it possible to confront the deeper roots of the problem. Simply sitting quietly in a chair in a relaxed state can free your mind and help you get in touch with your thoughts, feelings and creative powers. One by one, you let go of your tensions and they drop away, leaving you with a blessed feeling of profound calm, liberation, clarity, enhanced sensitivity and alertness. Sights, sounds, tastes, smells, feelings, all become more vivid. It becomes easier to think, understand, remember things and work out problems. New insights may result, together with a growing awareness of the spiritual dimension of life.

The benefits of relaxed sitting are so great that it is well worth devoting time to learn the art. At first you may have to concentrate more on the technique of bodily relaxation, but once you have mastered it you will be able to enter the relaxed state very rapidly and have full enjoyment of the intellectual, emotional and spiritual benefits it can bring.

Learning the Technique

Allow about twenty minutes for your initial sessions in order to give yourself time to experience deep relaxation. It is not a good idea to practice when you are in a hurry as this will inhibit you from fully relaxing. Don't practice soon after meals or when you are tired, as you are likely to fall asleep. Your sessions should be restful and will give you new energy, but if you try to use them solely as a form of rest when tired you will be unlikely to have the full experience of release and enhanced consciousness.

Choose a quiet place where you can be alone, preferably with subdued lighting, minimum distractions, and no background music. The room should have a comfortable temperature and be free of stuffiness, draughts and unpleasant associations. Arrange to have someone answer the telephone, or else disconnect it or use an answering machine. Wear comfortable clothing. Before you begin, relieve yourself if necessary, and if you like, freshen up by washing your hands and face. It may be helpful to do some gentle stretching and loosening movements before you start.

The sitting position is the most conducive to the mental alertness desired for clear thinking. Reclining positions may be appropriate for purely bodily relaxation. Rebbe Nachman mentions lying down with closed eyes for half an hour as an excellent form of rest (*Avanehah Barzel* #33). However lying on one's back is not an appropriate posture for spiritual work. One can easily become drowsy and fall asleep. (See also *Shulchan Aruch, Even HaEzer* 23:3.)

Choose an upright chair with a flat, firm seat, or, if you prefer, an armchair which gives support to the back of your head. Your feet may either be flat on the floor about six inches apart, or crossed at the ankles if you prefer. Sit well back on the seat so that the pelvis and lower back are supported (if necessary, place a small cushion against the lower back). Sit erect but not stiffly: allow your body to lengthen and expand naturally.

Your head should ride on the top of your neck in light alignment with the neck and torso, as if an invisible straight line extends downwards from the center of the skull through the spinal column. This way the head will be well supported on the neck, and will not fall forwards or backwards as you relax more and more deeply. The hands may be cupped in the lap or rest on the thighs, with the fingers loose.

Progressive Relaxation

There are two solvents that remove tension from muscles: awareness and trust. You shine your awareness like a flashlight on each part of your body in turn. First you focus your attention on what you are feeling there. Then you relax — by trusting HaShem. Relaxation is essentially simple. It comes through *non*-doing. You just *let go* of tension. Instead of trying to hold your muscles tight, trust in HaShem and hand the control over to Him, limb by limb. He will take care of you and fill your body with new energy.

When first learning relaxation, it is best to begin by tensing each group of muscles in turn and becoming conscious of how they feel when tense. Then release them and hand them back to HaShem, experiencing how they feel when relaxed. Later on, when you have learned the technique, you will no longer need to tense your muscles first: you will have the sensitivity to know when muscles are tense, and will get into the habit of handing them over to HaShem.

Close your eyes and slowly take a couple of deep breaths. Focus your attention on how your breathing feels. Your breathing will soon settle into a steady rhythm. After a few moments, make a tight fist with your right hand, hold for about five seconds and focus your mind on the feeling of tension. Unclinch and let the tension flow out, noting how different it feels.

Now do the same with your left hand (left-handed people may want to start with this hand). Then do the same with the muscles in your right upper arm (biceps) and shoulder, and then with your left upper arm and shoulder. Now move your beam of attention to your feet. Start with your right foot (or left if you prefer) and curl your toes. Then relax. Do the same with your other foot. Now contract the calf muscle at the rear of the lower right leg (if it begins to cramp, stop at once and rest for a minute, then try again less strongly). Then contract the calf of the left leg. Then relax. Now work on each of your thighs and buttocks in turn.

It is important to learn to relax the abdomen as it is an area that we often unconsciously tense in response to fear and anxiety, etc. Empty the lungs of air, pull the abdominal muscles back towards the spine, and release. Become aware of tensions in your lower back by arching your spine while keeping your pelvis and shoulders down, then lower your backbone to its resting position. Squeeze your shoulder blades together to tense the upper back, then release. Now take your shoulders forward, round your back and narrow your chest. And release. Shrug your shoulders, then allow them to drop down so that your arms seem to dangle from them.

The neck is another part of the body which reflects inner tensions. Tense your neck muscles and release. Finally, move your attention to your face. The facial muscles directly reflect your feelings, and may be the hardest to relax. Tighten your jaw muscles by clenching your teeth. And relax. Press your lips together, and release. Curl up your tongue and press it up and back against the roof of your mouth, and release. Keeping your eyes closed, swing your eyes as far as you can to the right, the left, up and down. And relax. Now bring your eyebrows hard down and squeeze your eyes tightly shut. And release. Finally, frown as hard as you can, and release the muscles of the forehead and scalp.

Physical Relaxation, Mental Attention

Next, take a few slow breaths, inhaling deeply and then allowing the air to drain slowly out of the lungs until you reach the natural end of the exhalation. Your body will automatically begin the next inhalation. Now hand your breathing over to Hashem. With each breath, allow all the air to drain out of the lungs, letting the exhalation come to an end by itself. Then let the inhalation take place by *it*self. Let your body breathe completely naturally, without interfering.

For the next few moments leave everything as it is. Enjoy the feeling of complete relaxation and bodily passivity. For the moment, do not try to direct your mind. Simply notice that you can be completely relaxed physically while mentally aware and attentive. At first the sensation may be strange. However, as you get used to it you will find that in these precious moments, time seems to stand still. If you choose, you can learn to direct your mind in virtually any way you wish. With experience, you will find that you can have some of your clearest understanding, creative thinking and inspiration in this state.

Finally, as you feel you would like to get up, think how you have enjoyed the peace and tranquillity of your session. Thank HaShem for the experience. Express your gratitude in your heart, or whisper some words of thanks. Now take four or five deep breaths. Start moving your fingers and toes gently, then your arms and legs, and, when you feel ready, get up.

Do not be surprised if you do not attain complete or lasting relaxation, clarity and insight during your first sessions. Even at the best of times, states of clarity and insight come and go. Spiritual awakening and insight are by nature spontaneous, and cannot be forced. You can make all the necessary preparations for a good relaxation session, only to find that you are as tightly locked in your tensions, worries, nagging thoughts and emotions as ever — perhaps more so, because now you *know* how tense you are!

Relaxation alone will not alleviate the underlying causes of mental constriction. However it can help to *ease* our tensions and other inhibiting factors sufficiently to put us into the right frame of mind for going deep into ourselves, working on the root causes, and making the far-reaching changes in habits and lifestyle that may be necessary if we really want to attain our true spiritual potential.

Applications

As you gain experience in the practice of quiet sitting, you should acquire a greater understanding of where your body tends to get the most tense and under what conditions. Knowing the likely locations of tension will enable you to relax much more quickly. Eventually the relaxation itself becomes less of an exercise, giving you greater flexibility in entering and using the relaxed state for the specific mental and spiritual work you want to do.

When you reach this stage, there is no longer any need to be rigorous about the length of your sessions, or maintaining a completely motionless position. Sometimes you may want a short relaxation period of just a few minutes. Other times you may want to sit for longer periods of contemplation. If, when sitting, you find you are getting restless but still want to continue, gently move around and stretch a bit, and then resume. If you find you are getting drowsy, take a few deep breaths and then continue with the work you want to do.

There are many ways of using this relaxation exercise to enhance your life and activities. A session of quiet sitting first thing in the morning can help you greet HaShem joyously and then face your day with greater calm and inner strength. After periods of intense activity, five to ten minutes of deep relaxation will enable you to recuperate your strength and continue with whatever you have to do next with greater poise and attention. At times when you are feeling particularly tense and nervous, a period of quiet sitting can help you unravel your thoughts and feelings, opening you to valuable insights about what lies at the root of the tension. If you have a particular problem or issue that needs working out, try thinking about it while sitting in the relaxed state.

The relaxation technique may serve as an invaluable preliminary to work tasks of various kinds, and especially to *Hisbodidus* — the regular meditation on one's life and activities that will be the subject of a full discussion later on (Chapter 6). Another important application would be as a preparation for Torah study and prayer. Thus we find that "the pious men of old would pause for a time before they prayed, in order to direct their hearts to their Father in Heaven" (*Berachot* 30b). Similarly, the sixteenth-century Kabbalistic master, Rabbi Chaim Vital, mentions a state of complete bodily relaxation as a precondition for deep meditation: "Close your eyes and strip your mind of all worldly thoughts, as if your soul has gone out of your body and you are devoid of all physical feelings" (*Sha'arey Kedushah* 3:8).

The Art of the Pause

After learning how to attain clarity and direction during periods of quiet sitting, the next stage is to cultivate this same state of mind in moment-to-moment living. The way to do this is by making a habit of taking short breaks and pauses of a minute or two, or at times even a few seconds, as you go through your daily activities.

Rhythms of activity and rest are an integral part of our make-up. We are awake, and then we go to sleep; bouts of activity, mental and physical, are followed by periods of rest and relaxation. Our moment-to-moment living is a subtle mesh in which activity and quiescence are constantly giving way to one another as successive thoughts and feelings, words, actions and movements come into being and pass away. Pausing is something we do quite naturally as we go about our lives.

We have the power to make conscious adjustments to our rhythms of activity so as to improve the quality of our performance. The tendency to delay or procrastinate over what we have to do is something we have to fight against if we want to succeed at anything. But creative breaks and pauses are far from being a lazy indulgence. They are a vital part of the process of achievement in all spheres.

Sometimes a few seconds may be all you need, sometimes a little more, perhaps a minute or two, and sometimes longer. How you use the time — whether for rapid relaxation, taking a few deep breaths, focusing on what you are doing, offering a prayer for help, etc. — depends on your special needs at each moment, whether before, during or after your various activities. Even when you're in a hurry, the best way to do things is not necessarily by rushing. With practice, even split-second pauses will be enough to release you from tension and prepare you for the next phase of the activity you are involved in, giving you a sense of calm and confidence even when working under great pressure.

Pausing is of special importance in all kinds of spiritual work. "When undertaking an act of spiritual devotion or a mitzvah, one should not enter into it suddenly and hurriedly, because the mind will not be settled and it will be impossible to reflect on what one is doing... One should take one's time preparing the heart, entering a state of contemplation in which one reflects on what one is going to do and before Whom. By concentrating in this way, it becomes easy to throw aside extraneous thoughts and motivations and focus one's heart on the correct and desired intention" (*Mesilat Yesharim* Ch.17, and see *Chayey Adam, Laws of Prayers and Blessings* 68:25.)

Before you recite a blessing or a prayer, pause briefly to focus your mind. When you are about to perform a mitzvah, stop for a moment and think about what you are going to do. The larger prayer books include various short meditations said before putting on the Tallit and Tefilin, entering the synagogue, reciting certain prayers, studying Torah, and fulfilling other mitzvot. (See *Yesod ve-Shoresh Ha-Avodah, passim.*) During hisbodidus, while saying your prayers, or during a study session, pause from time to time to relax and clear your mind. Remind yourself of your goals and refocus on what you are doing. When you finish your sessions and work tasks, etc., take a minute or two just to relax and let your mind range over what you have been doing, and thank HaShem for His goodness and wonders.

5

Crumbs and Bones

The Wise Man also pulled at crumbs and bones...

"Bodily health and well-being is one of the pathways to God, since it is virtually impossible to understand or know anything of the Creator if one is sick. Therefore one must avoid anything that may harm the body, and follow practices that are conducive to health and healing."

Rambam, *Mishneh Torah, Hilchot De'ot* 4:1

So far, even the subtle delights of quiet, contemplative sitting had little attraction for the Prince compared to the excitement of pulling at crumbs and bones. In order to bring him back, step by step, to being himself, the first thing the Wise Man did was to go right down to where the Prince was. The Wise Man also pulled at crumbs and bones — and he no doubt did this in his own wise way. For showing the Prince *how* to be a Turkey — how to live in his body — was one of the most important lessons the Wise Man had to teach him.

Body, Mind and Soul

Only when we sit down to try to clear our minds do we begin to realize how far we are from real clarity. People who experiment with the practice of quiet sitting frequently find themselves struggling with waves of drowsiness, restlessness, nervous tension and the like. Most of us suffer from similar problems in the course of other activities as well, but we may be so used to them that we just discount them. Not until we sit down and try to attain a state of heightened awareness do we become aware of their draining effect, not only on our efforts to be calm and think clearly, but on our lives in general. We may then wonder if there is anything we can do about them.

Among the many physiological and psychological factors that may contribute to such problems, our patterns of eating, breathing and exercise (or the lack of it) are among the most significant. The relationship between actual physical disorders and states of mind does not come within the scope of this work. However many people who are apparently in fairly good health find that problems such as lack of stamina, mental cloudiness, inability to concentrate, high tension, moodiness, negativity and depression, etc. tend to interfere with their efforts to lead a more spiritual life.

Sometimes these problems may be bound up with bad eating and breathing habits, or inadequate exercise. Even minor adjustments in these patterns can have a marked effect on physical stamina, mental clarity, efficiency and productivity, spirituality and general enjoyment of life.

Eating

"A righteous person eats for the satisfaction of his soul."

Proverbs 13:25

As soon as those luscious tid-bits would start raining down from the table, it was all go for the Turkey-Prince... darting here, racing there, snatching, grabbing, stuffing, gobbling... Gastronomic bliss is the acme of Turkey life.

The Prince's picking at crumbs and bones was more than just a symptom of his madness. It was one of the main factors keeping him locked into it. His compulsive feeding habits were just like a Turkey's, which in itself must have made him feel like one. More than that, the crumbs and bones and other junk food making up the Prince's diet merely provided more fuel for the Turkey states of consciousness that were gripping his mind, clouding over all awareness of his true essence.

In depicting how the crazy Prince spent his time pulling at crumbs and bones, Rebbe Nachman was emphasizing the relationship between bad eating habits and the lack of spirituality. "Eating properly subdues the tendency towards folly, enhancing one's intellectual and spiritual faculties... But when one over-indulges and eats like a glutton, folly will get the upper hand and overcome one's intellectual and spiritual faculties" (*Likutey Moharan* I:17,3).

Our culture is interested in the effect of diet on bodily health almost to the point of obsession. Far less attention, however, is paid to the effect of diet on the health of the mind and soul. Correct nutrition is crucial to the health of the body, and bodily health is a vital factor in mental and spiritual health. Moreover, the food we eat is not merely a physical substance. Everything in the creation contains "Divine sparks" — spiritual energy. When we eat and digest our food, not only does the body extract the substances it needs to build and fuel itself. At the same time subtle energies in the food rise to the brain and soul, influencing our states of mind, our thoughts, feelings, words and actions.

"Our states of mind," says Rebbe Nachman, "directly correspond to the food we eat. When the body is pure, the mind is clear and one is able to think properly and know what to do in life. But impurities in the body cause putrid gases to rise up to the brain, throwing the mind into such confusion that it becomes impossible to think straight" (*Likutey Moharan* I:61,1). So direct is the effect of what we eat on how we think and feel that Rebbe Nachman, speaking about the relationship of food and dreams, tells us that "if a person were to eat his second spoonful before his first, he would have a different dream" (*ibid.* I:19, end).

The kinds of food we eat, in what quantities, when and how we eat them, can all have a decisive influence on our energy levels, moods, attitudes, ability to think, feel and so on. Eating the wrong foods, or even the right foods in the wrong ways, can be responsible for excessive fatigue, drowsiness, general sluggishness, depression, mental cloudiness, nervousness, tension, anxiety, impulsiveness, excitability, etc.

What You Eat: Kashrut

Even the simplest foods have to go through many processes to remove substances that are unfit for human consumption. For example, in order to make bread, the grains of wheat have to be separated from the stalks, dirt and stones must be removed, the grains ground and the coarser bran sifted out. Only then can the flour be kneaded with water and baked.

There are parallel processes of purification on the spiritual level. The diverse and elaborate laws of Kashrut guide us as to how we may avoid taking into our bodies substances that are damaging to the soul, such as forbidden species of animals, fish and insects, the blood and forbidden fat of animals, mixtures of meat cooked with milk, and so on.

Anyone striving for mental clarity and spiritual purity would be well advised to pay careful attention to Kashrut. For example, a single small bug ingested with fruit or vegetables not properly inspected might give rise to damaging trains of negative thoughts, while closing off avenues of spirituality without one's even being aware of it. The same applies to other foods prohibited by the Torah or through Rabbinic enactment.

Take time to study the different aspects of the Laws of Kashrut, and consider how you can restructure your eating habits if necessary.

What You Eat: Diet for a Clear Head

Ensuring that our food is technically kosher is only the first step in eating for the good of our minds and souls. Traditional Torah sources make various references to foods which are generally healthy, others which are less healthy, and those which are extremely unhealthy. However, owing to the revolution in agriculture and in techniques of food production, preservation and transportation in modern times, most people now have access to a vastly wider range of foods than was available to their grandparents and great-grandparents. These include exotic foods, foods out of season, pre-cooked, ready and fast foods, as well as foods containing all kinds of preservatives and other additives. We therefore cannot expect direct guidance from the classic Torah sources concerning our food shopping today.

People's physical constitutions vary enormously. Different people have their own food needs, and may react to specific foods in very different ways. "Every individual should consult with medical experts to choose the foods best suited to his or her particular constitution, place and time" (*Kitzur Shulchan Aruch* 32:7). Those unable to turn to a competent nutritionist would be advised to consult texts offering sensible nutritional guidance. Aim to develop a diet that provides you with all your nutritional needs in a balanced way and gives you genuine and lasting satisfaction. To find out how you react to the different foods you eat, you could keep a notebook in which you enter what you eat and when, and then note down how you feel afterwards.

Coffee, tea and other stimulants are obviously inadvisable for those seeking to reduce tension and experience greater calm. Over-consumption of highly refined and processed foods can lead to nutritional imbalance, giving rise to a wide variety of problems. Consumption of refined sugar in large quantities causes rapid fluctuations in blood sugar levels and may often be responsible for fatigue, depression, lack of clarity, etc. An increase in the proportion of complex carbohydrates in your daily diet (derived from grains like millet, buckwheat, brown rice and rolled oats, vegetables, seeds, nuts, and fruit in moderate quantities) can help to stabilize blood sugar levels, leading to optimum functioning and eliminating cravings for sweet, rich and unhealthy foods. In general, it is advisable to eat foods in their natural, unprocessed form as far as possible. Not only *what* you eat, but also the way you *combine* various kinds of foods in your diet can have a significant effect on your energy levels throughout the day, and the way you think and feel.

Vegetarianism as such is not an integral part of the Jewish spiritual path, although some notable Rabbis of recent times have been practicing vegetarians. The Kabbalah teaches that the flesh of animals and fish contains powerful Divine sparks and should be eaten in great holiness in order to elevate them. We find that Rebbe Nachman advised some of his followers to abstain from eating animal products for twenty-four hours once a week (*Rabbi Nachman's Wisdom* #185).

When and How Much to Eat

1. Eat only when you are genuinely hungry.
2. Drink only when you are thirsty.
3. Do not eat to the point where your stomach is completely full — eat a quarter less than the amount that would make you feel completely full.
4. Drink a minimum with your meal. Only when the food has begun to be digested should you drink, and even then only just as much as you need.
5. Always try to eat sitting down in one place.
6. Do not engage in any form of strenuous physical activity until the food in the stomach is digested. Do not go to sleep directly after eating but wait three or four hours.

(Rambam, *Hilchot De'ot* 4:1-3, 5)

"Over-eating," says the Rambam, "is like poison to the body... The majority of illnesses are caused either because of eating harmful foods or through stuffing the stomach with excessive food, even good foods" (*ibid.* 4:15). "This is on the physical plane," says Rebbe Nachman. "On the spiritual level, a person who eats like an animal falls from spiritual understanding" (*Rabbi Nachman's Wisdom* #143).

Most people are aware that excessive over-eating may make them heavy, sleepy, depressed and unable to concentrate, but often do not realise that even moderate over-eating can also have a negative effect on physical and mental functioning and impair their spiritual sensitivity.

If you suspect that your present eating patterns may be having a negative influence on your energy levels, moods, alertness and clarity throughout the day, and especially when you want to concentrate, think clearly, study, pray, meditate and so on, try experimenting with your mealtimes and the kinds, quantities and combinations of foods you eat at different times of the day. Avoid scheduling study, prayer and meditation sessions soon after eating.

How You Eat: Please and Thank You

The table is compared to the Temple altar (*Berachot* 55a). Representatives of the mineral, vegetable and animal worlds were brought to the altar in the form of salt, flour, oil, wine, birds and animals. There they were sacrificed and transmuted into "a sweet savor to HaShem" (Leviticus 1:9). So, too, when we eat, our task is to elevate the energy in the material foods we consume, devoting it to Torah, prayer, mitzvot and the service of HaShem (see *Yesod ve-Shoresh Ha-Avodah* 7:2).

To spiritualize the act of eating requires concentration. One should prepare the table before beginning the meal and sit down to eat and drink in a composed state of mind. Where mandatory, as before eating bread, one should perform the ritual of washing the hands — the instruments of material action — raising them upwards toward the head to show that we wish to use them to feed our bodies for the sake of the soul.

The most important moments of the meal are when we recite the blessings before and after the food. Through these blessings we elevate the Divine sparks in the food. As you are about to say the blessing before food, pause and prepare yourself. Reflect on how this specific item came into being through the wonders of the Creator and how it contains energy that you will use to serve God through Torah, prayer and fullfilment of the mitzvot. As you say the blessing, think about God and your gratitude to Him for the food.

"Be careful not to gulp your food down hurriedly. Eat at a moderate pace, calmly and with the same table manners you would show if an important guest were present. You should always eat in this manner, even when you eat alone" (*Tzaddik* #515). Chew your food carefully, as this is the beginning of the process of digestion (*Kitzur Shulchan Aruch* 32:13), and it will also give you greater satisfaction. While you chew and taste the food, keep in mind how the spiritual energy in the food is being refined and elevated.

Many people forget about what they have eaten as soon as they have swallowed it (unless they get indigestion). Yet even after swallowing, the body continues to work dutifully to dissolve the food and distribute the nutrients as needed. On the spiritual plane, the processes of refinement and elevation also continue as the spiritual energy in the food is turned into our holy thoughts, words and actions.

Accordingly, we follow the act of eating with the appropriate blessings after food. We thank God for the food and the physical and spiritual energies it contains, reminding ourselves that God takes care of us and provides for all our needs. We pray for the spiritual restoration of the Jewish People and the holy Temple, thereby reaffirming our most precious hopes and aspirations in life.

If it often happens that you have to eat when rushed or under pressure, don't abandon your hopes of eating properly. Work out which snack foods will satisfy you and meet your working needs, giving you the best balance of nutrients. Try to prepare them in advance so that you don't have to make do with the wrong foods because that is all that is available at the snack bar. Even when you are in a hurry, it is always possible to take the few extra moments needed to say the blessings with appropriate concentration.

On the six weekdays our primary purpose in eating may be to nourish our bodies in order to function properly as we go about our working activities. However on Shabbat, the purpose of eating is entirely different: it is to delight the soul. Put particular care and effort into the beautification of the Shabbat table, and use the three meals of Shabbat as times to give special focus to the spiritual dimensions of eating.

Fasting

In earlier times, fasting was a prominent part of the Jewish spiritual pathway, but one of the innovations of the Chassidic movement was to take account of the greater physical weakness of later generations and use other routes to spiritual purity and devotion. Thus Rebbe Nachman explicitly told his followers not to fast — except, of course, on the set fast-days of the religious calendar (*Tzaddik* #491).

This does not mean that Chassidism gave a licence to eat without any discipline whatsoever. In some ways, the harder discipline is to eat moderately and with proper decency at all times. While complete abstinence from food and drink is no longer recommended, there are times when partial fasting for limited periods (e.g. only juices, or a carefully restricted diet) can be of great value for cleansing the body and clearing the mind. This should only be undertaken with expert guidance.

Look upon the set fast-days of the religious calendar as an opportunity to cleanse your body and soul. If you are careful about how you eat before the fast — not over-eating and not under-eating — it can help to make the fast itself easier and leave you with more strength and clarity of mind. One of the most important aspects of any fast is the way you break it: it is destructive and demoralizing to follow a good fast with a crazy binge.

Changing Food Habits

The link between eating habits, energy levels and states of mind is so subtle that it can take years of trial and error before one discovers the foods and eating patterns best suited to one's own unique constitution and life-style, and develops sufficient discipline to eat properly.

Never try to introduce drastic changes suddenly. You run the risk of doing more harm than good, and you may counter-react and regress even further into your old habits. If you are conscious that bad foods play too big a role in your present diet, it is not necessarily wise to try to cut them all out at once. The more sensible course is to find better foods that you can substitute for them. The easiest way to eliminate a bad habit is by developing a healthier one in its place. Do what you can, step by step, to improve your eating habits, but remember that you need God's help. Pray regularly for help in eating to satisfy your soul.

Breathing

"Man's vitality is the breath. If the breath is lacking, life is lacking."

Likutey Moharan I:8

In between pulling at crumbs and bones, the Prince would presumably sit down to rest. Before the arrival of his strange new companion, the Prince had perhaps spent these periods listlessly staring into the middle distance. But now there was something unusual to observe. The Wise Man, playing Turkey in his own way, would sit there for long periods of calm contemplation. And then, all that the increasingly curious Prince could observe was his long, deep breaths.

The Breath and the Soul

As long as we are alive, we all breathe, but how we breathe affects our bodily health and strength, our energy levels and states of mind and soul. Every one of the activities of life is bound up with this fundamental process, through which the oxygen vital to our body cells enters the blood, and carbon dioxide waste is eliminated.

The definition of living creatures is "all who have the soul of the breath of life in their nostrils" (Genesis 7:22). The life of man began when God "blew into his nostrils the breath of life" (*ibid.* 2:7). The intimate relationship between our mental and spiritual states and our breathing is reflected in the way the Children of Israel are depicted in exile in Egypt. They were too impatient and despondent to hear the spiritual message Moses was bringing them "because of *short-breathedness* and hard work" (Exodus 6:9). When we pray for spiritual regeneration, we ask God to "create within me a pure heart, and renew within me proper *breathing*" (Psalms 51:12).

"The soul of man is a lamp of God" (Proverbs 20:27). Chassidut explains the relationship between the heart and the body, the breath, the mind and the soul, through the image of an oil lamp. The light of the flame is the mind and soul. The wick of the lamp corresponds to the physical brain. The oil rising to the wick, fuelling the flame, symbolizes the vital oils and fluids of the body, which rise up to the brain and "burn" to fuel the activities of the mind and the soul.

Chassidut teaches that the steady burning of the lamp — the mind or soul — depends on the breath. The heart, with its driving passions, would burn up the entire body if it were not for the wings of the lungs fanning and blowing over it. The cooling effect of the lungs, drawing in cold air from the outside, prevents the heart from burning up all the body fluids, thus enabling the oils to rise up to the lamp — the brain — keeping it burning steadily in clear contemplation and understanding.

"The soul — the *neshamah* — of man is a lamp of God." The word *neshamah* is related to the Hebrew word *neshimah*, which means the breath. We can read the verse as if it says "The *breathing* of man is God's lamp," teaching us that when we breathe fully, the lamp burns brightly and the Godly soul shines in us. (See *Likutey Moharan* I:60,3.)

Controlling States of Mind Through Breathing

Our breathing is thus one of the most important ways through which we can affect not only our physical functioning but also our calm and clarity, and the state of our mind and spirit. Everyone knows that physical exertion causes rapid breathing and panting, and most people are also aware of the way nervousness, tension and the like are often accompanied by restricted breathing. States of rest and tranquillity, on the other hand, are associated with smoother, deeper breathing.

Not only does our breathing respond to temporary changes. In many people, complexes of behavior that have become part of their personality create distinctive patterns of distorted breathing which in turn affect their entire functioning and states of consciousnesss. Our frenetic, materialistic culture as a whole could be called the culture of the short breath.

In spite of the fact that air is one of the few things in life that is free, the overwhelming majority of the population has little or no awareness of the significance of the way we breathe. There is, of course, awareness of the damage caused by air pollution, especially in urban areas. Almost eight hundred years ago the Rambam, discussing air quality in the medieval city, wrote that "even the slightest change in the quality of the air will cause a far greater proportionate change in the quality of mental activity, and this is why you will find that many people function poorly in proportion to the poor quality of the air, i.e. they show signs of mental confusion, poor comprehension and reasoning abilities, and poor memory" (*Hanhagat Ha-Bri'ut* 4:2).

If this is the effect of poor air on our mental functioning, it is easy to infer the disastrous effect on consciousness of the poor breathing patterns exhibited by so many people — patterns that restrict the flow of available air to the lungs, sometimes drastically. The stressful conditions of contemporary living in general and our various private problems as individuals often tend to cause a stiffening and distortion in our posture. The exhalation of stale air becomes inhibited and the inhalation of fresh air inadequate.

Breathing is a self-regulatory function and has the capacity to recover from strain and malfunctioning automatically as soon as the situation that caused the disturbance is over. Unfortunately, what usually happens is that instead of allowing our breathing to return to normal in due course, we tend to interfere. Unconsciously and unintentionally, we often cling to the altered ways of breathing even after the events that brought on the disturbance have passed. Eventually they become habitual and our breathing does not regain its original undisturbed flow.

Although breathing is a self-regulatory organic process that is controlled by the involuntary nervous system, unlike other involuntary functions breathing is also partially under the influence of the voluntary nervous system. In other words, we have the ability to take conscious control of our breathing.

Breathing is therefore one of our most important physical means of influencing our spiritual and psychological states. Improved breathing can lead to a new world of well-being, bringing increased stamina, freedom from fatigue, inner calm, heightened sensitivity and greater clarity of mind.

Breathing in Kabbalah and Chassidut

Among the Kabbalistic meditation techniques practiced from the times of the Prophets until the Middle Ages, and, in a few closed circles, even today, are highly complex meditations in which contemplation on the letters of the holy Hebrew Names of God is associated with special breathing patterns. (See Rabbi Aryeh Kaplan, *Meditation and the Bible* and his *Meditation and the Kabbalah* esp. pp. 87-106.) A deep knowledge of Kabbalah is required even to begin to understand these methods, let alone practice them.

Chassidic teachings open up pathways of devotion that are accessible even without Kabbalistic knowledge, and in the writings of Rebbe Nachman, where breathing is a recurrent theme, the emphasis is on the long, smooth breath (see especially *Likutey Moharan* I:8, 60, 109, and II, 5 etc. and *Tzaddik* #163). The main focus here will therefore be on long, full breathing as a way to maximize our physical, mental and spiritual functioning.

Breathing Practice

In order to develop good breathing habits it is very helpful to have an understanding of the physiological process of breathing. It will be well worth your while to invest some time in a few sessions of exploration and practice in order to become sensitive to the different parts of the body involved, to become aware of any ingrained habits that may be inhibiting your breathing, and to learn and master better habits with which to replace them. (Those who are sick should not work with their breathing except under the supervision of a medical expert.)

Make the time to sit down and become aware of the way you are breathing. Concentrate on the breathing process. It is a good idea to close your eyes, as this will help you to focus on your feelings and sensations. Although in their healthy state it is impossible to feel the diaphragm and lungs themselves, it *is* possible to feel the effect of the breathing process on other parts of the body — especially the abdomen, which swells as the diaphragm contracts, and the chest-cage, which widens as it accommodates the air coming into the lungs.

The Exhalation

Good respiration begins with a slow and complete exhalation. This exhalation is the absolute prerequisite of correct and complete inhalation, because unless a vessel is emptied, it cannot be filled. Unless we first breathe out fully, it is impossible to breathe in correctly. Normal respiration therefore begins with a slow, calm exhalation accomplished by relaxation of the inspiratory muscles. The chest is depressed by its own weight, expelling the air. At the end of the expiration, the abdominal muscles help the lungs to empty as fully as possible by means of a contraction that expels the last traces of used air.

There is always a residue of impure air in the lungs owing to their spongy make-up, but we must attempt to minimize this residue because, together with the fresh air provided by inhalation, it makes up the actual air we are breathing. The more complete the exhalation, the greater the quantity of fresh air to enter the lungs, and so the purer the air in contact with the alveolar surfaces.

Observe the way you exhale. Are you aware of inhibiting your exhalation in any way, preventing the complete exhalation of stale, waste air? Giving a few sighs can help you to breathe out completely. Another simple way of overcoming incomplete exhalation is to practice counting slowly to three at the end of the exhalation before you breathe in again. Repeat this over a cycle of five to six breaths.

The Pause

Most people assume that our breathing function is a two-part rhythm of exhalation and inhalation, but this is not the case. The breathing rhythm has three components: the exhalation, a pause, and the inhalation. The pause gives us a rest from the effort of the exhalation, and enables us to rally the energy needed for the next inhalation. The pause is not an idle period when nothing happens, but a vital phase in the breathing process.

If we interfere with the length of the breathing pause, shortening it even slightly, we find ourselves feeling rushed and pressured. A full-length pause in your breathing rhythm will have a calming effect and engender a feeling of relief, eradicating the sensation of being under pressure. However you should not try to make the pause willfully, as its duration must vary with your different breathing needs at different times. What you should do is to try to become aware of any ways in which you might be inhibiting the pause, thereby generating feelings of stress.

The Inhalation

Inhalation is made up of three partial phases, which you should learn to distinguish when you first practice breathing. Note the muscular sensations associated with each phase.

Diaphragmatic breathing: this is abdominal breathing induced by contraction of the muscular fibers of the dome-shaped diaphragm, which flattens and lowers. This increases the volume of the lungs, drawing air into them through the trachea, nose and mouth. As the diaphragm contracts and the base of the lungs fills with air, the abdominal region swells. Abdominal breathing is the least faulty method of breathing. It may be easier to learn to recognize it at first by practicing lying down, since it is then easier to relax the muscles of the abdominal wall which serve to hold us upright when we are sitting or walking. Later on, you will be able to learn how to breathe from the diaphragm whenever required — even when walking or running.

Intercostal breathing: this is achieved by raising the ribs through dilating the thoracic cage or chest wall like a pair of bellows. The middle section of the lungs expands, causing air to flow in, but less than in abdominal respiration. Intercostal breathing also takes more effort. When combined with abdominal breathing it ventilates the lungs satisfactorily.

Clavicular breathing: this is breathing from the top of the lungs, produced by expanding the top part of the lungs through raising the upper part of the thorax — this we do by raising the collar-bones and shoulders. Shallow, high, upper-chest breathing is an inadequate method associated with slumped or rigid postures and with states of anxiety and tension.

Observe the way you breathe without trying to affect it at this stage. Do you tend to use one of the three methods of breathing more than the others? Are you in some way unconsciously inhibiting your body's natural instinct to use all three methods, restricting the free flow there should be from one to the next?

The Complete Breath

Good breathing incorporates all three methods of respiration integrated into a single, full and rhythmic movement. Unless you are congested, it is important to breathe in and out through the nose. Exhalation and inspiration should be silent, slow, continuous and easy. Don't blow yourself up like a balloon. Breathe easily without straining.

Allow your lungs to empty entirely. At the end of the exhalation there are a few moments of respite when we hold our breath with the lungs empty. Having completely emptied the lungs and paused for a few seconds, you will soon realize that your breathing is starting up on its own. Relax your stomach and allow the air to flow in.

Your abdominal muscles should be relaxed. Some people mistakenly believe they are breathing from the stomach because they are flexing their abdominal muscles, but in fact the air enters the lungs because of the flattening of the dome of the diaphragm. The sensation should be one of the natural swelling and rising of the abdomen... Next, expand the ribs without straining them... finally, allow the lungs to fill completely. Let the collar-bones rise by themselves without deliberately lifting up your shoulders. Avoid any tensing of the muscles of the hands, face and neck, particularly in this last stage of breathing.

Throughout this procedure the air should enter in a continuous flow without gasping. If your nose, throat, neck and shoulder muscles are relaxed, there should be no noise. When the breathing is slow, deep and complete, the interchange of gases in the lungs is at its optimum, with maximum absorption of life-giving oxygen and extrusion of waste carbon dioxide.

When the lungs are completely filled, breathe out by successively lowering the collar-bones and ribs and allowing the diaphragm to expand and drive the used air out of the lungs.

Hyperventilation

If in your practice you breathe more fully than you are normally accustomed to, it is quite possible that you will experience hyperventilation. This results from having breathed so deeply that you have more oxygen in your blood than you can handle just yet. You can recognize it by a slight sensation of dizziness or sometimes a sudden feeling of tiredness or slight malaise.

The remedy is to use up the excess oxygen with a few vigorous movements, such as getting up and walking around briskly or thrusting your arms out, fists clenched, a few times. As soon as your head feels clear, continue practicing. If you become dizzy again almost immediately, stop practicing for the time being. You may need to wait an hour or more, or even until the next day, before you continue.

As your breathing becomes more efficient and your vital capacity increases, you will develop a greater tolerance for oxygen and in time you will rarely, if ever, hyperventilate.

Breathing in Daily Life

You can practice breathing any time, whenever you think of it — at home, at work, while relaxing, waiting for buses or appointments, walking, travelling, etc. Be conscious of how you are breathing, and breathe as fully as possible. Gradually you will acquire the habit of complete respiration and your method of breathing will improve as you go on.

There is no single correct way to breathe valid for all people at all times. We have different breathing requirements at different times. Obviously, we need to breathe more rapidly during periods of physical activity, exercise, and so on, than when sitting concentrating, resting, meditating, etc. Even comparatively simple movements such as getting up from a chair necessitate an increase in the rate of breathing.

It is best to allow our breathing to adjust freely according to our specific needs at each moment. The goal should be to *remove breathing malfunctions* by eliminating tension and correcting the bad habits which cause us to inhibit the long, full, rhythmic breathing our bodies are instinctively geared for. Pay special attention to relaxing the muscles of the stomach and rib-cage.

Ten slow, deep breaths immediately after waking up in the morning will help banish drowsiness and heaviness and set you up for the day's activities. From time to time throughout the day, stop to re-energize with a few slow, long breaths. Breathe deeply and fully if you find yourself dozing just when you need to be awake. Include breathing in your pausing practice (see above pp. 70-1) as you go about your various activities.

Try to be conscious of your breathing as you work, study, pray and meditate. If you breathe long and full it will keep you fresh, alert and balanced and aid your concentration. Don't forget to breathe while interacting with others: use breaks in the conversation or times when the other person is doing the talking to breathe in and out fully a few times. Deep breathing before going to bed at night will relax you and prepare you for a restful, refreshing night's sleep.

Breathing in Meditation and Prayer

One way to develop the sitting relaxation practice (above pp. 66-70) is to sit for a period of breathing. Concentrating on your breathing is a way of entering a state of profound calm and contemplative clarity. During a session of sitting practice, after you have released all bodily tension and are fully relaxed, focus your awareness on your breathing. Watch each phase of the breathing process: the slow, long exhalation, the pause, the way the abdomen begins to swell and rise... Feel the cool air drawn into your nostrils and down into the lungs.

Hand over your breathing to God, letting your body breathe naturally, fully and deeply without any interference whatsoever. Think of the way the cool air entering the lungs is gently being fanned over the heart, allowing the rich, life-giving blood to rise up to and fuel the brain, causing the lamp of your mind, soul and consciousness to radiate.

When you are about to pray and you pause to focus before you begin, take a few deep breaths and think of how God is sending your life into you through your breath. Prayer is made up of talk and song — and we talk and sing with our breath. Think how your breathing is part of the universal song in which "the breath of all life will bless Your name, HaShem our God, and the spirit of all flesh will glorify and exalt Your memory at all times..." (from *Nishmat* in the Shabbat morning liturgy).

Be conscious of your breathing as you recite the prayers. With time you can teach yourself how to breathe rhythmically with the prayers, using the time of the inhale to pause and focus on the meaning of the words you are about to say, so that as you actually say them on the exhale they will be full of added significance.

At climactic moments during the prayer service, such as when reciting the Sh'ma and the Amidah, especially the first paragraph, take extra time to breathe fully and focus carefully on the meaning of the words. At times when you want to pray with special intensity, you may wish to take a whole breath for every sentence or phrase of the prayers, breathing in deeply and focusing before reciting it, then saying the words with fervor with the exhale.

Renewal: A *Kavanah* for Breathing

The root meaning of the Hebrew word *kavanah* is aiming or directing, as when an archer aims an arrow. In Jewish spiritual literature, a kavanah is a thought one has in mind while saying a prayer or performing a holy action, a mitzvah or good deed. One directs the mind by focusing on a particular thought.

Rebbe Nachman has given us a very simple kavanah for breathing — a thought we can have in mind as we breathe, a thought we can return to any time, as we go through our normal activities each day and in special periods of meditation.

The idea is to focus on breathing as renewal. We never stop breathing — we are constantly letting out stale air and drawing in fresh air. Rebbe Nachman tells us that the physical air we breathe in and out has a spiritual cognate. There is the good, fresh, holy air from which the Tzaddik draws energy, and the bad, stale, impure air that gives rise to sin.

In order to renew yourself and draw closer to God, you must separate yourself from the bad air and breathe in the good air. When a person dies, he gives a long sigh and the life goes out of him. In a sense, every exhale is a death: the death of the moment that has passed, as we breathe out the stale air. This death is a preparation for rebirth: the birth of the new moment.

When you breathe out, sigh and exhale all the stale air from within you, bearing in mind that you are releasing yourself from the bad air of impurity. Then, as you breathe in again, focus on how you are drawing in fresh, pure, good air and binding yourself to holiness and life. Sigh over the things you have done wrong in your life, and breathe out the stale, impure air that is inside you and affecting your mind. Breathe out your tensions and bad feelings. Breathe in the good, fresh air of holiness. Breathe in new life. This is a way to return from impurity to holiness (*Tzaddik* #163).

You can use this kavanah any time you focus on your breathing at various junctures in the course of your day, as discussed above. If you use it regularly, you will have a constant sense of revitalization as you become more and more alive with every breath and each new moment.

When you are in a session of sitting meditation, you could use this kavanah to release yourself from tension, negative feelings and deep-seated patterns of negative behavior. Bring your bad feelings into conscious awareness and as you exhale, put them all into the air you are breathing out. Sigh deeply and flush all the negativity out of your system. Then, when you breathe in, focus on positive thoughts and feelings, so that you bring goodness, holiness and purity into yourself with the fresh air you inhale.

Exercise

"Even if you eat good foods and take proper care of your health in other respects, if you sit back comfortably and do no exercise you will suffer from constant aches and pains and your strength will decrease."

Mishneh Torah, Hilchot De'ot 4:15

Yes, even turkeys seem to appreciate the importance of physical exercise. Seasoned observers know that turkeys have their own set times to fan out their tails, droop their wings, retract their heads, shake their quills and go strutting around till their heads turn blue and white.

The Wise Man probably followed a keep-fit routine of his own, because "exercise is the most important fundamental in maintaining good health and keeping up our resistance to the majority of illnesses" (Rambam, *Hanhagat Ha-Bri'ut* I:3), and the Torah commands us to "take the utmost care of your vital soul" (Deuteronomy 4:9).

Exercise improves blood circulation, brings more oxygen into every cell of the body, speeds up a sluggish metabolism, enhances the functioning of internal glands and organs, improves digestion, facilitates the removal of poisonous wastes from the body, reduces the risk of many diseases, keeps muscles fit, trim and flexible, builds coordination and balance, heightens reflexes, reduces stress, improves sleep patterns, increases energy, and helps maintain a relaxed body and a tranquil mind.

In the words of the Rambam, "There is no substitute whatsoever for exercise. Exercise increases the natural heat of the body and facilitates the elimination of waste products, whereas a purely sedentary lifestyle smothers the natural heat of the body so that while waste products are constantly generated, they are not expelled. Waste products are generated even if one eats foods of the highest quality and in exactly the right quantities. Exercise will rid the body of these wastes, and through exercise it is even possible to neutralize the damage caused by many bad habits" (*Hanhagat Ha-Bri'ut* I:3).

The Gemara states that "on Shabbat we do not exercise" (*Shabbat* 147a), thus implicitly recognizing the health benefits of exercise on the six working days. Cultivation of the physique for purely materialistic motives has been viewed negatively in Jewish circles ever since the third century B.C.E., when gymnasia were one of the main instruments used by the Greeks in their attempt to subvert Torah culture. This, together with the fact that hundreds of years of exile and persecution gave Jews little opportunity to take proper care of their bodies, may partly explain the widespread lack of attention to exercise in observant Jewish communities today.

Nevertheless, outstanding Torah teachers of recent generations, including Rabbi Yisrael Meir Kagen, the "Chofetz Chaim," have been highly conscious of the great importance of exercise for spiritual well-being, and encouraged their students to get out and take walks, etc. R. Yisrael Salanter, founder of the Mussar Movement, is known to have had a regular exercise routine, and followed the instructions of an exercise manual recommended by his doctor in scrupulous detail (*T'nuat Ha-Mussar* Vol I, p.342).

An exercise routine of some kind is virtually indispensible for sound physical health, and should therefore be a part of the Torah life-style. Practice of the mitzvot at every juncture in life takes energy and stamina, while study, prayer and meditation are activities requiring a clarity and concentration that can only properly be sustained when the body is fit and functioning optimally. Exercise releases body tensions, facilitating deep relaxation — often a valuable preliminary to meditation — as well as promoting a general sense of calm and well-being that should accompany all spiritual work.

What Kind of Exercise?

"Not every bodily movement is 'exercise'," says the Rambam. "Exercise is defined as any form of movement — whether vigorous, gentle, or a combination of both — that involves some effort and causes an increase in one's rate of breathing. Anything more than this is hard exercise, and not everyone can bear hard exercise or needs it either" (*Hanhagat Ha-Bri'ut* I:3).

Someone whose daily life involves a fair amount of physical activity may not need to devote much time to formal exercise, but anyone who spends much of the day sitting in an office or Yeshivah should definitely endeavor to schedule an exercise routine of some kind at least three or four times a week.

The kind of exercise required depends on your state of health and fitness and other individual factors. No-one should begin any program of exercise without first consulting a doctor, physiotherapist, etc. The body is a most wonderful, subtle, delicate instrument that has to be treated with the utmost care and respect. If you have not exercised for a long time and are out of condition, you must be very patient and gentle as you slowly encourage stiff and lazy joints and muscles to start working again.

People sometimes try to find a short-cut to fitness by straining themselves, but this can be physically dangerous, and there is the risk of causing an injury that could prevent one from exercising altogether. It may be right to push yourself beyond the point where the Turkey says it's time to take a break, but don't ever try to carry on if the Wise Man tells you to stop.

The Rambam's above-quoted definition of exercise seems to correspond to what we would call aerobic exercise — a steady, non-stop movement that leads to an increased pulse rate yet without putting strain on the cardiovascular system. Examples of aerobic exercise are walking — the most natural and oldest form of exercise, which utilizes almost all your muscles; running — preferably on grass or a dirt track to reduce stress on the muscular/skeletal system and internal organs; swimming, and cycling.

The perfect form of aerobic exercise is Chassidic dance, in which all parts of the body are moved with grace and joy in praise of the Creator. Why not put on a recording of your favorite *nigunim* — holy melodies — and dance free-style as gently or as vigorously as you like, expressing your inner self through the various movements of your body!

Another important component of a fitness program would be a series of stretching and flexing exercises in order to keep your muscles well toned. The more flexible and strong your body, the more protection you have against pain and injury. The fitness section of a good bookstore should include a choice of graded programs that combine aerobic, stretching and loosening exercises, requiring little or no equipment. These can be carried out in even a limited space in the privacy of your home, and need take no more than twelve to fifteen minutes or so per session.

Describing the ideal exercise procedure, the Rambam writes: "One should discipline the body and exercise every day in the morning until the body begins to be warm. One should then relax a little until one is calm, and then eat. Washing in warm water after exercise is good: afterwards, rest a little and eat" (*Hilchot De'ot* 4:2).

"The best time for exercise," says the Rambam, "is at the beginning of the day, after one wakes up from one's sleep... One should only exercise on an empty stomach and after relieving oneself... One should not exercise in extreme heat or extreme cold... As good as it is to take exercise before a meal, so it is harmful to exercise after eating" (*Hanhagat Ha-Bri'ut* I:3).

While people with vision problems should consult an eye specialist, those blessed with good vision can help maintain it with simple, gentle eye exercises.

The Soul and the Body

Cultivating healthy living habits can be the beginning of spiritual self-reclamation.

"When a person does not direct himself to the true goal of life, what is his life for? The Godly soul constantly yearns to do the will of the One who formed her, but when the soul sees that the person is not leading a spiritual life according to the will of God, she yearns to return to her Source and starts drawing herself away from the person's body in order to leave it. This can make the person physically ill, because the power of the soul becomes weakened as a result...

"The reason why a person returns to good health as a result of medical treatment is because the soul sees that this person has the ability to force himself to go against his bodily appetites and habits. He may be accustomed to eating bread and other foods, but now he controls his appetite and submits to treatments and bitter medicines for the sake of his health. The soul sees that he is able to control his excesses for the sake of a higher goal, and she therefore comes back to him in the hope that he will control his appetites in order to pursue his true purpose in life — to do the will of his Maker" (*Likutey Moharan* I:268).

Especially for those who have tended to neglect themselves, cultivating good eating, breathing and exercise habits can be a pleasurable process of self-discovery. Initially you are very likely to encounter various minor problems as you experiment with new practices and adjust to unfamiliar patterns. But within a short time, you should find yourself experiencing higher energy levels, and a growing feeling of general well-being, relaxation and clarity.

The whole purpose of caring for the body is to make it a fit vessel to receive the soul. Physical health is one of the most important foundations for successful spiritual work, but that does not mean that one can only begin work on the soul after achieving perfect physical fitness. On the contrary, the motivation and personal discipline required to develop a genuinely healthy life-style come only through spiritual work, in particular regular prayer and meditation.

Sensible patterns of eating, breathing and exercise should therefore be an integrated part of a total spiritual pathway in which Torah study, prayer and meditation have pride of place, for these are the key to everything else.

6

"Who Are You and What are You Doing Here?"

The Prince asked the Wise Man, "Who are you and what are you doing here?" The Wise Man replied, "And what are *you* doing here?" "I am a turkey," said the Prince. "Well I'm also a turkey," said the Wise Man. The two of them sat there together like this for some time, until they were used to one another.

"One should ask people 'What?' People don't think about their purpose in life. What? After all the frustrations and distractions, after all the complaining and all the empty excuses you give for being far from God, when everything is over, what is going to be left of you? What are you going to do in the end? What will you answer the One who sent you? What are you if not a visitor on this earth? Life is vanity and emptiness, a passing shadow, a vanishing cloud. You know this. What do you say?"

Rabbi Nachman's Wisdom #286

The Wise Man is under the table. The Prince is sitting there looking at him. Eventually the Prince breaks the silence and asks the first question that comes to mind when two people meet for the first time: "Who *are* you, and what are you doing here?"

But the Wise man doesn't answer. He doesn't just tell the Prince who he is, or that he's a Turkey. The Wise Man has no intention of getting drawn into conversational pleasantries. Instead, he turns the Prince's question back on him. He wants the Prince to ask *himself* this very question. "Who are you? What are you doing here?" This is the most important question you have to ask yourself in life. Who are you really? What is life about, and what are you doing with it?

"What?"

There are times when life itself forces you to ask these questions. Perhaps a difficult situation puts you with your back to the wall, or events cause you to wake up with a start. These challenges are sent to prompt *you* to search for the answers and look for God. Thus the Hebrew word *KaShYA*, a difficulty or question, consists of the initial letters of the words *Sh'ma HaShem (YKVK) Koli Ekra* (Psalms 27:7): "God, hear my voice — I call." The difficulty is sent to make you call out to God.

Only when you are willing to confront these questions will you become free. Instead of indiscriminately accepting the answers you have absorbed and inherited from your family, friends and the surrounding culture, you decide what *you* want to do with your life. Many people assume they are free because they do whatever they feel like, but actually they are prisoners of their own hearts, compulsively pursuing goals dictated to them by parents, educators, opinion-leaders, entertainers, the demands of fashion, and the like.

Freedom is the ability to choose your own goals with wisdom, and then act decisively to pursue them, without being shackled by the dictates of others or your own weaknesses. The first step to freedom is to confront yourself frankly and honestly and become aware of who you really are.

What are you doing with your life? Where does your time go? What are the thoughts that pass through your mind all day? What are your typical behavior-patterns, attitudes and reactions? What do you *want* to achieve in this life? What are your ultimate goals and values? Is your daily routine taking you closer to your goals? Or do you often act indecisively, ineffectively, or even at cross-purposes with yourself? How can you release yourself from the compulsions that imprison you? What will you have to do in order to reach your goals?

Meditation

In order to take responsibility for your life and become free, you must make a serious effort to confront these questions. The work involved in answering them takes time. You have to make that time. The only way to advance is by *fixing* special meditation times for yourself in which you settle your mind, think calmly about your life and goals, and work out how to attain them. This is *Hisbodidus*, the most important, practicable and relevant form of Jewish meditation in our time. "Hisbodidus is the highest level. It is greater than everything" (*Likutey Moharan* II:25).

The word "meditation" is problematic, because different people attribute different meanings to it. Some still use it in the classic sense of serious and sustained reflection or contemplation, especially on religious truth. Others, however, use the term to refer to a technique of calming the mind that may have no spiritual significance. For many people today, "meditation" is no more than a synonym for deep relaxation.

In the sense of spiritual devotion, meditation was and is an integral part of Jewish mysticism. Among the different methods discussed in the Kabbalah are elaborate meditations involving Hebrew letters in complex combinations, Yichudim relating to Holy Names, Sefirot and Partzufim, and so on. These meditations can be meaningfully practiced only by people who are deeply steeped in Torah life and thoroughly conversant with Biblical and Rabbinic teaching, and who have spent years not only studying Kabbalah but subjecting themselves to the rigorous personal discipline it demands. For deeply pious and learned Jews who have reached advanced levels of knowledge and spiritual development, these meditations are an integral part of the devotional life of prayer, Torah study and mitzvah-observance.

For most of us, however, the central spiritual issue is how to practice the very basics of Judaism amidst the daily challenges of life in the contemporary world. As we seek God through the fundamental patterns of Torah life — Tallit and Tefilin, the daily blessings and prayers, Shabbat and the festivals, Kashrut, family purity, charity, personal integrity and so on — we often face powerful inner barriers, not to speak of the external obstacles created by the people around us and the prevailing society and culture. The way to overcome them is with hisbodidus.

Hisbodidus:

Time for Your Self

The word *hisbodidus* (pronounced *hitbodidut* in Ivrit*) derives from the Hebrew root *bod*, meaning separate or alone. *Hisbodidus* is the reflexive form, signifying "making oneself alone": you separate yourself from other people and activities for a period of time in order to direct your focus inwards. A good way of translating *hisbodidus* might be "private time," or "time for your self." The idea is not to become a hermit, but to take regular breaks from the pressures of life in order to come back and face them from a position of far greater strength — through clarifying your goals, and working out how you can pursue them more effectively.

*Although all other transliterations of Hebrew words in this book are based on their Ivrit pronunciation, in the case of *hisbodidus* the Ashkenazic form has been retained since it is the most widely used.

The goal of hisbodidus is more than mere relaxation — although those who practice it regularly may certainly feel more relaxed and confident about life. A calm, clear mind is the most desirable state in which to practice hisbodidus, and part of the time of hisbodidus may be spent on preparing and settling the mind. However hisbodidus is far more than a method of passive relaxation-meditation. It takes more than deep relaxation or contemplation of a simple word or phrase to attain connection with God and personal transformation.

Hisbodidus would be classified as an *inner-directed, unstructured, active meditation.*

— Inner-directed, because the subject is *you*. You turn your focus of attention on yourself and your life, asking where you are now standing in relation to God.

— Unstructured, because the kind of work you do in your hisbodidus sessions at any given time depends to a large extent on you. Where are you right now, and how much of a commitment are you willing to make to develop yourself spiritually? As you examine and learn more about yourself, *you* create the structure of your sessions in relation to your individual situation and current needs.

— Active, because although the purpose of examining yourself is to become more self-aware, heightened awareness is only the beginning. The main goal is to actively *work* on yourself in order to develop yourself and bring yourself closer to God.

The Power of Words

Right under your very nose is your most powerful tool for spiritual growth — your mouth! The Prince's innocent question — "Who are you and what are you doing here?" — was a normal everyday conversational ploy. He was using language the way the majority of people use it most of the time: to talk to another human being. But the Wise Man turned the question back on the Prince. "Who are *you?*" He wanted him to ask *himself* the question. The Wise Man was teaching the Prince a different way of using language: to speak to our selves, to search for our selves and *grow*.

Hisbodidus is private time for working on yourself. The most important way of actually doing the work is through talking. You speak to yourself and to God in your own words. The idea is to express and articulate different facets of yourself out loud: who are you, what are your deepest yearnings, what are you striving toward, what is it that is holding you back, and how can you overcome the obstacles and attain what you want? Through the spoken word you turn the potential into the actual, making distant, barely-articulated dreams, hopes, wishes and intentions into concrete ideas leading you to practical action and achievement.

Some of the time, you need to speak directly to yourself in hisbodidus, talking out what is on your mind and in your heart, telling yourself what you want of yourself, encouraging yourself and gearing yourself for action. At other times, you must call out *beyond* yourself to the very source of the self, to God, crying and praying for help.

Obviously talking is not the only thing you should do in hisbodidus. There is no need to chatter like a parrot from the beginning to the end of every session. There are times when you may need to just sit, relax, breathe, and settle your mind. You must observe yourself, and think about your general behavior and activities. This is the way to get in touch with your thoughts and feelings, and come to know yourself. Hisbodidus time may thus be used for many kinds of spiritual work, from deep thinking and contemplation to singing, dancing, laughing... But the essential tool for search, development and change is language.

Talking to Your Self

People think talking to yourself is mad, but in fact it's the best way to make the Prince sane.

The Torah tells us that when God created man, He breathed life into him, "...and the man was a living soul" (Genesis 2:7). Onkelos, the Aramaic translator of the Bible, renders the words "living soul" as "*speaking* spirit," teaching us that language is the defining feature of man.

The use of language for communicating with one another is something we are all familiar with. We talk to one another in any number of ways, from the most simple and direct to the most subtle and sophisticated, telling one another what we want, giving orders, making requests, sharing or asking for information, expressing our thoughts and feelings, and so on and so forth. But the use of language to communicate with ourselves, our souls and with God is largely unexplored in contemporary culture. Yet the fact is that our hearing apparatus is arranged in such a way that not only do we hear what others say; we also hear what we ourselves are saying. We are set up to talk to ourselves!

Most small children talk to themselves aloud quite naturally, expressing whatever they feel, simply and directly. Often, they successively play out all kinds of different roles, reflecting various patterns of adult behavior as they see them in the world around them. Dialoguing with themselves is an important part of childhood growth and learning, and one of the principle ways in which children develop their sense of self.

However the growing child soon learns that in the adult world, talking to oneself out loud is suspect. It is associated with madmen and eccentrics. Only on stage do heroes soliloquize. For the majority of "normal" people, the natural dialogue within the self becomes silenced some time during childhood. The dialogue continues in our minds as thought follows thought, but usually in ways we are barely aware of.

Still, people do talk to themselves — possibly more than most would be willing to admit. It is fairly common to hear people muttering audibly to themselves as they go about their business. Some people are constantly telling themselves what they want to do or not do. Sometimes people reprimand themselves. Another common phenomenon is giving vent to strong feelings under one's breath or in private, especially when unable to display them openly to the people who actually arouse them, such as parents, spouses, rivals, bullies, the boss, etc.

When people feel that their lives and development are being excessively restricted by those around them or by social convention in general, they may go to a therapist to talk out their problems. Having someone there to hear them is important, and the feedback of the therapist may be very valuable. Most important of all, however, is the process of actually talking things out. By expressing our inner problems and feelings, we gain deeper insight and begin finding solutions.

Today there is a growing interest in the use of language as a means of working on oneself. There is the salesman who stands in front of the mirror each morning and gives himself a pep talk. People who want to quit smoking, lose weight or change themselves in other ways are learning the value of repeating affirmations to themselves. And so we are on the way to rediscovering something that religion has taught for thousands of years: prayer.

Prayer

Prayer is a grossly misunderstood activity. The primary connotation of the English word "pray" is to request, and this has led to a widespread image of prayer as being centered around asking for things — health, wealth, success, and so on.

Prayer is often thought of as a form of quasi-magic resorted to by the primitive and ignorant in an effort to overcome their helplessness in the face of overwhelming natural forces. For many people religious prayer rituals are meaningless, antiquated, formal ceremonies conducted in a language they do not understand, and having nothing to do with their inner selves and personal issues.

It is largely forgotten that up until our great-grandparents' generation many people found it quite natural to talk directly and spontaneously to God in their own native language, discussing all their needs and pouring out their hearts. For the majority of people today, the very idea of talking directly to God in your own words is mystifying, awkward, and unreal. God is so awesome and far away. How are you supposed to talk to Him? How could God be interested in all our petty needs and problems? In any case, if God knows everything, including our thoughts, why is it necessary to talk to Him? Besides, what kind of conversation is it? When you talk to a person, you see their reactions, and hear what they have to say. How does God answer?

But "it is not in the Heavens... The word is very close to you, in your mouth and in your heart to do it" (Deuteronomy 30:12-14). Prayer does not have to mean speaking to God "out there." It can be as direct and intimate as talking to your own heart. If you look at the actual content of many of the Psalms and prayers of the Siddur, although prayers of request and petition, especially for spiritual illumination, have a prominent place, they are only one aspect of prayer. There are also many descriptions of God's works and activities in nature and history — praises, thanks and acknowledgement — because recognizing God's active presence in our lives and the world around us is one of the most important ways of experiencing our connection with Him.

In addition to prayers *to* God or statements *about* Him, the Psalms in particular give intimate voice to the innermost thoughts and feelings of the spiritual seeker in every phase of the search — introspection and self-judgment; happiness about the good in oneself, regret about the bad; the struggle with evil instincts; fears, doubts and questions; the joy of devotion; reverence, love, awe and yearning for God, and so on. Another important part of prayer is affirmation: we repeatedly remind ourselves of our faith, hope and trust in God; we exhort ourselves against fear, demoralization and despair; and we set our minds on the qualities of justice and righteousness, kindness and mercy that we want to cultivate in our lives.

God's first words to Avraham, founder of the Jewish People, were: "*Lech lecha* — go to your*self*" (Genesis 12:1). The essence of the spiritual journey is to go deep into ourselves in order to discover and draw out the Princely higher self from where it is buried amongst our Turkey identities, thoughts and feelings — to draw it out, express it and bring it to perfection. We accomplish this through prayer — talking directly to the heart and soul, that is to say, the self, in our own words.

Ultimately prayer and self-communion must meet, because the self — the soul — derives from God: the soul is "a part of God above" (Job 31:2). Thus the more we discover and develop our spiritual side, the more the Divine Presence manifests itself in us, and we begin to experience just how intimately we are bound up with God in our essence, and how close at hand He is in our thoughts and feelings and consciousness.

In the works of Rebbe Nachman, our main source of teaching about hisbodidus, the practice is often called *sichah beino le-vein kono* — conversation between oneself and one's Owner. (See *Likutey Moharan* II:25, etc.) One might say that the conversation is always somewhere *in between* ourselves and God — sometimes more with ourselves, sometimes more with God.

Thus in one discussion, Rebbe Nachman characterizes our relationship with God during hisbodidus as that of "a child pleading with his father... complaining and pestering him. How good it is when you can awaken your heart and plead until tears stream from your eyes and you stand like a little child crying before its Father" (*Rabbi Nachman's Wisdom* #7). Elsewhere, Rebbe Nachman suggests that we should talk to God "like a person speaks to his friend" (Exodus 33:11, see *Likutey Moharan* II:99) — discussing things frankly and earnestly, heart to heart, in order to work everything out. In another lesson, Rebbe Nachman tells us to try talking directly to ourselves, literally addressing the different parts of ourselves and even the limbs of the physical body, guiding and training ourselves to do what we want and live as we should (*Tzaddik* #442).

Out Loud

One of the essential problems we all face is a multitude of conflicting voices. The whole world confronts us with a clamor of cries and messages demanding our attention — from the people around us to the ringing telephones, beepers, adverts, signs, slogans... "Hey there! Stop! Go! Come here! Do this! Don't do that!" One may try to close out the external distractions by going to a quiet location. But as soon as one looks inside one's private inner world, there is an endless parade of thoughts, images, sensations, impulses, needs, desires, anxieties, fears, strategies, plans, etc.

The Prince in us sends one set of messages, but the Turkey vies for our attention with a constant stream of urgent messages of its own. One wants to study... but suddenly one has an irresistible urge to eat, sleep, or read the papers, etc. One wants to pray and meditate calmly... but all kinds of things need attending to, so one has to rush. One wants to be kind and patient with others... but somehow there seem to be so many good reasons for getting irritated and angry. The most insidious inner talk the Turkey feeds us is endless negative commentary about our life experiences, the people we encounter and the things they do, or, worst of all, about our very selves.

The way to overcome the Turkey voice is by raising *your own voice* — the voice you really want to hear and follow. By repeating out loud the things you know to be true — what you want most deeply in life, how important your goals are to you, and how you plan to achieve them — you strengthen the very aspects of your personality that you want to cultivate, and lead yourself to where you need to go. "*Hakol me'orer et ha-kavanah* — the voice arouses attention" (*Kitzur Shulchan Aruch* 6:1). When you raise your voice, your attention follows: the words you say aloud become the focus of your thoughts.

At times you may need to *find* your true voice, because your true self, the self you are searching for, may be buried behind years of repression, shyness, embarrassment, poor self-esteem, negativity, self-neglect and the like. You have to fan the flames of your nascent self, learning to express new, tender, unfamiliar feelings. Sometimes you may have to dredge out voices from way back in your past, or experiment with new voices. One of the most important voices to search for is the voice of song — your own song of joy, love and devotion to God.

When you speak out loud, it is not only the talking that's important, but also *hearing* what you say. If you only think your thoughts, they may fly through your mind so quickly that they remain vague and incoherent and eventually just disappear. When you say them out loud, the very act of articulating them forces you to clarify them. You hear what you have said and it makes an impact. Sometimes when you hear what you are saying, you realize it isn't quite right. You have to develop the idea further, express yourself more clearly. You redefine what you want to say and examine it again, until you are saying exactly what you want to say. This is the way you learn to think and talk more clearly and effectively.

In mystical literature, speech is called *malchut* — rule and power. Not only can you use words to tell others what you want them to do. You can also use them to direct and program yourself. When you want to think about a given issue, formulate a question and say it over to yourself, as the Wise Man had the Prince ask himself, "Who are you?" This is a method of concentrating on the issue you want to think about. As you work out which aspects of yourself you most want to develop or change, express what you want to achieve in simple formulas and use them to direct yourself toward your goal. For example, when you want to relax your body, you can shine the torch of your consciousness to each of your muscle groups in turn and gently whisper "Relax." If you want to change your eating habits, develop affirmations that you repeat to yourself in the kitchen or at the table, and so on.

Use your voice to create the atmosphere *you* want to live in. Even when you find yourself surrounded by negativity, you can whisper positive messages to yourself: "Peace, calm, kindness..." When you want to elevate your spiritual awareness and heighten your consciousness of God, simply say "God," "HaShem" or "Ribono shel Olam" etc. out loud to yourself again and again. Hum your favorite melodies of joy and devotion. Listen to the melody as you sing: let it fill your entire consciousness, and lift you to a higher plane.

Hisbodidus in Practice

Wherever you go, your mouth goes with you. Talking to your soul and to God is something you can do practically any time of the day or night. At any juncture, you can use words, laughs, cries, songs and other vocal means any way *you* choose, to influence your moods, focus your attention and lead yourself to deeper spiritual fulfillment.

But for steady personal growth and spiritual development, hisbodidus should be practiced for set periods of time on a regular basis. Hisbodidus then becomes the center of your spiritual discipline, the time when you experiment and develop ways of talking that are most effective for you. Ideally you should fix special times to go somewhere that will give you privacy and the freedom to express yourself uninhibitedly. The more regular and persistent you are with hisbodidus, the more progress you will make.

How long?

If possible, the length of your regular hisbodidus sessions should be what in Hebrew is called a *sha'ah*. How long is that? The word *sha'ah* is translated as "an hour," but that does not have to mean an hour of exactly sixty minutes. In Torah literature we find that the length of a *sha'ah* is flexible: for example, although the length of day- and night-time varies according to the seasons, for halachic purposes the day and night are always divided into twelve *sha'ot* each. This means that in the summer the daytime hours are long and the night-time hours are short, while in the winter the reverse is the case.

So the "hour" of hisbodidus need not necessarily be one clock-hour: it may be more and it may be less. What really matters is that you should allocate sufficient time for your hisbodidus sessions to settle and focus your mind and do serious spiritual work. If you had important business to discuss with your doctor, lawyer, accountant, etc. you would want enough time to explain all the relevant details calmly and fully, and work out with them exactly what steps you need to take next. This is the approach you should take with your hisbodidus sessions. In Hebrew, *sha'ah* is also a verb having the connotation of "turn to, pay attention to" (as in Genesis 4:4). Make your *sha'ah* of hisbodidus long enough to be able to turn to God and give your full attention to the all-important work of spiritual growth.

Sixty minutes of hisbodidus is a long time. Some people will find they can benefit from daily sessions of this length and fill each one with useful work. Others may feel this is too much for them. They may find they run out of things to say, or feel they simply cannot invest the time. If a full clock-hour is excessive for you, this does not mean you should not practice hisbodidus at all. Even shorter periods of hisbodidus are very valuable. You can accomplish a great deal in as little as ten or fifteen minutes — and it is certainly better to settle for shorter periods and *do* it than to promise yourself a full hour and never get around to it.

There has to be an upper limit to hisbodidus as well, or else it becomes counter-productive. Chassidic literature contains accounts of exceptionally pious people who would spend hours and hours, and even days, in secluded prayer and devotion. Some beginners who have time on their hands become so enthusiastic that they think they can do the same. This is a mistake. Without years of preparation and practice, excessively lengthy hisbodidus sessions on a regular basis are likely to become obsessive and result in self-absorption and depression. (*Likutey Moharan* II:96 and *Rabbi Nachman's Wisdom* #41.)

There are times when it may be appropriate to make a somewhat longer hisbodidus session — for example in the month of Elul, in preparation for the High Holidays, or when confronting a serious personal problem, an important decision, etc. At such times, you might want to take extra time to go to a park or country area and work intensively either for one long period or a number of shorter periods separated by interludes for relaxation. For those who are able to take a few days' retreat away from the pressures of life, this can be very conducive to spiritual regeneration.

However the purpose of hisbodidus is not to escape from life but to take a temporary break from other business and afterwards return and live more fully and effectively. It often happens when people start hisbodidus and begin to understand its power, that they realize how much of a backlog of personal work they have after years of neglect. They imagine that extended sessions will help them clear this backlog more quickly. That is an illusion. More important than the length of one's sessions is the work one does to integrate the insights they bring into practical day-to-day living.

How often?

To make continuous progress with hisbodidus, it is best to practice every day. The daily hisbodidus session is comparable to the daily meeting between the director and staff of an organization. Its health and success depend on the care with which they monitor its activities and progress and work out what each department has to do in order to achieve the overall goal. They need to conduct their business thoroughly but briskly, and then, as soon as the meeting is over, get back to work with new direction and energy.

If you feel you are presently unable to invest in a full-length session of hisbodidus each day, start with shorter sessions. Could you manage fifteen to twenty minutes a day, or at least a few times a week? On days when you cannot allocate a substantial block of time, try to find even as little as five minutes just to sit down, close your eyes for a short while, say a few words to God, and affirm your desire to practice hisbodidus regularly. This will help you maintain the continuity of your spiritual work.

When?

If you understand the value and importance of hisbodidus and seriously want to make it a regular part of your life, take some time to consider how you can fit a hisbodidus session into your daily schedule. Try to find a convenient time when you are not too tired. Hisbodidus is a serious project: to make the most progress you need to give it your full attention.

Everybody has his own schedule, and each day is different. Be realistic. What parts of your schedule are fixed and unchangeable, and where is there room for flexibility? Are you utilizing all of your time wisely? Are there ways you could rearrange some of your existing activities? Are some of the things you are doing now *less* important than hisbodidus?

If your schedule varies unpredictably from day to day, there may be no alternative but to snatch time for hisbodidus whenever you can. Could you consider getting up twenty minutes earlier in the morning? If you are not too tired, could you consider taking a few minutes last thing at night before going to sleep? People with more flexibility might consider two twenty-minute sessions a day, one in the morning and one late at night. This can be a very good way to start the day on a good footing and then round it off by making a reckoning and getting back in touch with yourself.

Rebbe Nachman says the ideal time for hisbodidus is after midnight! (*Likutey Moharan* I:52). Even today there are Breslover Chassidim who go to bed soon after night-fall, sleep for five or six hours, and then get up at two or three in the morning for hisbodidus. The workaday grind is at a halt and most of the world is asleep. In these sweet, hushed moments it is possible to attain complete calm and detachment from the stresses and tensions of daily life and focus clearly on the ultimate goal of life.

For many people, hisbodidus at such a time may seem an unattainable goal, but don't dismiss the idea out of hand. You may be able to get up an hour or so before dawn once in a while, and even if you can't, it's worth trying to imagine the calm and quiet of those night-time moments in order to understand the ideal of hisbodidus. Even by day, when you sit relaxing and preparing for hisbodidus, you can close your eyes and *envisage* yourself sitting in complete quiet in the hush of night. This in itself might help you to attain a degree of calm.

Where?

The best place to practice hisbodidus is in a place where you will not be disturbed and where no-one will hear you if you talk, call out or cry out loud. This way you will not feel inhibited, or worried that others will get to know the details of your inner life.

Rebbe Nachman tells us that the ideal place for hisbodidus is somewhere isolated that people do not go to (*op.cit.*) or in the woods and meadows (*Rabbi Nachman's Wisdom* #98). If there is a safe place of this kind within easy reach of you, it is the most conducive for giving vent to your true feelings, experimenting with shouts and cries, and drawing out and developing deeply buried parts of the self. Even if there is nowhere like this that you can go to regularly, could you make a special journey to somewhere suitable in the countryside, at least from time to time — perhaps in the company of a friend?

Rebbe Nachman also recommends practicing hisbodidus in a private room (*Rabbi Nachman's Wisdom* #274) and this is where the majority of people are likely to practice hisbodidus most of the time. If you have an option, choose the room you feel most at ease in. Try to minimize potential distractions in the room itself: put away newspapers, magazines and anything else that might tempt you to interrupt your hisbodidus. Arrange with others in the house not to disturb you during your session. If possible, have someone else answer the telephone, or switch on your answering machine if you have one. If you feel apprehensive about what others might think if they hear you talking out loud, you might consider explaining to them what you are doing.

Even if you do not have access to somewhere private, you can still practice hisbodidus. Can you find a corner of the house where no-one will disturb you for a while? Do you have a yard or garden? Rebbe Nachman suggests that by draping a Tallit over your eyes you can create your own room and converse with God as you desire! You can talk with God in bed under the covers, as King David did ("Each night I converse in my bed..." Psalms 6:7), or whisper to God while sitting in front of an open book. Let others think you are studying! Surprisingly, public places where nobody knows you can sometimes give privacy of a kind. With a little imagination you should be able to find many places where you can practice hisbodidus.

Generally speaking it is preferable to hold your regular hisbodidus sessions in the same place: this helps to give your work continuity. At times, however, going somewhere different for a change — to a park, the woods, a quiet synagogue etc. — may provide a new stimulus. It is interesting to try casual hisbodidus wherever you happen to be — in the car, the office, the supermarket, and so on. It can give you a powerful sense of the presence of God and lead to deeper self-understanding, increased confidence and greater freedom.

Posture

Most people associate meditation with special postures such as the lotus position or the erect seated posture discussed above (Chapter 4). However there is no specific posture for hisbodidus. Whatever postures you personally find most conducive to your own *yishuv ha-da'at* are the ones you should use in your hisbodidus.

In the Sh'ma, we say: "You should speak on these things when you *sit* in your house, and when you *go* on your way, and when you *lie down* and when you *rise up*" (Deuteronomy 6:7). Sitting, walking, reclining and standing up are all suitable postures for hisbodidus.

Sitting: We have seen above (Chapter 4) that sitting is directly associated with *yishuv ha-da'at*, and the majority of people are likely to find this posture the most conducive to the calm and concentration desirable for hisbodidus. If you wish to practice sitting relaxation and breathing as a preparation for hisbodidus, you can then move directly into hisbodidus without having to change your position. Many people associate meditation with physical stillness, but this is not necessary for hisbodidus. Sit however you feel most comfortable, and move about as and when you want to. The important thing is to be able to think clearly and express yourself. For some people in some phases of hisbodidus, sitting still in the relaxation posture can be very helpful. Others may find the steady, gentle swaying often associated with Jewish prayer conducive to concentration and devotion.

Walking: Some people find walking about an aid to concentration, others find it a distraction. This is an individual matter. If you find that walking around in a park or the woods, or even pacing up and down in your room, helps you to think and express yourself, then do it!

Reclining: Lying on one's back is not an appropriate posture for spiritual work (see above p. 65) but lying on one's side is quite in order, and as mentioned above, King David himself practiced hisbodidus in bed at night. Speak to God last thing at night, before you drift off to sleep. Your whispered prayers and affirmations to yourself about your goals in general and what you want to do tomorrow are powerful instruments of growth and change.

Standing: If you are able to posture yourself comfortably so that you are relaxed and clear-headed, standing before God is one of the noblest and most appropriate positions for hisbodidus.

Procedure

Hisbodidus is by definition an activity that you practice by yourself. Prayer and meditation groups of two or three or more can be very powerful, and when practicing hisbodidus in the woods etc. it can be very helpful and supportive for friends to go out together. However the essential work of hisbodidus — introspection, talk and prayer — is something each one can only do by him- or herself, and when you practice hisbodidus you are most likely to be alone.

Working by yourself takes a certain amount of self discpline. Hisbodidus has its up's and down's (see below pp. 137-9) and when the going starts to become a little difficult there is no-one to stop you from getting up and abandoning your session. It can help to have a watch in front of you, decide how long your session is going to be, and tell yourself: "For the next *x* amount of time I am in hisbodidus." Promise yourself that you will not get up before that time expires, no matter what happens in the hisbodidus — even if nothing happens, or you get drowsy and fall asleep, etc.

As you begin a session of hisbodidus, it is very helpful to give charity (*Shulchan Aruch, Yoreh De'ah* 249:14, and see *Likutey Moharan* II:4,2). Keep a charity box where you have your sessions and give a small coin each time you start — later on you can donate the money to any cause you choose. As you give the money, pray to God to open the gates to your prayers and meditation.

Mark the start of your hisbodidus with an affirmation that you want to make a new beginning and come close to God:

"Ribono shel Olam, Master of the World, I want to come close to You and serve You. I want to start *now!* Please help me."

Closing one's eyes during hisbodidus can be a great aid to focusing and concentration. One turns away from the external visual world and its many deceptive images — the world of "Under the Table" — in order to focus on the inner world and search for the light of truth. Keep your eyes closed only if you feel comfortable doing so — it is helpful but not essential. If you are not accustomed to keeping your eyes closed for extended periods of meditation, you could try to do so for short periods. Don't feel discouraged if you open your eyes from time to time!

What do you do in hisbodidus?

What you actually do in your hisbodidus sessions is up to you. In its very nature, hisbodidus is an individual practice. Hisbodidus is private time for your self. It is *your* time to work on yourself, your life and your growth. What you do may vary with your individual needs and interests at different periods in your life and development, and even from day to day. The possibilities are endless. A single session may be used for several different kinds of work, one after the other.

For some people, the most important aspect of hisbodidus may be the opportunity it gives them to simply relax and free themselves from their everyday tensions in order to calmly survey their various activities and involvements and get a better perspective on their lives.

Hisbodidus can also be used for creative work. Someone wanting to develop a new project (whether private, business, community, academic, literary, artistic or of some other kind) might wish to devote one or more sessions to "brainstorming" — exploring different ideas and approaches and developing plans. Another application of hisbodidus would be to think and pray intensively about specific problems one faces — whether personal, social, financial, business, career, health, etc.

For those interested in their personal growth and development, the possibilities range from cultivating particular aptitudes or resolving specific problems — fears, lack of confidence, addictions of various kinds, etc. — to the most far-reaching self-analysis and transformation. People working on personal issues in conjunction with a counsellor or therapist may wish to use hisbodidus for follow-up work. This can help when seeking to apply the insights gained in joint sessions to practical life, and, even more importantly, to develop the ability to cope with the challenges of life independently and maturely.

Above all, hisbodidus is the time for spiritual exploration and development. The literature of Mussar and Chassidut offers many different pathways of devotion, whether through looking outwards and contemplating the surrounding wonders of the Creation and their Source, or by turning inwards — "from my flesh I will see God" (Job 19:26). It is in hisbodidus that one can experiment and endeavor to follow these pathways in practice, exploiting the awesome power of words, cries, sighs, prayers and songs to elevate one's consciousness and lift oneself closer to God. Hisbodidus can bring one to the highest levels of love, awe and Godly devotion.

Sitting, Breathing and Awareness

Unless you have a clear idea of exactly what you want to do in a particular session, one of the best ways to begin a hisbodidus session is by sitting down and going into deep relaxation. Especially if you are tense or have been preoccupied with mundane thoughts and activities, relaxation will help to still and open your mind and enable you to see yourself and your life in a far broader perspective.

As you become more relaxed, you may wish to practice long, deep breathing for a while in order to clear your mind of heaviness, fuzziness and interference. Softly humming an appropriate melody of devotion can also help put you into the right frame of mind for hisbodidus.

Then, as you sit quietly, simply be aware of what is going on in your mind, without as yet trying to direct your thoughts in any way. Many different kinds of thoughts and feelings are likely to come into your mind in a jumble — some profound and highly significant, some trivial and meaningless, some having no apparent relevance at all. Instead of trying to define and analyse your thoughts and feelings, simply observe them. What is going on?

Getting in Touch

Because of the pressures of day-to-day living, we tend to suppress the Princely higher self from our normal consciousness. We are often so busy doing all the things we have to do each day that we do not have the time to listen to what our conscience is saying. Moreover, there is a significant part of us that often does not *want* to listen.

On one level, we may feel regretful about, wounded by, or otherwise sensitive to things we or others have been doing, but we may be so involved in the practical business of living that we are not able to deal with these thoughts and feelings, or even admit them into consciousness, and they go underground. Hisbodidus is the time to allow them to surface, to explore and work through them.

When we study Torah and yearn to follow its high ideals in every detail of our lives, we may often feel that we have failed the test of actually applying them in real situations. The higher self wants to do the right thing — to study and pray well, eat correctly, do business honestly, talk and behave properly, etc.

However, outside pressures and the inner Turkey push us into doing things we know to be wrong. One of the most characteristic responses of the Turkey is to evade and deny the sense of guilt and wrong-doing and push it out of consciousness. But the wound remains, and the Prince feels it.

Confession

Hisbodidus is the time to admit our guilt about the things we have done wrong and to work through it. It is no good living with regrets: we need to be positive, not negative. But the only way to free ourselves of regrets is to confront them openly. Until we face up to them, they will always continue to nag at us one way or another.

Get into the habit of admitting the things you did wrong. You will find it will give you a great sense of relief. Cast your mind over your various involvements and activities. If you are conscious of having done something contrary to what you know to be right, or neglected something you know you should have done, admit it honestly. Have the courage to accept responsibility for what you do. Remember the details of what you did, and say or whisper out loud: "I did (or failed to do) such and such, and I know it was wrong — it goes against what I know to be right. I regret what I did, and I fully intend not to do this again."

Our suppressed feelings are often more subtle and complex than simple regret. As you sit in hisbodidus, listen carefully to your inner voices, and try to draw them to the surface. Express out loud what you are feeling inside. Even if you think some of your private thoughts and emotions are unacceptable, admit them honestly before God. If they are offensive, ask God to cleanse you and help you let go of them. If you feel stifled cries and screams inside you, let them come out: cry and shout out loud. Who is it calling out? What are you trying to say?

Surface Patterns, Deeper Causes

Confessing — admitting to the things you do wrong. things that go against your own goals and standards — is only the first step. In order to make meaningful changes in your life, you need to ask *why* you do things that violate your own standards: what impels you?

Don't simply think about specific things you have done in a piecemeal fashion, or express your inner thoughts and feelings as if they are disconnected. Try to develop a more general picture of your personality by observing *patterns* in the various areas of your life. Don't just say, "I ate so much last night, I was too sleepy to learn," but "I tend to over-eat in the evenings — what makes me do that? Under what circumstances do I reach out for unnecessary food? What are the characteristic thoughts and feelings I have as I do so?" Don't just say, "I had a furious argument with *x* today," but "I tend to get angry in the following kinds of situations. What do they have in common? How does my anger develop? At what point do I tend to lose control? What really is it that makes me so mad?"

In Hebrew this is called *cheshbon ha-nefesh* — the balance-sheet of the soul, or spiritual accounting. It means deepening your understanding of your life and activities, and evaluating them against the yardstick of Torah. This is obviously not a project that you can complete in a single session of hisbodidus. You will need weeks and months at the very least in order to build a clear, honest picture of yourself. For some people, sorting through and understanding their different sides can be one of the major tasks of hisbodidus. It is a task greatly complicated by the fact that some aspects may be in conflict with others, while the on-going process of growth and change itself keeps our personalities in a state of constant flux.

Something that may help you in your self-exploration is to take a pen and paper and make a kind of "map" of yourself. List the different areas of your life — e.g. physical functions: eating, sleeping, etc.; personal relationships: with family, friends, others; work; money matters; spiritual pursuits: study, prayer, meditation etc.; leisure-time activities, and so on.

Now consider each of the different areas in turn and ask how you function in each. What, if any, are your goals in this area? To what extent do you live up to them? Do you sometimes do things that are in conflict with your avowed goals? Why? Note particular issues that come up for you in any given area.

Take a general look at yourself. What kind of a person are you? What images do you have of yourself? Are they positive or negative? How would you define what your life is about? What motivates you? When do you feel good, and when do you feel bad? What are your better qualities? What are your main faults? What messages do you give yourself? Do you encourage or discourage yourself? How do you react to problematic situations? Are you easily thrown off course, or do you persist and keep going? How do you relate to other people? Easily, or with difficulty? What are the main problems in your life and what are you doing about them? What are you afraid of? What has made you the way you are?

Briefly note down your answers using key words and phrases, and think about how your various character traits relate to one another. Keep this map of yourself so that you can refer back to it in successive hisbodidus sessions, redefining, expanding and developing it as your self-understanding grows.

Your Goals

Ask yourself about your purpose in life. Think about your various activities and involvements and ask yourself what you are trying to achieve. Do you do the things you do because *you* want to, or because they have been imposed on you by others.

What are your obligations to others? What are your obligations to yourself? What are your obligations to God?

If you don't *know* the purpose of your life, admit it. Tell God frankly and openly that you do not understand why you were created, and ask Him to help you know what He wants of you.

Make it a regular part of your hisbodidus to define and clarify your goals. Keep a detailed list, starting with a definition of your overall purpose in life. Note down the things you think you *ought* to aim for, those you would *like* to aim for, and the goals that your current activities and involvements are in fact geared to. To what extent is your present life-style in harmony with the goals that are most important to you? Are your various goals in harmony with each other, or do some of them conflict with others? To what extent are your goals practicable? How will you be able to realize them?

How can you attain what you want?

It is impossible to work on everything at once. There may be many things you want to change in your life, and much that you want to accomplish. However if you try to achieve too much at once, it can be counter-productive. Follow the example of the Wise Man (see above, Chapter 3). To cure the Prince, he went project by project, step by step.

Think about what your most important priorities should be at the present juncture, and come to a decision about what you should concentrate on for the time being. Affirm that this is your decision. Say out loud: "I have decided to work on *x*, *y*, and *z*." Next, decide which project you need to work on first.

Now concentrate your thoughts on this project as intensely as you can. Focus every faculty of your mind on your goal, spelling out in detail each of the different steps you will need to take in order to achieve it. What will you have to do in the external world? And which changes will you have to make in yourself? What about the things you can do nothing about? Can you learn to live with them and even turn them into advantages? Work out all the different things you will have to do in the fullest detail. In what order will you have to do them? What is the very first step you will have to take? When and how are you going to do so?

"For example," says Rebbe Nachman, "you can concentrate on the fact that you want to study all four sections of the *Shulchan Aruch* in their entirety. You can calculate that if you study five pages a day, you will finish all four sections in a single year. Picture in your mind exactly how you will go about this course of study. Concentrate so strongly that you are literally obsessed with the thought. If your desire is strong and your concentration intense enough, your plans will be fulfilled" (*Rabbi Nachman's Wisdom* #62).

The methods Rebbe Nachman suggests — working out the steps that have to be taken, visualizing yourself taking them, and concentrating intensely on your desire to do so — can be applied to accomplish anything in life.

Praying to God and Talking to Yourself

We are taught that God controls the entire universe, yet at the same time, man has free will. If God is in complete control, this would seem to mean that we should depend on God for everything. In that case, why do *we* have to work and make an effort to achieve our goals? Why do we even have to pray? On the other hand, if man has free will, this would appear to indicate that anything we attain is up to us. In that case, what sense does it make to pray for God's help when everything is in fact in our hands?

How can it be that God controls everything, yet man has free will? Rebbe Nachman teaches that this is a paradox that is simply impossible for us to resolve or even comprehend in this life. Indeed it is our very inability to grasp this enigma that gives us our free will. Rather than making fruitless efforts to fathom the unfathomable, Rebbe Nachman tells us that we must have faith that things are in our hands *and* that at the same time, God is in control of everything. (See *Restore My Soul* pp. 73-9 for a fuller discussion.)

Whatever you want to achieve in life, you must have faith that only God can bring it about, but at the same time you must know that it is entirely up to you to make every effort and take all the necessary steps in order to attain it. This basic principle of faith affects the way you should pray in hisbodidus when working out how to achieve your goals. As you concentrate on the details of what you want to accomplish, list every step in turn and ask God to help you with each one.

But while praying to God, you must also act as if everything is up to you. You must therefore also talk to yourself in hisbodidus, gearing yourself for action. Affirm your goals and explain to yourself exactly what you want to accomplish. Encourage yourself. Remind yourself how important your goal is, and talk yourself into working toward it wholeheartedly. Take yourself step by step through your project, telling yourself what you will do in each progressive stage.

However, if you feel that something is beyond your power to achieve for whatever reason, do not conclude that it is pointless to try, and that you should not ask God to help you. You may have distant hopes and ambitions that seem unreachable at present, or indeed ever. You may feel locked in situations which seem unchangeable. But God is all-powerful. Tell God of your yearnings. Plead with Him again and again to help you. Never lose faith in God's power to work miracles!

Maybe you are attracted by the exalted levels of spiritual service described in Chassidut, but dismiss them as being way beyond your capability in this lifetime. Perhaps they are — right now. But it does no harm to heave a sigh and tell God how you *wish* you could achieve such levels, and how greatly you value and yearn for them. Who knows? For God, everything is possible. Some of the most amazing accomplishments in the spiritual history of mankind started off as mere pipedreams — only the people who dreamed them were bold enough to pray for them. Be daring! (See *Rabbi Nachman's Stories* #9 "The Sophisticate and the Simpleton.")

Your Pen is Your Friend

"Get yourself a friend" (*Avot* 1:6). The Hebrew, *k'neh lecha chaver*, can also be translated as: "Your pen is your friend."

Unless you have a spiritual teacher or a very good friend in whom you can confide about your hisbodidus, most of the time you will have no-one to guide you directly or keep track of your work and progress. One of the best aids for hisbodidus, and spiritual growth in general, is paper and something to write with.

At the start of your hisbodidus session, make a brief agenda of the various topics you want to work on. You might want to note down a number of general headings (e.g. livelihood, health, family, spiritual pursuits, people to pray for, and so on) listing specific items under each one (e.g. livelihood: ways of increasing income, improvement of performance at work, job-change, charity donations, etc.)

In the course of the session, when you are trying to work out complex issues, it may help you to note down ideas as you think and talk, though be careful not to turn your hisbodidus into a diary-writing session. The essence of hisbodidus is the spoken word: the purpose of writing is to *aid* your thinking and praying.

To give continuity to your spiritual work, conclude your hisbodidus sessions by looking back over what came up, and making brief notes about particular insights you may have gained, issues and questions you want to go into in greater detail another time, etc. If you are praying to God for answers to specific questions, keep a record of your questions and then, in the days and weeks ahead, note down all the relevant ideas that come to you. You should begin to see how your questions are being answered.

Keep your list of your goals and refer to it frequently so that you can check your progress. Get into the habit of listing the various things you have to attend to. What do you plan to do today? This week? This month? Over the course of the coming year? List what you have to do in order of priority. Organize your papers in a special file and look over them regularly.

The Process of Hisbodidus

"Acknowledge God for what is past and cry out about the future."

Berachot 54a

The present is where the past and the future meet. As you sit in hisbodidus, you are at the interface. The questions the Wise Man turned back on the Prince — "Who are you and what are you doing here?" — point to both the past and the future. The past — because who you are, and what you are doing in your life right now, are bound up with all that has happened with you until now. And the future, because "Who are you?" also means, Who are you potentially? Who is the real you, your authentic higher self — your future self? And "What are you doing here?" can mean, What is the purpose of your life, and what *should* you be doing with your life?

These questions, pointing as they do to both your past and your future, are the guiding questions of the growth process, and thus of hisbodidus. You have to ask and define who you want to be and what you want to attain. This is how to define your goals and work out how to move toward them. But you must also gain a deeper understanding of who you are already — your present behavior-patterns and what lies behind them.

Only by acknowledging yourself as you really are can you begin to work out what you must do in practical terms to change yourself and become what you want to be.

Paradoxically, to go freely into the future you must first go into your past. This is why hisbodidus begins with confession and acknowledgement of what you are. "Who are you?" — "I'm a turkey — I've done this and this..." The effects of the mistakes we make in life remain with us and exert an influence over us whether we like it or not. Only when we confront our mistakes frankly and regret them can we free ourselves of the hold of the past.

"Acknowledge God for the past and cry out about the future." The Talmud's directive about prayer is the key to hisbodidus. What is now — the present — is the result of the past. The first thing is to "acknowledge it" — to be frank and honest about who we are and what we have made ourselves into, and to try to understand what lies behind our existing patterns of behavior. Where we are unaware of this, we must dig down beneath our defenses to uncover factors we may be denying. Then, with an understanding of what we are and what we have to change, we have to "cry out" about the future — to use words and cries to our souls and to God in order to bring the potential self into being.

Your efforts to develop your self-understanding through hisbodidus will obviously increase your self-awareness as you go through your life day by day. And this awareness will in turn feed into your hisbodidus. Similarly, the more you think about and clarify your goals in hisbodidus, the more effective you will be in pursuing them. As time goes on, you will need to spend much less time trying to understand your basic make-up and long-term goals. The main work will then be "fine-tuning" yourself to pursue your chosen goals more effectively, so that you can steadily bring more and more of yourself into the service of God, until you love God "with all your heart and all your soul and all your might" (Deuteronomy 6:5).

Getting Started & Keeping Going

Imagine the scene under the table as the Prince and the Wise Man first started getting to know one another. Before the ice began to thaw, things were probably very slow and stilted. Perhaps the Prince strutted around a bit and gave a few of his best turkey yelps just for show, until curiosity began to get the better of him. Should he speak? Shouldn't he speak? Do Turkeys speak? Finally he put his question: "Who are you and what are you doing here?"

"And who are you?" asked the Wise Man. "Me? I am a turkey." "Are you really?" said the Wise Man. "What a coincidence! So am I! I'm also a turkey." The Prince may have found his new companion somewhat peculiar, but their frank mutual confession did provide a good basis for a relationship.

During the royal mealtimes, the Prince and the Wise Man probably did little talking: with crumbs and bones plopping down on all sides, the Prince had plenty to do. But then the king and all the other diners would leave the table. The royal butlers would clear away the plates and cutlery, and the royal sweepers would clean up all around, pretending not to notice the two of them under the table. Finally the lights would be turned down for the night, and the Prince and the Wise Man would be left to themselves.

It was probably during the long hushed nights that the Prince and the Wise Man achieved the intimacy and trust that became the foundation of the Prince's cure. The Prince will have learned that he really could confide in this father figure-cum-friend and talk about his deepest problems. He will have been able to tell him things he had never told anyone else — about what it was actually like to be a Turkey, how those irresistible urges really felt, how much pain and anguish lay beneath them, the terrible frustrations of Turkey life, his secret fears and gnawing despair... How the Prince must have cried... and then laughed in relief... and talked more... and more...

People trying hisbodidus for the first time sometimes find it hard to start talking. How do you begin? The key to talking to God is to say exactly what you think and feel. Shortly before Rebbe Nachman passed away in 1810, he was seriously ill. His four-year-old grandson, Yisrael, came into him. The Rebbe said: "Pray to God that I should become well again." The little boy went aside and said: "God! God! Let my *zeida* be well!" The adults in the room started smiling, but Rebbe Nachman said: "This is how we have to ask things of God. What other way is there to pray?" The essence of prayer is total simplicity: to speak to God like a child talking to his father, or the way a person talks with a friend (*Tzaddik* #439).

Let's assume you have gone somewhere alone with no-one to disturb you. You have made the time; you have nowhere to run to. How do you begin?

Sit comfortably. Relax and take a few breaths. Some people are well aware of their problems and the issues they want to work on, but if you don't know how to begin, try the following:

Say out loud: "Who am I and what am I doing here?" Simply say the words.

Do you feel funny about talking out loud? Some people find it strange hearing themselves talk to themselves for the first time — though it isn't very different from looking at yourself in a mirror!

What do *you* feel? Say out loud what you feel. If you feel this is crazy or funny, say so. Laugh! Then ask yourself again: "Who am I and what am I doing here?"

Speak to God. "God. Why did You create me? What is my purpose in this world? What do You want of me?"

Think carefully. What answers come to mind? Try and formulate an answer. Say it out loud. Listen to yourself saying it. If you see that what you said is not really the answer, rephrase it.

"God, what do I want to do in my hisbodidus? What are the things I want to talk about? Help me to order my thoughts and speak about what I want to speak about, subject by subject..."

If you find it hard to address God, try to visualize yourself talking on the telephone to someone you have never seen — someone very wise and understanding who can help you face up to the major issues in your life. Or visualize yourself talking to a wise counsellor or a very good friend that you really trust.

You cannot expect to hear direct answers from God, but keep your questions in mind over the coming days and weeks. If you are sincere and really want to find answers, you will probably find that in the course of your thinking, studying, conversations with various people and other experiences, answers will begin to dawn in your mind.

Someone once complained to Rebbe Nachman that he found it hard to talk in hisbodidus. The Rebbe replied: "You are like a warrior who girds his loins to overcome a mighty wall. When you come to the gate you find it blocked with a spider's web. Can you imagine anything more foolish than returning in defeat because of a spider's web blocking your path?

"You can meditate in thought, but the most important thing is to express it in words. You may find it difficult to speak with God, but it's really laziness and shyness. Be daring. You are ready to use your speech to overcome the great battle against the evil within you. You are on the verge of victory and are about to break down walls with your words. The gates are ready to fly open. Should you then not speak because of mere shyness? Should you hold back because of a minor barrier like this? You are about to break down a wall. Will you be discouraged by a spider's web?" (*Rabbi Nachman's Wisdom* #232).

"I'm a Turkey!"

People beginning hisbodidus frequently experience a tremendous sense of liberation and insight the first few times, but as soon as they start trying to practice on a regular basis, they suddenly find themselves facing all kinds of obstacles both from the outside world and from within themselves.

You may make careful plans to schedule your sessions, only to find the most unexpected things suddenly cropping up out of the blue to prevent you carrying them out — a sudden flood of work, things going wrong in the house, urgent problems, etc. etc. Everything seems to be conspiring to make you put off your hisbodidus for a day, two days, a week, a month and even longer. Suddenly it seems to be the hardest thing in the world to snatch just a few minutes to sit calmly by oneself.

Even more insidious are the resistances from within. There is a full fifty per cent of you that does not *want* to practice hisbodidus, certainly not in a way that could bring you to wake up spiritually and fight the Turkey inside you. One part of you may want to sit calmly in hisbodidus, but another side is struggling to break away — to get up and eat something, browse through the papers, make a telephone call, go out somewhere, do something... anything but meditate!

Here you are trying to become calm and clear, and suddenly it seems as though you've never been so tense! You feel uncomfortable, restless, moody, impatient; your mind darts from one thing to another; you are plagued with a succession of bodily desires; all of a sudden you feel unbelievably heavy and drowsy. All you want to do is to go to sleep... You try relaxing, breathing, talking, praying. Nothing seems to work. You may well start thinking you were far better off before you started hisbodidus.

This kind of reaction can erupt in the middle of a session as well, just as things seemed to have been going very well and you were feeling calm, clear, joyous and connected. Eternity was just around the corner... and then, suddenly, it all breaks down and you feel cast into the mud, your mind is in turmoil and everything is out of control.

This can happen after practicing hisbodidus regularly for months and even years. You may have had great success and feel that at last you have succeeded in making hisbodidus an integral part of your life, only to find yourself suddenly in a dry patch where you feel you are getting nowhere. You find your hisbodidus boring and fruitless, you start missing sessions, and before you know it you have stopped.

The reason for all this is that hisbodidus is about fighting the Turkey. Things may have seemed calmer before starting hisbodidus. This is because the Turkey was well entrenched and felt no need to fight for survival. The moment you begin to question your Turkey habits and try to stir the Prince or Princess in you, the Turkey digs in and prepares for battle. As soon as the Wise Man raises the question of identity — "Who are you?" — the Turkey replies with a resounding *No!* "I'm not a Prince, I'm a *Turkey!* Always have been and always will be. Turkey! Turkey! Turkey! No way am I going to change!"

The Turkey side of us resists facing the very issues that are at the center of hisbodidus: What is the truth of our condition in this world? What should we be doing with our precious time? How can we wean ourselves from the crumbs and bones of this world and follow the Torah and mitzvot with all our hearts? One of the hardest things to face up to in life is regret, because we know life is short, and it is painful to recognize how much of it we have wasted. The Turkey runs to the crumbs and bones in order to escape from the truth.

Rebbe Nachman said: "A pot of water may seem perfectly clear, but when it is placed on a fire and begins to boil, all its impurities are brought to the surface. One must stand by and constantly remove these impurities. The original purity was actually an illusion. With a little heat the impurity surfaces. But when these impurities are finally removed, the water is truly pure and clear.

"The same is true of a person. Before he begins serving God, the good and bad in him are all mixed together. The impurities are so closely united with the good that they cannot be recognized. But when this person begins to burn with passion for God, he is touched with the heat of purification and all the evil and impurities come to the surface. Here again one must stand by and constantly remove the dirt and impurities as they appear. In the end the person is truly pure and clear" (*Rabbi Nachman's Wisdom* #79).

When Things Are Going Against You

1. Know that all the different obstacles, internal and external, are coming up just *because* your hisbodidus is so important. They are being sent to challenge you and goad you into marshalling all your inner resources to overcome them and win mastery of yourself. You *can* succeed. Remember that in your essence you really are the Prince or Princess: the higher self is your innate heritage. You should know that the resistances are at their strongest when you are on the verge of a spiritual advance.

2. Look on the obstacles you encounter as a reminder to call out to God for help with your hisbodidus. Remember that hisbodidus is the *key* to your spiritual growth and fulfillment. Every day, offer a short prayer to God to bring you to practice hisbodidus regularly. Ask God to help you make time for hisbodidus today!

3. Don't say you tried hisbodidus and it didn't work. Give yourself positive messages. Tell yourself you are going to make hisbodidus a regular part of your life. Even if you dropped your hisbodidus for a day, a few days, a week, two weeks, a month or even years, don't feel you can't do it any more. The past is dead and gone. This present moment is the beginning of the rest of your life. Start afresh.

4. It is often better to find ways around problems than to try to confront them head on. Use your intelligence to *anticipate* external obstacles to your hisbodidus sessions and work out ways of circumventing them. Don't assume that if you cannot practice hisbodidus exactly the way you feel it ought to be practiced, it means you must not practice it at all. If you can't manage a full session, try a shorter one — fifteen minutes, ten minutes, even five. If you can't become calm, try saying a few words of prayer anyway. Even if all you do is repeat a single word, that's also good! "Ribono shel Olam, Master of the World!" If you can't talk, try breathing. If you can't breathe, just sit!

5. Turn your very problems into the subject of your conversation with God. Explain to God that you cannot talk to Him, and ask Him to help you open your mouth.

6. They say that half the art of anything is showing up! There may be times when the mere thought of sitting down to face your tired, old problems all over again is very upsetting. Don't even try! Picking away at them is not going to help. For today's hisbodidus just sit yourself down for a few minutes without trying to do anything. Sitting is the simplest thing. Just relax and enjoy. Often the very insight you've been waiting for will pop straight into your mind.

7. Don't *expect* your hisbodidus to produce amazing spiritual experiences and dramatic breakthroughs in personal growth, only to be disappointed when it doesn't. If you are hoping for

mystical experiences, you must understand that by definition, such experiences are mystical: they steal over us when we least expect them. You cannot force them. There are times when spiritual growth is very rapid, but real gains are usually gradual, and you may only notice them when you look back and see how far you've come. Have you ever watched a plant and seen it grow in front of your eyes? Come back in a few weeks and take another look!

The Honest Truth

At times you may feel imprisoned by your Turkey self. You may have made genuine efforts to work on your baser impulses and bad habits, only to find that they are as strong and persistent as ever. You may come to think that you will never change, and it is hopeless even to try.

The way to escape from this prison is through the truth. Encountering the bad side of yourself is in fact one of the most important elements in getting to know yourself. Many people go around with all kinds of illusions about themselves. In actual fact they do many things they would be the first to criticize if they saw others doing them, but a certain blind-spot prevents them from seeing these faults in themselves.

Don't deceive yourself in life. Have the humility to admit that you are less than perfect. To the best of your ability, be honest with yourself about what you are and the way you actually behave. Try to look at yourself the way others might see you. As far as you can, examine yourself as an unbiased observer, and call your traits and actions by their proper name. If indeed you are a compulsive Turkey it is a major achievement if you know it. Don't be one of the people "who call bad good and good bad" (Isaiah 5:20).

Take responsibility for what you do. Don't deceive yourself about why you are the way you are or do the things you do. Don't blame your parents, wife, husband, family, teachers, boss, society or the rest of the world for everything. It's no good to constantly make excuses. Other factors may play a part, but beware of using them as a rationalization to avoid changing parts of yourself that you can in fact change. Confronting your problems honestly is the first step towards solving them.

God tells us, "I planted you as a seedling that is all the seed of truth" (Jeremiah 2:21). Deep down in all of us is a part that is not at all deceived by our illusions and self-evasion, but knows the truth and yearns for it to be revealed within us. This is the Princely Soul, the child of God. Truth indeed is the seal of God Himself (*Shabbat* 55a, *Yoma* 69b). By being truthful you will find your way to the Prince in you, your higher self, and to God.

As you look at yourself in hisbodidus and sift through your life, pour out your whole heart to God. Tell Him exactly what you feel — your impulses and desires, your fears and worries, your frustrations, your pain and your grief. You can tell God things you would never dream of saying to other people, down to your most private shame and pain.

"When you succeed in turning to God with truth, genuine honesty and sincerity, you will be able to express yourself with words of deep reverence and love springing from the depths of a heart truly aroused. Then your radiant words will break through all the barriers. When you come to the truth, it is as if God's own light is clothed in you, because truth is God's seal" (*Likutey Moharan* I:112, and see *Tsohar, passim*).

The Truth Need Not Hurt

Even if you see bad in yourself, don't look on yourself as being worse than you really are. That's not the truth either. The truth does not have to be harsh. Examining yourself truthfully does not mean that you must indulge in merciless self-criticism and condemnation.

Although the Prince in our story had gone crazy, he still had enough of the Prince in him to be honest. When the Wise Man asked him who he was, he admitted his craziness quite candidly. "I'm a turkey."

How did the Wise Man reply? "I'm *also* a turkey!" At first sight you may take the Wise Man's reply at face value: "I'm a Turkey just like you are — all Turkey and nothing more." But there is another way of interpreting the Wise Man's words, "I'm *also* a Turkey": "I'm a Turkey *in addition to whatever else I am.*"

The Wise Man is teaching us a lesson about truthfulness. Even if we look at ourselves and see a lot of Turkey, we should know and have faith that we are *also* turkeys — turkeys and something else besides. Buried within us is the good point that is our inalienable heritage. Even the wisest, saintliest people have their Turkey side. We are all human beings. When the Wise Man examines himself, he sees darkness. But he knows that this is not *all* there is. There is a good side too, even if it is deeply buried. The way to retrieve it is through the truth.

Being truthful means looking for the good within you and all around you. When you examine yourself, don't only concentrate on the bad. Look for your good points. Look at the good all around you, and thank God for it. When you "acknowledge God for what is past," thank Him for all the blessings and miracles you have enjoyed from the moment you were born until today — your health, your vision, your hearing, breathing, co-ordination, digestion... your parents, family, teachers, friends... your food, clothes, house, livelihood, and so on.

God is present all around you. Even when confronted by obstacles, try to think why God is putting these barriers across your path. What positive aspects can you find in them? God Himself is present in all of them, and His only reason for sending them to you is to prompt you to call out to Him for help. If you have a *KaShYA*, a difficulty, remember that it is a prompt to you to call out: *Sh'ma HaShem (YKVK) Koli Ekra* "Hear, God, my voice — I call" (Psalms 27:7). The truth is that God can do anything. God can help you. All you have to do is open your mouth and talk to Him.

"A person who wants to turn away from evil but sees that there is no truth in the world should make himself like a madman" (*The Aleph-Bet Book, Truth* 31). People who talk to themselves are normally thought to be crazy, but in fact, talking to your self, your soul and to God is the sanest thing you can do.

"Even if many days and years pass and it seems that you have accomplished nothing with your words, do not abandon it. Every single word makes an impression. 'Water wears away stone' (Job 14:10). It may seem impossible that mere water dripping on a stone could make an impression. Still, after many years, it can actually make a hole in the stone, as we know. Your heart may be like stone. It may seem that your words of prayer make no impression on it at all. Still, as the days and years pass, your heart of stone will also be penetrated" (*Rabbi Nachman's Wisdom* #234).

7

Putting on the Shirts

Then the Wise Man gave a sign, and they threw them shirts. The Wise Man-Turkey said to the king's son, "Do you think a turkey can't wear a shirt? You can wear a shirt and still be a turkey." The two of them put on shirts.

The Turkey-Prince might have been quite content to while away the time chatting endlessly with his new friend. However the Wise Man did not only want to get to know the Prince, he wanted to elevate him. Conversation alone was not going to be enough. When the time was ripe, the Wise Man had to take the initiative and get the Prince to *act*. He had to get him to put his shirt on. "The Wise Man gave a sign, and they threw them shirts."

The Limits of Meditation

Hisbodidus is made up of conversations — between the Prince and Wise Man within ourselves, or between ourselves and God. Hisbodidus can be a very powerful practice, leading to profound self-understanding, and at times an amazing awareness of God's intimate closeness. But for a lasting connection with God, hisbodidus by itself is not enough.

Certain schools of meditation hold that complete self-realization and intimacy with God can come through meditation alone. One of the greatest dangers of such approaches is that they can easily leave those who follow them locked within their own subjectivity. The altered states of mind that meditation can produce are sometimes very impressive — so much so that those experiencing them for the first time may be quite convinced they have found the ultimate truth of existence. Having had a taste of a higher state of consciousness, people sometimes spend years trying to recapture it. But the mere fact that certain meditational states may be very entrancing does not mean that those who have experienced them are genuinely close to God. Exclusive attention to a single technique can lead people to ignore major problems in their lives and personalities that may, in fact, be keeping them from God.

The Torah teaches that our purpose in this world is to "know this day and take to your heart that HaShem is the only God in heaven above and on the earth below" (Deuteronomy 4:39). "Know this day" implies knowing God not only during moments of intimacy in meditation, but through all the different phases of the entire day. "Take to your heart" means that it is not enough to have isolated religious experiences from time to time: we must draw our knowledge of God into our very hearts, so that all of our activities are suffused with a yearning for connection with God.

Much of the work of hisbodidus is concerned with making the connection between the head and the heart. We may have noble ideals about the way we would like to be, but they will always remain theoretical — in the head, as it were — until we work to marshal the motive forces of the heart, the seat of the will, in order to realize them. This work is vital, but even so, it is still only a preparation for the final stage, which is to put our ideals into practice through *action*.

The Hebrew word for the knowledge of God is *da'at*. *Da'at* means far more than mere intellectual knowledge. Not only does *da'at* include the profound states of insight and connection that can be attained through prayer and meditation. It has a still broader reference. To "know this day..." means to be aware of and connected with God in every fiber of our being and in all of our activities, down to the most mundane.

The only way to attain this connection is through carrying out the mitzvot, the commandments of the Torah, in practice. We have seen that the mitzvot apply to every sphere of human activity, and on every level of behavior — thought, emotion, speech and action. Each mitzvah is a detailed pathway of practical action relating to a particular facet of life, and leading to its own particular form of connection with God. The word *mitzvah* is thus related to the Hebrew root *tzavat*, which means "connect." (See above pp. 28-32.)

The mitzvot are the royal "clothes" of the "Prince," the Godly Soul. Thoughts, feelings, words and actions of any kind are "clothes" through which the personality is expressed and actualized in different ways. The mitzvot are detailed patterns of divinely prescribed thoughts, words, feelings and actions, oriented toward God and connecting us with Him. It is through carrying out the mitzvot — "putting on" these royal "clothes" — that the "Prince," the Godly Soul, becomes revealed in this world, and our potential spirituality becomes actualized.

Torah Study

"The greatness of Torah study is that it brings one to practical action."
Kidushin 40b

"The Wise Man gave a sign, and they put down shirts." The very first mitzvah a young boy is introduced to is that of Tzitzit — wearing the four-cornered, fringed garment that covers the upper part of the body. Tzitzit is also the first mitzvah of the day for every Jewish male: immediately after getting up in the morning, one puts on the *Tallit Katan*, the small, fringed garment worn throughout the day. The "shirts" in our story suggest this upper garment: when the Wise Man wanted to get the Prince to dress himself, this was where he began.

The purpose of the Tzitzit (the fringes) is that we should "look at them, and remember all the mitzvot of HaShem" (Numbers 15:39). The numerical value of the Hebrew letters of the word TziTziT is six hundred, which together with the eight threads and five knots of the Tzitzit makes a total of six hundred and thirteen. This corresponds to the six hundred and thirteen mitzvot of the Torah. The Tzitzit thus alludes to the entire Torah, which we are to "look at and remember" constantly, studying it whenever possible, and inscribing the knowledge of the Torah in our memories and our very hearts.

"Putting on the shirts" can therefore be interpreted as an allusion to studying the Torah, which is as important as all the mitzvot of the Torah put together (*Pe'ah* 1:1). Indeed, Torah study is the *key* to fulfillment of all the other mitzvot, since it is impossible to practice them unless you know exactly what they are.

Only in conjunction with Torah study is it possible to come to a closer connection with God through hisbodidus. Some people believe that meditation alone can lead to spiritual illumination. They put forth their questions and then listen to their own inner voices, or to what they may think of as spirits channelling information from somewhere outside of themselves. But without objective criteria to evaluate the messages they hear, how can they know if they are truthful and not merely what a part of them *wants* to hear? Those who profess to channel spirits may simply be projecting the outpourings of their own unconscious onto an external source. People have used meditative "insight" to justify the most wanton acts of selfishness and destruction.

Exclusive reliance on subjective intuition can only lead to self-deception. The Torah teaches us that the creation of the universe was planned in such a way as to place us in a situation of challenge, so that we can then exercise the highest faculty we have: free will. On every level, goodness and truth are therefore mixed up with evil and falsehood, often in the most subtle ways. Our task is to sift and search until we uncover the good — earning goodness through our own work and efforts.

Just as good and evil are mixed up in the outer world, so they are in the inner world of the mind and soul. We have all kinds of thoughts, ideas, hopes, wishes, dreams, desires, impulses, intentions, instincts, etc. Some of them are good — they can lead us closer to God — while others are bad, pulling us further away. Not only do the Princely parts of the soul dwell side by side with the Turkey in us, but to make the challenge even greater, the Turkey masquerades as the Prince, blunting our sensitivity to what is truly good and desirable and what is not.

Without objective criteria for distinguishing between fantasy and truth, we have no protection against the weaknesses of our own judgment. The purpose of hisbodidus is to find the Prince and Princess in ourselves — to sift out and develop the good, while cleansing ourselves of our bad, Turkey aspects. But the Turkey has its own ideas about what is good and desirable. Without the objective guidance of the Torah it is impossible to escape from our own subjectivity and find the truth.

The primary purpose of Torah study is not to develop our intellectual acumen or acquire knowledge for its own sake, but to connect with God. Every word of the Torah is a revelation of the will of God. The goal is to fill our minds and hearts with God's teaching in order to fulfill it and do it. The purpose of study is to bring us to practical action. It is therefore most important to learn Torah only from works by Rabbis genuinely devoted to the fulfillment of Torah, and not from outside sources.

The Torah is unlike any worldly body of knowledge which we can verify through accepted canons of scientific validation. The Torah is a revelation from beyond this world, and connects us with levels of reality which cannot be experienced and explored directly with our five material senses. The Torah has its own logic (such as the Thirteen Hermeneutical Rules of Rabbi Yishmael, etc.) and has to be taken on trust.

We thus speak of *kabbalat ha-Torah* — *receiving* the Torah. When someone gives you a gift, you receive what is given without trying to dictate what they should give you. The only way to receive the Torah is through *Emunah*, faith in God, and *Emunat Chachamim*, faith in the saints and sages of all the generations, who labored in the Torah in holiness and purity day and night and transmitted it to us.

What to Study

Halachah: "The Academy of Eliahu taught: Everyone who studies *halachot* every day is assured he will be in the World to Come" (*Megilah* 28b). The first priority in Torah study should be practical *Halachah*, the detailed laws of the mitzvot applicable in everyday life — Tzitzit and Tefilin, blessings and prayers, Shabbat and festivals, Kashrut, relations with other people, purity of speech, charity, lovingkindness, honesty in business, family purity, etc. Even if you have no time to study anything else, you should make a point to study Halachah every day. On a day when you are very pressed, still study at least one practical Halachah.

Not only is it vital to know the details of the mitzvot in order to fulfill them properly. Study of Halachah is also one of the main elements in separating the Prince from the Turkey. "When a person transgresses, good and evil are mixed up. A legal decision is a clear separation between the permitted and the forbidden, the clean and the unclean. When you study religious law, good is once again separated from evil and the sin is rectified" (*Rabbi Nachman's Wisdom* #29).

A wide variety of clear and easily understandable halachic texts is available in English covering all the mitzvot of everyday life. Make a list of the main areas you should be familiar with and work through the relevant texts one after the other until you have covered them all. Start with simpler works and go through them steadily, one by one. When you have been through them all, go through them again. When you are fully familiar with them, move on to more comprehensive works. Make daily halachic study a lifelong practice.

The Halachah consists of many fine details, and you may feel you cannot remember much of what you study. Don't be discouraged. By merely reading the words aloud, you have fulfilled the mitzvah of *studying* Torah, even if you later forget what you have learned. (See *Rabbi Nachman's Wisdom* pp. 126ff.) In fact you probably absorbed more than you are aware of. The more you review what you have studied, the more you will remember.

Mussar: Mussar is Torah literature on the theme of spiritual growth. The classic Mussar texts include the *Mesilat Yesharim* ("The Path of the Just"), the *Orchot Tzaddikim* ("Pathways of the Righteous"), the *Chovot HaLevavot* ("Duties of the Heart"), etc. Recent works, such as *Strive for Truth* by R. Eliahu Dessler, and *Gateway to Happiness* by R. Zelig Pliskin, present traditional Mussar teachings in a more contemporary form. The field of Mussar also includes the classic texts of Chassidism, such as the *Tanya*, *Rabbi Nachman's Wisdom*, the *Aleph-Bet Book*, *Likutey Moharan* and *Advice*, etc.

The Turkey is powerfully entrenched in all of us, and "someone in fetters cannot release himself from prison by himself"

(*Berachot* 5b). The only way to free ourselves is with Torah, which is the spice created by God for the specific purpose of tempering the evil inclination (*Bava Batra* 16b). Most of us have so many worldly involvements that it is all too easy to get distracted from the real purpose for which we were brought into this world — to get to know and serve God. Regular study of Mussar can help to keep this purpose uppermost in your mind and inspire you to follow the Torah path with all your energy. Find the Mussar works that speak to you most directly in order to get clear guidance on how to advance along the Torah pathway of spiritual growth.

Chumash: The Five Books of Moses are the heart of the Torah. Every week you should go through the Torah portion that will be read in the synagogue on Shabbat. If you know Hebrew, you should aim to read the entire portion twice, preferably with the Aramaic Targum and the commentary of Rashi. If you are learning Hebrew, try to study at least part of the weekly portion in the original, and in any event read through the English translation. Familiarity with the text of the Five Books of Moses is the best foundation for all Torah study.

Other Studies: Everyone should aim to acquire a basic understanding of the main principles of faith and the Torah way of life, as explained in the *Derech HaShem* ("The Way of God") by Rabbi Moshe Chaim Luzzatto, and other texts.

It is possible to be a pious Jew without being a scholar (see *Zohar* I:59b and *Rabbi Nachman's Wisdom* #76), but deep perception can only be attained with Talmudic scholarship. Broad knowledge of NaCh (Prophets and other Biblical writings) and Mishnah is the best foundation for Talmud study. You may look at the many volumes you would like to cover — the *Talmud Bavli* and *Yerushalmi*, *Shulchan Aruch*, *Midrashim*, the *Zohar* and the Kabbalah of the ARI — and wonder how you will ever get through them. At the very least, pray about it regularly and tell

God you would *like* to study them all. Follow the example of the Wise Man and *make a start* with small, easy steps. Even if you go through only a few lines every day without fail, your skills will increase with time, and within a few years you will be able to cover far more ground than you ever thought possible.

When to Study

The most important thing is to *fix regular times* for Torah study. Rebbe Nachman points out that the Hebrew word for "fixing" — *keva* — also has the connotation of stealing (as in Proverbs 22:23). One has to *steal* time from one's other activities in order to make time for Torah study! Make sure to set regular study sessions, whether you study alone, with a study-partner, or in classes.

In order to fulfill the prescription to "meditate in the Torah day and night," (Joshua 1:8) you should fix at least one study session during the day and one at night — even if you can devote no more than a few minutes. If possible, try to schedule at least one of your daily sessions at a time when you are fresh and alert, for example in the early morning. If you are unable to allocate much time for study during the week, schedule longer study periods on Shabbat. When circumstances arise that cause you to miss one of your regular sessions, still try to take your study text off the shelf, open it and read a phrase or two, then close and kiss the book and return it to the shelf.

Every word of Torah study is a mitzvah: utilize a few spare moments to open a book and learn even a short passage. Make it a habit to carry a small book with you wherever you go. Choose something you enjoy studying. In this way you will be able to put to good use even the minutes you spend waiting for buses, trains, appointments, etc.

How to Study

It is best to hold your regular sessions in a Beit Midrash if possible — "whoever learns in a synagogue or study hall will not forget quickly" (*Yerushalmi Berachot* 5). Alternatively, study anywhere that you find comfortable and where you will not be disturbed. (It goes without saying that it is forbidden to think Torah thoughts in the bathroom, etc., let alone bring Torah literature to such a place.)

Treat your study sessions with the utmost respect. Do not allow anything to interrupt you except a real emergency. When you learn, you are studying the words of God and His sages: how do you feel when you are in the middle of an important discussion and someone interrupts you for something trivial? Use your intelligence to avoid potential interruptions where possible. Relieve yourself, have a drink or snack, etc., *before* you start studying.

A private undertaking to try not to talk about anything except Torah for the duration of your session is beneficial to concentration. Before you begin learning, take some moments to sit, relax, breathe deeply and clear your mind. Offer a few words of prayer to connect yourself to God through your study, and ask for success. (Many Siddurim include the special prayer to be said on entering the study hall.) Spend a moment or two reflecting on what you are about to study. Remind yourself *why* you want to study, in order to motivate yourself. Bringing to mind what you already know about the subject can help you focus your mind. Where did you leave off last time? Are there specific questions you would like to have answered?

If you are in a class, try your best to focus on what the teacher is saying, and reserve your questions until the teacher has had a chance to explain the material. If you are studying with a partner, let one of your goals be that your partner should get as much as possible out of the session. Explaining a point clearly to a partner or student is one of the best ways of getting it straight in your own mind.

If you are studying by yourself, read the words of your study text out loud, for "they are life to those who pronounce them aloud, and healing to all their flesh" (Proverbs 4:22 and *Eruvin* 54a). Saying the words out loud helps you to focus your mind and brings them into your soul. If you are studying in Hebrew, even if you understand the language, it is still very beneficial to translate into your native tongue as you go along.

Where the Halachah, Mishnah or Gemara discusses a particular case, try to envisage the case in concrete terms. For example, if you are studying the laws of damages in *Bava Kama*, try to visualize the hoof of the ox, the hole in the ground, the camel munching someone else's produce, the fire spreading into someone else's field, etc. The same applies whether you are studying the laws of Shabbat, Kashrut, purity of speech or any other area of Torah. Can you think of situations in your own experience that parallel the instance under discussion? After reading the text inside, look away from the text and try to formulate the concept or go back over the argument in your own words out loud.

When you come upon a passage that you find incomprehensible, if you simply read it over several times the meaning will often become clearer. If not, try to pinpoint your main problems in order to determine what you need to investigate further. If you find it impossible to understand, simply leave this passage aside and go forward. Often, something you learn later will throw light on what you could not understand earlier. In the long run, you will make more progress by covering a lot of ground, even without going into depth, than you will if you try to go into every single detail over a narrow area.

If you find your attention wandering during your study session, try to give yourself new energy through deep breathing.

At times it may help you to get up and walk around a bit, or to close your eyes and relax for a minute or two. From time to time take a short break to clear your mind, refocus, repeat your prayer for success and connection with God, and so on.

As you study, ask yourself how the subject-matter applies to your life. What practical guidance can you derive? When you come across a teaching that is directly relevant, say it over to yourself a few times and *make a prayer* out of it using the words of the text in front of you. "God, help me to fulfil *x*, *y* and *z*." This applies particularly to the study of Mussar and Chassidut, which are primarily concerned with personal spiritual growth. When you find a passage in Mussar or Chassidut that addresses your current growth issues directly, use some of your learning time to say it over and over again. This is how the words will penetrate your heart and consciousness until the spirit of the holy sage who taught them will come into you, lift you and bring you to true holiness.

When you come to the end of a study session, pause for a moment or two and cast your mind back over what you have been learning. Thank God for His Torah and the opportunity to learn it. (A prayer when leaving the study hall is also printed in many Siddurim.) Use spare moments after your session (e.g. on your way home from the Beit Midrash, or while eating, etc.) to review what you studied in the session.

The hardest thing about learning is getting to the session. Even when you feel tired and unable to concentrate, you can still learn a little. Take one small step — open the book. Just say over a few words, even if you don't understand them. This is also learning.

"You can wear a shirt and still be a Turkey!"

Contemplating the vast literature of Torah, you may ask, "Where do *I* come into all this?" The six hundred and thirteen commandments confront us with an awesome code of detailed regulations and prohibitions reaching into every corner of life: Torah commandments, enactments of the Rabbis, customs and stringencies with the force of law, opinions and counter-opinions... all contained in thousands upon thousands of pages laden with dense commentaries and supercommentaries...

"Is this the way to *find* myself, or am I being asked to give *up* my individuality, my spontaneity and personal creativity and take on a heavy burden that will crush any hopes of ever enjoying life?"

It may be easy enough to offer answers, and explain how the mitzvot provide the clothes that enable the inner Prince and Princess to come forth in their true radiance and beauty. (See above pp. 28-32.) God created the souls. The Torah is His infinite wisdom. The mitzvot that make up the Torah are tailored to all the souls that have ever been and ever will be. Each soul is the unique child of God. In a royal court, the beautiful costumes of each of the royal children are individually styled and tailored. So too, for each one of us, the six hundred and thirteen mitzvot that are the garments of the Godly Soul have their own unique meaning and significance.

"Rabbi Chanania ben Akashia says: The Holy One, blessed-be-He, wished to confer merit upon Israel and He therefore gave them Torah and mitzvot in abundance" (*Maccot* 23b). The endless treasury of Torah includes opportunities for the development of every level of aptitude and ability, joyously and creatively, for the glory of God — whether in the pursuit of spirituality, cultivation of the intellect, emotional growth, the development of skills, interpersonal relationships, domestic and family life, social and communal activity, agriculture, manufacturing, engineering, business, the professions, administration, scientific research, arts, crafts, music, literature, care of the sick, elderly, handicapped or underprivileged, travel, sports, entertainment and anything else that comes into the realm of the permissible.

Even fulfillment of the regular daily and periodic mitzvot is not supposed to resemble a performance of the longest-running play. Each day and each moment is new: it never has been and never will be. Let today's Sh'ma be different from any other. The Divine sparks in this fruit will come into your thoughts, words and deeds in an entirely original way, the like of which will never be again: put unique energy into the blessing you make over it. Next Shabbat will have a spirit quite different from that of last Shabbat. A young boy's Seder night could never be the same as his grandfather's...

Answers like these may be good for Princes and Princesses, but what about Turkeys? For the Turkey, submission to the mitzvot may certainly entail a surrender of individuality — if that means eating anything one *wants* to eat in whichever restaurant takes one's fancy, lying in bed as long as one likes instead of having to get up to pray, spending all of one's money exactly the way one wishes, doing anything one wants over the weekend instead of having to think about Shabbat, and so on.

Even when we are basically willing to follow the mitzvot, we may still have many contrary feelings. The next step in deepening our observance may be staring us in the face, yet we may still feel unwilling to take it because of apprehensions concerning the extra commitment involved. We may be well aware of what we are supposed to be doing, yet we keep putting it off until eventually we either do it cursorily or neglect it completely.

After years of mitzvah-observance there can still be days when it seems the hardest thing to open the Siddur and begin the prayers, to put one's hand into one's pocket and give a little charity, to smile at someone we had an argument with... God's plan is to give us complete freedom of choice about the mitzvot. No matter how much the Prince desires to keep a mitzvah, the

Turkey is likely to be there almost every step of the way with resistance and opposition of some kind: arguments against, other things to do, sudden irresistible impulses, fatigue and heaviness. The very holiness of the mitzvot may overwhelm us: "Who am I to put on the garments of the Prince?"

Look how the Wise Man got the Prince to put on his shirt.

After all the sitting and talking and getting to know each other, when the time was finally ripe "...the Wise Man gave a sign."

What does this sign symbolize? We can look at it as an allusion to what Chassidut calls "the arousal from below."

Everything in the world is in the hands of God, yet God has given us free will. We are surrounded by Godly opportunities and invitations; within our minds, holy thoughts and impulses come up all the time. These are God's call to us. They are what is termed "the arousal from above." But we are given the freedom to respond or not respond. When offered a prompt, it is up to us to decide whether we will follow it or not. More than that, we have it in our power to take the initiative. We ourselves can make the first move, turning to God in order to receive His blessing. The move we make to lift ourselves spiritually is called "the arousal from below."

The question may be asked: if everything is in the hands of God, how can we make an "arousal from below" without having had some "arousal from above" to stir us beforehand? In that case, the "arousal from below" is not really our own initiative. Do we have free will or don't we? This is a paradox that we do not have the understanding to resolve in this world. (See above pp. 129-31.) We cannot know why some holy thought or impulse enters our mind "out of nowhere." What is important is that we do our part: when faced with a prompt, whether from within ourselves or the surrounding environment, it is up to us to stir ourselves and make a practical response.

When the path we have to take is right ahead of us, the first thing to do is to point ourselves in the right direction. Our initiative may be the slightest action: not wanting to get out of bed on a winter's morning, but still pulling off the cover; not feeling like praying, but opening the prayerbook anyway; having no energy to do what one knows one has to do, but still whispering a few faint words of prayer: "God, help me to do this!" Such initiatives are like the "sign" the Wise Man made. With it he indicated that he was ready to have what he needed next sent down from above.

The Prince's shirt is there on the floor beside him. How does the Wise Man get him to put it on? He *talks* him into it! We too must use words to spur ourselves into action. Let the Wise Man in you talk to the Turkey. "Do you think a turkey can't wear a shirt? You can wear a shirt and still be a turkey." You may feel like a complete Turkey — interested mostly in just having things easy and pleasant, while negative about the idea of doing the mitzvah, overwhelmed with heaviness and apathy. The part of you that wants to do the mitzvah may seem weak and uninspired. Still, give voice to it, even in a whisper: "I *want* to."

The Wise Man doesn't try anything too ambitious. He doesn't try to get the Prince to put all his clothes on at once. A single shirt is all he wants him to put on. One small, easy step. You can do that. Give voice to the Wise Man in you. "This is all I want to do right now. I may feel heavy and uninspired. I don't undertake that I'll do any *more* than this, but this much I can do. I can do this and still stay myself." Starting off with small, easy steps is a fundamental rule in doing anything in life, from beginning your physical exercises in the morning to learning the Kabbalah of the ARI.

It is in fact impossible to put on all the clothes at once and practice all the mitzvot perfectly in one step. The mitzvot come from the Infinite God: they are pathways of overwhelming power. Trying to go too quickly can be a recipe for disaster. Getting involved with the life of the spirit can be very heady. People who start experimenting with intense prayer and study, hisbodidus, diet, exercise and so on may be tempted to try to take on too much too soon. One day they may be filled with a desire for holiness and purity, only to fall back the next day and drop to a lower level than the one they started on. Aim to be the best Jew you can be, but don't try to take on burdens that could break you.

"Do not be hurried. You may find many kinds of devotion in the sacred literature and ask, 'When will I be able to fulfill even one of these devotions? How can I ever hope to keep them all?' Don't let this frustrate you.

"Go slowly, step by step. Do not rush and try to grasp everything at once. If you are over-hasty and try to grasp everything at once, you can become totally confused. When a house burns down, people often rescue the most worthless items. You can do the same in your confusion. Proceed slowly, one step at a time. If you cannot do everything, it is not your fault. One under duress is exempted by God.

"Even though there are many things you cannot do, you should still yearn to fulfill them. The longing itself is a great thing, for 'God desires the heart' (*Sanhedrin* 106b)" (*Rabbi Nachman's Wisdom* #27).

8

The Trousers

After a while the Wise Man gave another sign and they threw them trousers. Again he said, "Do you think if you wear trousers you can't be a turkey?" They put on the trousers.

"After a while..."

The Wise Man wanted to dress the Prince much more than the Prince wanted to get dressed. Even so, the Wise Man did not let his enthusiasm get the better of him. It was not until "after a while" that he gave the signal for the trousers. He knew that after an advance as great as putting on the shirts, there must always be a pause, even a regression, before advancing further.

In Ezekiel's prophecy of the Divine Chariot, the *Chayot* — the vital forces of creation, the "angels" — are described as "running and returning" (Ezekiel 1:14). They rise up in yearning to transcend their limitations as created beings and to merge in unity with their Creator: they "run out" of themselves... But then they "return" to themselves and their separate existence, because it is the will of God that they should continue to be independent creatures.

So it is with human beings. We may have moments of self-transcendence and intimate closeness with God — "running." Nevertheless, they are always temporary. God's will is that as long as we remain in this world, these moments of merging with God should be followed by a "return" into ourselves and our everyday states of mind. Our purpose in this world is to transcend ourselves and attain closeness to God of our own free will. It would go counter to this purpose if God simply did this for us. We have to "return" to our separate selves in order to continue with our work, until the time comes for us to leave this world.

The whole of this life is made up of rhythms of "running" and "returning." We wake up from our sleep in the morning and come back to life and activity — "running." But eventually we get tired and have to "return" and we go to sleep again. Similarly, we eat and fuel our bodies and for a time we are full of energy. But eventually all the energy is spent, and we get hungry and have to eat again.

In order to live to the full, it is very important to be sensitive to the rhythms of life. Learn to recognize and respect the rhythms of your body. You may function better at certain times of the day than at others. Where possible, try to schedule your various activities accordingly. Know your limits. After a reasonable period of activity, you need to relax. If you take intermittent breaks from tasks involving intense concentration, you may be able to accomplish more than you could if you were to work uninterruptedly for the same length of time. Remember that if you take a rest, you may need to limber up gently before resuming vigorous activity.

People's nutritional needs also vary according to the time of day. For some, it is better to eat light in the morning and more substantially later on, while others have different needs. Try to learn what foods, and in what quantities and combinations, will help you to function optimally at different times of the day.

It does not pay to push yourself beyond your physical limitations. While you should not give in to your bodily whims and appetites, you should respect the genuine needs of your body. Get to know what they really are by careful trial and error. Rebbe Nachman said, "Sleep well and eat well. Just don't waste time!" (*Kochvey Or* p.25).

Learn your own limits, when is enough and when is too much, whether it be in Torah study, hisbodidus, work, social interaction, or anything else. One of the ways the Turkey tries to sabotage our spiritual life is through excessive enthusiasm. At times we may feel so inspired that we throw ourselves into spiritual work — riding on the crest of the wave as if we could go on for ever — until we simply exhaust ourselves and fall down.

It is no good staying up to study so late one night that you oversleep the following morning and then have to go through your prayers like an express train, or spending such an inordinately long time on your prayers one day that you never get to do the other things you want to do. Learn the proper balance in all things.

The Wise Man was an expert in the fine art of good timing. After the two of them had put on the shirts, he waited. Not until "after a while" did he give the sign for the trousers.

The Trousers

What do the "trousers" signify?

We have seen that the "shirts" can be understood as a reference to the Tallit, the fringed upper garment, and that the Tzitzit, the fringes of the Tallit, allude to the six hundred and thirteen mitzvot of the Torah, and to study of the Torah. (See above pp. 147-8.) The "trousers" can be seen as a reference to the Tefilin, the phylacteries, and to Prayer.

The order of the daily service of the Jew is first to put on the Tallit and then to put on the Tefilin. The Wise Man followed the same order when he started getting the Prince dressed. He began with the "shirt" — the Tallit. He then continued with the "trousers" — the Tefilin. Thus, the Tefilin are called a "garment" (see *Tikkuney Zohar* 69 interpreting "garments of leather" [Genesis 3:21] — "these are the Tefilin"). The Tefilin are particularly associated with Prayer. We wear them while praying, and the very word TeFiLin is connected with the Hebrew word for prayer, TeFiLah.

Our Rabbis speak of prayer itself as a "garment" covering the "legs" — i.e. the "trousers." Thus the verse in the Song of Songs (7:2) says: "How beautiful are your feet in shoes, noble daughter, *the circles of your thighs are like ornaments of gold, the work of the hands of the craftsman.*"

Commenting on this verse, the Rabbis said (*Mo'ed Katan* 16b): " '...the circles of your thighs are like ornaments, the work of the hands of the craftsman.' — Just as the thighs are covered over, so are the mysteries of Torah covered over." (The verse is comparing the thighs and the ornaments to one another. We know that the "ornaments" are the mysteries of the Torah, because we find at the end of the verse that they are called "the work of the hands of the Craftsman." This is the Torah, which is the handicraft of the Creator of the World. See Rashi *ad loc.*)

Just as the thighs are covered over, so too the mysteries of the Torah are covered over. What is the garment that covers the mysteries of the Torah? The prayers. The prayers may at times seem simple, but beneath the surface of the words and letters lie the profoundest secrets of the Torah. The prayers are "garments" that clothe these mysteries. The mysteries of the Torah are covered over exactly the way the thighs are covered over. What is the garment that covers the thighs? The trousers. As a garment, the prayers correspond to the trousers. (See *Likutey Moharan* I:15, 5-6 and I:73 etc.)

We thus see that the "trousers" with which the Wise Man now proceeded to dress the Prince can be taken as a symbol for prayer!

Prayer

"Know that prayer is the main way to become connected with God and attached to Him. Prayer is the gate through which we enter to God and come to know Him."

Likutey Moharan II:84

"Prayer stands at the very summit of the universe, yet people treat it lightly."

Berachot 6b and Rashi *ad loc.*

Many people think of prayer as a magical way of asking for things that is irrelevant in a world where everything is governed by natural causes. Why is it necessary to pray for our livelihood when it is up to us to go out and earn a living? Why pray for healing — go to the doctor! Either he can do something about it or he can't, in which case, what's the use of praying? For many people, the prayer services are little more than meaningless, tedious relics to be hurried through with minimal attention.

The idea that prayer is a matter of "asking for what I want" is a Turkey notion. The Turkey in us — the self-seeking ego — believes that it is only "my strength and the power of my hands" (Deuteronomy 8:17) that makes anything happen in our lives. Under normal circumstances, the Turkey assumes that whatever one gets in life depends on a combination of one's own efforts and pure chance. Only when things get out of control and the Turkey feels helpless does he suddenly cry out, "God help me!" — like an enraged child who imagines he can elicit what he wants by the sheer force of his screams.

In fact, the purpose of prayer is not to force God to do what we want, but rather to *open* ourselves to the Godly blessing that is constantly pouring forth, and to *channel* it to ourselves and the world around us. The great prestige of science in our culture has led people to assume that everything in the universe is subject to the laws of nature. But in fact natural law is only one of the ways in which God governs the universe. The more aware of God we become, the more we see that the entire fabric of life within us and around us is made up of all kinds of *nissim* — "wonders." The Hebrew word *ness* means a flag or banner that reveals and declares the sovereign power of God.

The essential work of prayer is to become conscious of God's hand in all the processes of life, and to channel Godly awareness and blessing to ourselves and the world as a whole — all through *words*. The words of our prayers are the "vessels" through which Godly blessing flows down to us.

A vessel is a container which holds something else. A cup may hold water; a pipe is a vessel that will channel the water from one place to another. The physical sounds that make up a word are a "container" for the meaning of that word. By uttering the word, one can "channel" this meaning from one's own mind, via one's mouth and through the air, across to the ear of the listener and into his mind. The message that gets across, and the effect it has, depends upon which words we use and how.

Words may seem insubstantial, but you can change the world with them. Lovers, flatterers, advertizers, politicians and many others know and exploit the power of words. Try saying one word over and over to yourself. "Hate!" Now repeat a different word. "Love!" And now, with reverence and awe, repeat the word "God." The more skilled you are with words, the more subtly you can manipulate the influences you want to have dominance in your life and environment.

When we pray, we are using words to channel Divine influences into our lives. It is because we are part-Turkeys living in an under-the-table world that we need to do this work. To create our challenge in this life and bring us to our destiny, the world around us and our own inner make-up were designed in such a way as to conceal Godliness from us. In our everyday states of consciousness it is natural for us to assume that things depend either on "my strength and the power of my hands" or on chance.

In order to recognize the truth that lies beneath the surface appearance of this world, the Torah teaches us to work on ourselves and our consciousness. "And you shall *work* for Him" (Deuteronomy 6:13). The work referred to is the work of the *heart* — sifting out and developing our higher, Princely consciousness, while learning to dispense with Turkey notions. "Which is the work that one does in the heart? It is prayer" (*Ta'anit* 2a).

The work of prayer involves learning the limits of our worldly egos. Not "*my* strength and the power of *my* hands," but "*Yours*, HaShem, is the power and the sovereignty over every head. Wealth and honor are from You, and You rule over everything. In Your hand is power and might, and it is in Your hand to make anything and anyone great and strong... You, HaShem, are alone. You made the heavens, the heavens of the heavens and all their hosts, the earth and all that is upon it, the seas and everything that is in them, and You give life to all. The hosts of the heavens bow down to You" (I Chronicles 29:11-12 & Nehemiah 9:6).

It is common for people to say that God Himself has no need for our prayers, it is we who need them. This is true to some extent: one of the main reasons for praying is that we should be aware of God and come to know Him. But it is only part of the truth. In a sense God *does* need our prayers, because He created the cosmic order in such a way that the prayers of the Jewish People are an integral part of the chain through which blessing flows into the world as a whole.

"The twelve tribes of Israel correspond to the twelve constellations, and each tribe has its own style of prayer and a special gate through which its prayer rises. The effect of each tribe's prayers is to arouse the power of the corresponding constellation, and then the constellation radiates below and gives energy to the vegetation and all the other things which depend upon it" (*Likutey Moharan* I:9,2).

The Fixed Prayers

The art of prayer is to use the right words and combinations of words in order to channel Divine power and blessing. The Hebrew language is called the Holy Language, because Hebrew is the language of God's revelation in the Torah, and the letters and words of the Hebrew language are the perfect vessels to reveal and channel Godliness.

From the beginnings of Jewish history until the destruction of the First Temple and the Babylonian Exile (586 B.C.E.) Hebrew was the native language of the Jews, and the pathways of prayer were widely known among the people. Until that time, the overall spiritual level was very high — hundreds of thousands of people in every generation were actively involved in the practice of meditation and prophecy (*Megilah* 14a). Besides reciting the Sh'ma, Psalms and other Biblical passages, each person would use his or her own words to express what was in their heart (*Mishneh Torah, Hilchot Tefilah* 1:2-3).

During the Babylonian Exile, however, a new generation grew up speaking the vernacular of the countries of exile, and their knowledge of Hebrew deteriorated. People no longer knew how to exploit the unique power of the Holy Language by themselves in order to channel Godliness. It was in response to this new situation that Ezra and the Men of the Great Assembly — the supreme legislative court of the time — instituted a standard form of prayers and blessings for all occasions (*ibid.* 4).

Together with certain Biblical passages and Psalms, these prayers and blessings form the basis of the Siddur, the prayer-book, as we have it today.

The Men of the Great Assembly who composed these prayers included outstanding prophets, such as Chagai, Zechariah, Malachi, Daniel, Nehemiah and Mordechai. They had Divine inspiration in arranging the twenty-seven letters and ten vowels of the Holy Language into the sequences that make up the fixed prayers and blessings. Each word of the Siddur has a clear, simple meaning that even a child can comprehend. At the same time, it is enough to glance at the Kabbalistic writings of the ARI, or a Kabbalistic Siddur such as that of Rabbi Shalom Sharabi (the RaShaSh), to get a glimpse of the awesome depths of every single word and the worlds upon worlds of significance that hang upon every single letter and vowel. "Prayer stands at the very summit of the universe" (*Berachot* 6b).

In a sense the prayers do not have one single meaning: they mean something different to each individual, depending on his or her level of knowledge, understanding and devotion. The fixed prayers include everything that anyone needs to express formally to God. Rebbe Nachman evokes this idea in one of his stories, where he tells of a great king who had a secretary to whom many people came, some with praise for the king, others with petitions. "I take all their messages," said the secretary, "and condense them into a few words that I tell the king. The few short words of mine contain all their praises and petitions" (*Rabbi Nachman's Stories* p.401).

The fixed prayers composed by the Men of the Great Assembly were never intended to supercede private prayer in one's own language — hisbodidus — but to *complement* it. Today we need both. (See *Rabbi Nachman's Wisdom* #229.) Because of the low overall spiritual level, we would no longer know the correct way of approaching God or how to channel Godly blessing into ourselves or the world as a whole without the fixed prayers, which were designed to do just this. Through their daily recital, we establish our connection with God and keep certain essentials at the forefront of our minds: God's awesome majesty, His overwhelming love and kindness, and His might and power.

At the same time, each one of us has our own individual issues which we need to work out with God. Each of us has our own unique way of reaching out to God: we need to do this in our native language, in our own individual words, songs, cries, moans, sighs and other forms of self-expression. This we do in hisbodidus. It is in the private, intimate conversations of hisbodidus that we can attain the greatest heights of personal communion with God.

The Set Prayers: How to Pray

There is an extensive literature on the subject of the set prayers. The first volume of the *Shulchan Aruch* is largely taken up with the rules governing all the various blessings and prayers recited both regularly and occasionally. The details of these rules are elaborated in a wide range of commentaries and derivative works. Literature on the meaning of the prayers is a field of its own, with commentaries at every level, ranging from simple, straightforward, step-by-step explanations to profound devotional texts and Kabbalistic explorations involving complex *kavanot* — mystical intentions — on the highest of levels.

The rules governing the recital of the regular prayers — what to say when, postures, when it is permitted to interrupt and when not, when to pray out loud and when to pray in a quiet whisper, etc. — are printed clearly and simply in most Siddurim. A variety of excellent translations of the Siddur is available, many of them accompanied by commentaries giving information about the background and significance of the various prayers.

Invest in a quality Siddur of your choice that you will enjoy using. If you are not familiar with the most frequently recited blessings, such as the blessing after attending to one's needs and those before and after food, you could copy the relevant blessings onto a slip of paper and take it around with you, unless you prefer to carry a pocket Siddur. (A Siddur should not be taken into a bathroom, but if you have a sheet with blessings written on it in your pocket, bag or wallet, etc., it is permissible to enter without removing it.)

Beginners for whom saying all the blessings and prayers in full would be beyond their present ability are advised to consult with a competent Rabbi as to which they should emphasize first. It is a Torah mitzvah to pray daily, to recite the three paragraphs of the Sh'ma in the morning and after nightfall, and to say Birkhat HaMazon (Grace) after eating bread. Over the course of time, aim to familiarize yourself with the words of the basic prayers and as much of the translation as you can understand. Study works about the prayers and their meaning.

Praying in Hebrew

Even those who do not understand any Hebrew should aim to recite the Sh'ma and a few basic prayers and blessings in Hebrew. This is not to say that you should not pray in your native language if you wish. However, even if your Hebrew is rudimentary and halting, there are advantages to reciting the prayers in Hebrew. Simply by articulating the Hebrew letters and words in order, even without comprehension, you are forming vessels that are channelling Godliness into the world. Personal prayers may also be introduced at certain points in the set prayers. When you weave your private offerings in with the holy prayers of the Siddur, you are forming a most powerful connection with God.

You do not have to understand how a telephone works in order to make a call. All you have to know is the number of the party you want to speak to and how to dial it. If you dial the wrong number, you will not get through, regardless of how sincere you may be in wanting to make the call. The prayers of the Siddur are the codes for getting through to God. All we have to do is to say them!

The set prayers influence cosmic processes whether we understand them or not. Similarly, you may not have the faintest idea of how the inside of a computer works, but you can operate it perfectly simply by punching out the requisite letters and symbols on the key-board. The computer will do exactly what you tell it, neither more nor less. To get the desired results, you must punch out the correct commands. Otherwise, you will get a "Bad command or file name" message back.

If you do not understand Hebrew, the prayers you take upon yourself to recite are the most selfless service you could offer to God. In the time of the Baal Shem Tov, founder of the Chassidic movement, there was one illiterate boy who knew nothing but the letters of the Aleph Bet. While everyone else in the synagogue was praying fervently, he repeated the Aleph Bet over and over again. Then he said to the angels of prayer: "I don't know the words of the prayers. All I know is the Aleph Bet. *You* take the letters and form them into the proper words." The Baal Shem Tov said this boy's prayers broke through all the barriers and lifted up the prayers of all the others in the synagogue. Say what *you* can and leave it to HaShem to bring blessing into your soul and the whole world.

Praying with a Minyan

One should make every effort to pray in a properly constituted synagogue together with a minyan of ten adult males. Prayer is more than a personal religious experience. Most of the set prayers are phrased in the plural, because when we stand before God, it is as members of the community of Israel. We are praying not only for ourselves, but for the Jewish People and for the entire world. "When ten people pray together, the Divine Presence rests among them" (*Berachot* 6a). Those who are unable to pray with a minyan regularly should endeavor to do so from time to time.

A frequent problem experienced by people trying to pray with proper devotion is that they find it difficult to keep up with the minyan. For whatever reason, many minyanim go through the prayer services at a brisk pace. If you cannot find a nearby minyan that prays at a comfortable pace, could you find enough people with similar interests to make one? You might try to form a group that would get together to pray once a week or once a month, etc. As a first step, you might consider trying to organize a regular study circle on themes related to prayer.

In the event that you have to pray regularly in a minyan that you find unsatisfactory, still try to make every effort to judge everyone positively. Think how long it took you to reach the stage where you want to pray with devotion. Remember that each person develops at his own pace. Don't expect to be able to change others: you will save yourself a great deal of frustration if you learn to tolerate people the way they are. When the Wise Man wanted to change the Prince, he didn't try to clothe him forcibly. He taught him *by example*. The Wise Man put on his own shirt and trousers, allowing the Prince to follow in his own good time.

No matter how the others may pray, make it your goal to pray with as much concentration as you can. Consult a competent, sympathetic rabbi as to how you should conduct yourself if you constantly find yourself falling behind the rest of the minyan, yet want to fulfill your halachic obligations and make all the necessary responses (Barchu, Kaddish and Kedushah). The halachah gives detailed guidance about when you may interrupt the prayer you are saying in order to join in the congregational responses if the minyan is at a different point in the service.

If you find the behavior of other members of the minyan a distraction, there is no need to feel that you have failed because you cannot rise above such distractions. It is very natural to be disturbed by others. In the words of Rebbe Nachman: "People say that if you have true feeling and are really bound up in your prayers, you should not hear any disturbance. Your devotion should be enough to block out everything else. But the truth is that this is no argument. The greatest Tzaddik may pray with great strength and attachment to God, but he can still be disturbed, no matter how great his enthusiasm, no matter how deeply he is bound up in prayer.... All his feeling and emotion will not prevent him from being disturbed and distressed" (*Rabbi Nachman's Wisdom* #284).

Take time to look around the synagogue and find a place where you will be able to pray regularly with the minimum of distractions. If the synagogue is crowded and you find you are pushed and jostled, try to move to a place where this will be less likely to happen. Avoid the temptation to watch other people: look only at your Siddur, or close your eyes and imagine you are praying in a forest! (*Yesod ve-Shoresh Ha-Avodah* I:10).

Despite this, you may still hear things that disturb you or that you find inappropriate in a synagogue. Rebbe Nachman taught that the solution to this is to erase one's ego completely until one is aware of nothing but the presence of God: "When a person stands in the palace of the King, nullifies himself completely and sees nothing there but the King, then certainly when he hears something shameful, he will find a way of interpreting it in a way that actually enhances the greatness of the King" (*Likutey Moharan* I:55,7).

Having Faith and Making Time

Prayer is intimately bound up with belief. One of the main reasons why people feel they get little out of praying is because they do not have enough faith in the importance of what they are doing. They think God is not interested in their prayers. Since they underrate the activity of praying, they give it little time or attention. They hurry through the prayers unthinkingly, and consequently find them dry and uninspiring. Strengthen your belief that God is listening to your prayers, and that every word and letter is most precious. The more you understand the meaning of the prayers and the exalted spiritual work you are doing by simply saying them, the more enthusiastic you will become and the more you will enjoy praying.

In practical terms, one of the first prerequisites is simply to make the necessary time. If it takes *x* seconds to mumble a blessing or prayer without feeling, and *y* seconds to say it clearly and deliberately, the only way to say it properly is by taking the extra time. This applies equally to the incidental blessings and the fixed prayer services. That is not to say that the only way to pray with attention is to go slowly. Not everyone finds this necessary. Some people are able to pray fast and maintain their full attention. What is important is to pray at the pace *you* need to pray at in order to concentrate.

Work out how much time you can devote to the daily prayer services: how long can you spend praying in the morning, how long in the afternoon, and how long at night? Consult with a competent rabbi, if necessary, to work out how much of the full service you should say, given your present rate of reciting the prayers. If you feel that, owing to lack of time, you will have to compromise and recite only part of the service, doing this at a pace that enables you to concentrate and say the words properly may be better than rushing through the entire service inattentively and without enunciating the words properly.

Before you begin your prayers, try to put yourself in a cheerful mood. Sing a happy tune on your way to the synagogue. At the entrance to the synagogue, pause to compose yourself, then enter with reverence. Before beginning one of the main weekday prayer services, give some charity according to your means. If you cannot put the money in a suitable charity box or give it to someone immeditately, set it aside from your other money and give it later.

Affirm out loud that you take upon yourself the mitzvah of "love your friend as yourself" (Leviticus 19:18). Affirm that you bind yourself to all the true Tzaddikim. Binding oneself to the Tzaddikim means looking to their teachings and example for guidance and inspiration, both in one's prayers and one's life in general. The Tzaddikim have general souls, in which all the individual souls are rooted. By binding yourself to the Tzaddikim you connect yourself with all the souls. This gives added strength to your prayers. (See *Likutey Moharan* II:1, 1-3.)

Out of the Mouth, Into the Ear

"Let your ears hear what you are saying with your mouth."

Berachot 13a

The essential work of prayer is twofold: to articulate the words of the Siddur clearly, one after the other, and to listen to what you are saying. This applies equally to the daily prayer services and to the various other blessings and prayers recited at different junctures during the day. "True devotion is listening very carefully to the words you are saying" (*Rabbi Nachman's Wisdom* #75).

People sometimes ask if it is possible to "use the blessings and prayers as meditation." In order to answer this, it is necessary to be clear in what sense the term "meditation" is being used. If "meditation" is being used in the sense of a method of stress reduction and relaxation, clearly it would be a grave insult to the blessings and prayers to look upon them merely as this. It may be that those who put effort into their prayers do become more relaxed as they deepen their trust in God, but prayer is far more than a means of reducing tension.

Another definition of meditation is "thinking in a controlled manner... deciding exactly how one wishes to direct the mind for a period of time, and then doing it" (R. Aryeh Kaplan, *Jewish Meditation* p.3). In this sense, the fixed prayers and blessings are unquestionably a form of meditation. We could call them "guided" meditations, in the sense that the goal is to direct the mind along a series of thoughts as expressed in the words of the prayers.

As we have seen (above p. 94), the Hebrew term for directing the mind is *kavanah*, from the root *le-khaven*, meaning to aim or direct, as when an archer aims an arrow. Thus people speak of "praying with *kavanah*" — proper attention and inner feeling. A specific thought or intention that one has in mind while saying a word, phrase or entire prayer, or while performing a mitzvah, is also called a *kavanah* (plural, *kavanot*). There is an enormous literature on the *kavanot* of the prayers, from the simple meanings and allusions of the words to the profoundest Kabbalistic devotions, as set forth in the writings of the ARI and derivative literature.

To pray with proper attention and inner feeling means that "the person praying should inwardly concentrate on the meaning of the words that he is saying with his lips" (*Shulchan Aruch, Orach Chaim* 98:1). Not only is it unnecessary to know or use the Kabbalistic *kavanot* of the prayers in order to pray with inner feeling, but for anyone who lacks the requisite depth of knowledge and spiritual purity, it can be highly confusing to try to do so. (See *Tzaddik* #526 and *Rabbi Nachman's Wisdom* #75.) Rebbe Nachman said: "Perfect prayer is having in mind the *simple meaning* of such words as *Baruch Atah HaShem* — 'Blessed are You, O God' " (*Rabbi Nachman's Wisdom* #75).

"Let your ears hear what you are bringing out of your mouth" (*Berachot* 13a). This fundamental Talmudic prescription about prayer means that one should physically listen to the sounds one is making with one's mouth. In addition, the idea of *hearing* what you are saying implies *understanding* the words and hearing their *message*. (Thus when King Solomon prayed for wisdom, he asked God to give him "a heart that *hears*" — I Kings 3:9.) Letting "your ears hear what you are bringing out of your mouth" thus means exactly the same as what the Shulchan Aruch says: concentrating on the meaning of each word as one says it. As you say each word, think of the literal translation of the word, and listen to its message.

Devotion

> *"The person praying... should feel as if the Divine Presence is directly before him."*
>
> *Orach Chaim* 98:1

"I imagine You, I address You, even though I do not know You" (from *An'im Z'mirot*). God in Himself is unknowable, yet all our prayers are directed to God, the Source of all existence.

HaShem literally means "the Name," referring to the Tetragrammaton — the essential name of HaShem: Y H V H. (Tetragrammaton is Greek for "the name of four letters.") It is strictly forbidden to pronounce the Tetragrammaton as it is written: even when one has occasion to say the letters in the order they are written, one says Yod *K*e Vav *K*e so as not to come even close to pronouncing the Name of God.

Nevertheless, it is not forbidden to contemplate the Name of God: on the contrary, much Kabbalistic teaching is concerned with the meaning and significance of the Name and its letters. God's Name is bound up with the Hebrew root *HaVaH*, meaning "is" or "exists." We could say that the "meaning" of the Tetragrammaton is "the One that brings existence into being" — i.e. the Source of existence.

When reciting prayers and blessings, the Tetragrammaton (or the conventional Yod Yod often printed in Siddurim in its place) is pronounced as "Adonoy" — "Lord." (When merely quoting a phrase containing the Tetragrammaton, as opposed to reciting it in a prayer, we say "HaShem" in order to avoid taking the name of God in vain.)

All our prayers and blessings are woven around the Name of HaShem, the Source of all existence. The different prayers and blessings contain all kinds of statements, descriptions, praises, affirmations and requests and so on, but essentially all of them revolve around and return to HaShem. In our prayers we affirm how all the manifold phenomena of existence derive from HaShem. With each blessing, praise or request we offer, we should think of how the specific item which is the subject of this blessing, etc. derives from God. Similarly, when reciting the Sh'ma we should have in mind that we are binding ourselves to the Source of our existence.

During the recital of any prayer or blessing, try to keep your awareness focused on the fact that you are speaking to and about HaShem — that the Divine Presence is directly before you. When pausing to relax, breathe and focus prior to each prayer service or blessing, this is the thought you should try to bring to mind. Then, as you start to say the words, try to keep your attention on the simple meaning of each word.

The word *Baruch*, "Blessed," is related to the Hebrew word *breichah* meaning a pool in which the waters of a stream gather, and from which all our various needs for water are supplied. When saying *Baruch* you should recall that you are drawing from the Source of all blessing. The word *baruch* is also related to *berech*, which means a knee. When we bend the knees, the head is lowered. When we humble our hearts and thank God for His blessing — "*Baruch*" — we are making it possible for the Source of Creation, the "Head," to descend, as it were, bringing blessing to the very place where we are.

Atah — "You." When we address God directly we should be aware that the Divine Presence is before us. The word *ATaH* includes Aleph and Tav, the first and last letters of the Aleph Bet, through which God created the Universe. *Atah* signifies that from beginning to end, through all the diversity of creation, "You are One."

HaShem: When saying *Adonoy* in prayer, we should have in mind that this word means that HaShem is *Adon Kol* — Master of All. When reciting the Sh'ma and, if possible, in other places where the Tetragrammaton appears in the prayers, we should also have in mind that the Name of HaShem signifies: "Was, is and will be," i.e. God is eternal (*Orach Chaim* 5, and see *Mishnah Berurah ad loc.* 3). When saying *Adonoy* one could thus think: "Eternal Master of All."

Elohim: (When pronouncing this name of God other than in prayer, it is customary to pronounce it as Elo*k*im so as not to profane the Name.) *Elokim* is usually translated as "God" — and *Elokenu* means *our* God. The Divine name *Elokim* refers to God's power as manifested in the Creation. Thus grammatically *Elokim* is a plural form, although when referring to God it is almost always used with a singular verb. All the various powers manifested in the diversity of the Creation derive from the unitary God. When saying *Elokim* or *Elokenu*, have in mind that God is "mighty and omnipotent" (*ibid.*).

The ultimate connection with God in every prayer and blessing is when we address HaShem directly. However in this world it is not possible to remain constantly in a state of direct communication with God. After "running" forwards and addressing God directly, we now have to "return" to ourselves and the world we live in. The blessing continues to speak *about* God in the third person, and about the things He creates, etc. Having had a glimpse of the unity of God at the moment of direct connection, the task now, in the continuation of the blessing or prayer, is to try to experience His unity even amidst the plurality of the created world.

Melech HaOlam, "Ruler of the Universe": The word *Olam*, universe, is related to the Hebrew root ALaM, meaning "conceal." We look around at the visible universe but we do not see God. The very creation of the universe could only come about through the concealment of God's light. But in speaking of *Melech HaOlam*, "Ruler of the Universe," we remind ourselves that even though God may be concealed, making the world seem independent, in fact the Universe and everything in it has a Source and Ruler: beyond the diversity is the unitary God.

In practice, it is very difficult for anyone to maintain his concentration on every word throughout the recitation of the prayers. In any event, one should make every effort to concentrate at least while reciting the first verse of the Sh'ma and the first blessing of the Amidah, the silent Standing Prayer.

One of the main problems encountered by everyone who prays regularly is the tendency to repeat the prayers by rote. Try to prevent this by pausing from time to time during your prayers in order to remind yourself of the importance of prayer. The best way to concentrate on the meaning of key words and phrases in the prayers is to pause briefly *before* saying them. Look at the word or phrase on the page, and give yourself a moment to think what it means. "*Think* the word before you bring it out of your mouth, as taught in the Psalms (10:17): 'prepare the heart...' — first, and then: '...make the ear hear' " (*Iggeret HaRamban*).

Distracting Thoughts

Ideally, "the person praying should remove all distracting thoughts until his mind is clear and his attention fixed on his prayer" (*Orach Chaim* 98:1). In practice, however, most of us find it virtually impossible to achieve this. The important thing is not to *worry* about distractions. "You may be distracted by many outside thoughts when you pray. Ignore them completely. Do your part and say all the prayers in order, ignoring all disturbing thoughts. Do what you must, and disregard these thoughts completely" (*Rabbi Nachman's Wisdom* #72).

Rebbe Nachman tells us that these disturbing thoughts actually benefit our prayers. "There are tremendous powers denouncing our prayers. Without distracting thoughts, prayer would be impossible. Outside thoughts disguise our prayers so that they are ignored by the Outside Forces. They do not denounce the prayers, which are then allowed to enter on high. God knows our innermost thoughts. We may be distracted, but deep in our hearts, our thoughts are only to God... God knows what is in your heart, and sees this innermost desire. He sees through the disguise, and accepts the prayer in love" (*ibid.*).

"It may be impossible to go through the entire service with proper devotion, but each person can at least say a small portion with feeling." Rebbe Nachman explains that this is because in the root of their soul, each person is associated with a particular part of the prayer service. When he comes to the part of the service pertaining to his soul-root, he is aroused to great devotion. "You may sometimes pray with great devotion, but then the feeling departs and the words begin to seem empty. Do not be discouraged, for you have merely left your area... Continue the service, saying each word in absolute simplicity" (*Rabbi Nachman's Wisdom* #75).

Even though it may be impossible to pray the entire service with devotion, you should still "force yourself to say each word of the service. Make believe that you are a child just learning to read, and simply say the words... Follow the order of the service even without feeling. Continue word by word, page by page, until God helps you achieve a feeling of devotion. And even if you complete the entire service without feeling, it is not the end. You can still say a Psalm. There are other prayers to be said" (*ibid.*).

After all your efforts, you may still feel like a Turkey. If so, remind yourself that "I may be far from God because of my many sins. Let it be. If this is so, there can be no perfect prayer without me. The Talmud teaches us that every prayer that does not include the sinners of Israel is not a true prayer. Prayer is like an incense offering. The Torah requires that the incense contain galbanum, even though by itself it has a vile odor... Just as the vile-smelling galbanum is an essential ingredient of the sweet incense, so my tainted prayer is a vital ingredient of the prayers of all Israel. Without it, prayer is deficient, like incense without the galbanum" (*Rabbi Nachman's Wisdom* #295).

Fervor

Rapturous prayer is a sweet and amazing experience. You are totally involved in the prayer: the only reality for you at each moment is the word you are now at in the Siddur. The word comes leaping off the page and into your mouth: it comes forth from your mouth as if through a spirit that is beyond you, yet speaking through you. Each word cries out the magnificent glory of God. You stand in your place, but you are lifted up. Suddenly you see a world you do not see most of the time: the world all around you, transformed into oneness. Every familiar object and person is shouting the glory of God in unison — the other daveners, the chairs, the tables, the walls, the windows, the buildings and trees, the skies...

How does one attain the intense, ecstatic fervor of the true Chassidim — lovers of God? How does one come to pray with leaping joy, with profound awe and amazement at God, with shaking and trembling, dancing and singing, tears and radiant happiness? Does such prayer come by itself, or do you have to *make* it come? Are you supposed to force yourself to feel the prayers intensely, or perhaps even *pretend* you feel them intensely?

Two hundred and fifty years ago, before the birth of the Chassidic movement, Rabbi Moshe Chaim Luzzatto had this to say about *Chassidut* (devout religiosity): "Chassidut has come to have a bad odor in the eyes of the broad run of people, including the more intelligent, in that they assume that Chassidut involves empty and irrational practices, or simply means reciting many lengthy supplications and confessions to the accompaniment of a lot of tears and violent swaying and bowing, and strange forms of asceticism" (*Mesilat Yesharim* ch.18).

Today, it often happens that even those who feel drawn to fervent Chassidic prayer are confused by the externals they see in some Chassidic circles: vigorous physical movements, loud cries, hand-clapping, jumping and the like. They wonder if the only way to become true Chassidim is by imitating these externals. Are they a necessary part of Chassidic prayer? Should you sway, clap and shout while praying, even if you don't feel like it?

Maybe when we find ourselves half asleep and want to arouse ourselves, one way to do it is by moving about vigorously and praying loudly so as to "warm up." However the true inner emotion of Chassidic prayer does not come merely by imitating the external movements. Sincere emotion when praying is certainly desirable, but it is a mistake to try to force it. For example, speaking of tears when praying, Rebbe Nachman says: "When a person is praying, if he keeps on thinking he should cry and is waiting for the tears to come, this so confuses him that it makes it impossible for him to say his prayers sincerely and whole-heartedly... The thought that he is going to cry at any moment distracts him and prevents him concentrating on what he is saying... If you weep, very good. If not, not" (*Likutey Moharan* II:95).

True emotion is not something you can force. If it comes, it comes. The essence of the work of prayer is not to affect emotion but always to concentrate on the words and their meaning. Regarding whether to sway or not to sway in prayer, do whatever comes to you most naturally. Sometimes you may want to sway, at other times you may prefer to stand (or sit) still. Some people find gentle swaying from side to side, or backwards and forwards, soothing and an aid to concentration; others find it a distraction.

The same applies to whether one should pray loudly or softly, and whether one should speak or sing. You should always be able to hear the words you are saying, including during the Amidah prayer, when your whisper should be audible to *you*. But how loudly you pray is entirely up to you — as long as you are not disturbing others. There may be times when you may wish to pray more loudly, especially when you want to arouse yourself. At other times you may want to put your entire focus on hearing the letters and words in your mind and heart, and you will not pay attention to the volume of your physical voice.

The main thing is to "detach yourself from every outside thought in the world and only direct your attention to the words you are saying to HaShem, just as a person speaks to his friend. Your heart will then easily be aroused by itself... *Say the words sincerely to HaShem* without any other thoughts whatsoever" (*ibid.*).

It is not one's emotions that one should force, says Rebbe Nachman, but one's concentration on the words and their meaning. "There are some who say that prayer must come of itself, without being strained, but they are wrong, and one must do everything in one's power to force oneself... *True devotion is the binding of thought to word.* If you listen to your own words, then strength will enter your prayers by itself. All your energy anticipates the time when it will be drawn into words of holiness. When you focus your mind on the prayers, this strength rushes to enter the words"(*Rabbi Nachman's Wisdom* #66).

"You can be a Turkey and still wear trousers"

Some people may feel ecstatic prayer to be light-years away from where they are currently holding with their own daily Turkey gobbledygook mumblings. Even those who make a regular effort to concentrate on their prayers frequently go through periods when they feel like uninspired Turkeys, finding it impossible to get involved. Every day challenges us with new and old distractions from this most exalted spiritual service.

Don't be discouraged. No matter how badly you may think you pray, the fact that you say your prayers every day, no matter how, is more important than anything. Once the Baal Shem Tov bitterly reproached a preacher who had denounced someone. "Will you speak evil of a Jew? Know that a Jew goes to work every day, and in the late afternoon he starts trembling and says to himself, 'It's getting late for Minchah'. He goes off somewhere to pray Minchah, and he doesn't know what he is saying, *and even so, the heavenly angels quake at his prayer*" (*Shevachey HaBa'al Shem Tov* #132).

Every day, three times a day, we pray. You may feel unable to give any more time and attention to your prayers than you do already. You may feel you cannot concentrate properly on even a single word. Perhaps you think you are the vile-smelling galbanum and you'll *never* be able to pray properly. That doesn't mean you cannot make an effort just once — perhaps one day when you happen to be in a place where nobody knows you, or in a moment of great seriousness one Yom Kippur, or at a quiet point one Shabbat...

"You can be a Turkey and still wear trousers." Just pronounce the words on the page of the Siddur, one by one, like a child learning to read.

"Anyone with sense and understanding should pray all his days to be able to say one true word to God the way he should — even *just once in his life*" (*Likutey Moharan* I:112).

9

From Strength to Strength: Joy and Song

In the same way, they put on the rest of their clothes, one by one.

"Joy in HaShem is your tower of strength."

Nehemiah 8:10

It must have taken a long time for the Wise Man to get the Prince to put on the rest of his clothes. He must have come up against resistances practically every step of the way. The Prince was probably wondering what a Turkey was doing wearing all these clothes. Maybe putting on a shirt and trousers had been fun at first, but now the Prince must have been re-experiencing the same old negative feelings that had driven him into his madness in the first place. He must have felt more like a Turkey than ever.

Still, the Wise Man continued with his work undaunted. He kept his eyes on the good in the Prince. He had his plan, and he patiently carried it out. Each garment he could persuade the Prince to wear was a victory in itself. More than that: putting them on, one after the other, kept the Prince moving forward, creating a rhythm. Getting the Prince drawn into this positive rhythm was the best way to circuit around the negativity in him and eventually overcome it completely.

Keeping active and positive has a power similar to that of music. You may be feeling extremely lethargic and uninspired, and if you try singing a lively melody to yourself, you might find it very hard to get into it. But if you force yourself to keep on singing, before long you'll start getting into the swing. Soon the song will be carrying *you*, and you won't want to stop.

The same applies to developing a positive outlook on your life in general. If you have had a tendency toward pessimism, it can be difficult to stir out of it at first. But if you push yourself for a while and make a real effort to look at things differently, you'll soon find that they really are better than you thought they were, and before long a new joyous spirit will lift up your entire life.

Nothing is more destructive to spiritual growth than negativity and depression. Genuine growth is a long, slow process with many ups and downs. It is harder to change than to stay the same. It is harder to strive for excellence than to be content with mediocrity. Almost every step of the way, there are likely to be obstacles of some kind, whether from outside circumstances and other people, or from entrenched forces within yourself. Obstacles can be very discouraging, but if you allow yourself to become demoralized, it could push you off the path completely.

No matter how much progress you make, encountering problems is an integral part of the process of growth: in fact, it is the efforts you make to overcome them that cause you to grow. Do everything in your power to avoid becoming demoralized. A happy, positive attitude will give you the inner strength to overcome all obstacles. How does one develop such an attitude? Before we try to find an answer, let us first look a little further into the problem.

The Yoke of Torah

The more seriously one takes one's Torah obligations, the more the Turkey is likely to rebel. The first encounter with Jewish spirituality may be as an enjoyable experiment, but sooner or later every Jew must come to terms with the fact that the path of the mitzvot involves commitment. Certainly the mitzvot are a pathway of individual spiritual growth, but they are also much much more. Accepting the mitzvot means taking on responsibility, not only to oneself but also to the rest of the world, whose welfare depends on them, and to God.

Most of the self-help practices currently popular in our culture leave their practitioners with an option: if you feel like meditating, exercising, eating macrobiotic, and so on, you do; if not, no-one is likely to force you. For a Jew, however, the Torah and mitzvot are not voluntary. Judaism is service. The Torah and mitzvot are called a "yoke" — like the yoke that keeps the ox harnessed to the plough, forcing it to work whether it wants to or not. The Torah and the mitzvot are obligatory.

You may have entered the spiritual path in the hope of getting *free* of Turkey madness, only to find yourself feeling more and more *restricted* by the numerous obligations and prohibitions of the Torah. Trying to lead a spiritual life day by day — observing the mitzvot, studying Torah, praying intently, practicing hisbodidus, taking care with your diet, exercising, etc. — while at the same time working for a living, spending time with family and friends, and doing all of the other things we all have to do, you may well feel like a juggler trying to keep too many balls up in the air at once.

The very pathway of hisbodidus that is supposed to transform us into joyous, spiritual achievers can at times feel like a heavy weight. Hisbodidus involves honest self-confrontation. You know that you cannot fool God or yourself. There is no retreat. Going back to being a Turkey ceases to be an option.

You look at your faults and shortcomings. You know you have to fight them. But at times they seem more indomitable than ever.

The Princely side of us longs to draw close to God and keep the entire Torah. Often we set ourselves the highest goals, but when we fail, it is dangerously easy to become despondent. Some blame external factors, railing at the people and circumstances they believe to be preventing them from observing the Torah the way they feel they should. Others blame themselves. They look at themselves and the way they repeatedly violate their own high standards, and judge themselves guilty.

Frustration, anger, self-condemnation and similar responses trap people in vicious cycles of negativity and depression that can stunt all growth and change. Feeling they are bound to fail no matter what they do, they stop trying. They allow themselves to slip back into their old ways, gratifying their baser appetites as a way of forgetting their misery. Knowing how far they have fallen makes them even more frustrated and depressed. And so the syndrome continues, until they may end up further away than ever, locked in a cage of despair.

Looking for the Good

It is vital to make every effort to steer clear of negativity and depression, and cultivate a positive outlook. You may look at the people and circumstances that seem to be holding you back and feel frustrated and bitter. You may look at your own faults and shortcomings and feel strongly disappointed at your lack of progress. You may wonder if anything will ever change.

The solution is to learn to look at things differently. There may be little you can do to alter external circumstances or deeply-ingrained features of your inner make-up, but you can change the way you *view* them. In many cases, a simple change in outlook and attitude can transform even the toughest obstacles into powerful allies.

What you actually see when you look at something is largely governed by what you are looking *for*. If you expect to see bad, that is almost certainly what you will find. If you look hard enough for the good, you will eventually see it. This applies to the way you look at yourself, other people, the situations you face, and life in general.

Someone who is upset and angry about the way things are is really angry with God for making them so. This is one of the worst forms of arrogance there is. The angry person is saying "Why aren't things the way *I* think they ought to be?" Looking for the good requires an act of humility: "Maybe *I* am wrong in my ideas about how things ought to be."

People often imagine that the barriers they experience in their efforts to come close to God are so great that they will never be able to overcome them. But the truth is that God only sends people difficulties that are within their capacity to overcome, if they fight with enough determination. All obstacles, whether external or internal, are sent by God. Every impediment is therefore a veil for God Himself. In reality there is no obstacle at all.

God put you where you are because this is the best possible place for you to be. He made you the way you are because this is how you can eventually experience God's goodness to the fullest extent possible, by rising to the challenge He has set you. Even when you feel under great pressure, make every effort to find God and turn to Him within the very situation in which you find yourself. Can you think of a positive reason why God should have sent you this problem? How can you benefit from it?

One of the chief influences on the way you look at life is the way you talk. If you keep on telling yourself that things are grim and unpleasant, that people and circumstances are against you, that you are unsuccessful and everything you try fails, then regardless of what may actually happen in reality, you are cued to notice only those segments of reality that fit in with your preconceived notions. The experiences you then have will simply confirm your worst expectations.

The foundation of positive thinking is belief in God and faith in His goodness. "God is good to all, and His tender kindnesses are over all His works... God is just in all his ways" (Psalms 145:9 & 17). The first step toward thinking positively is to try to *talk* positively, even if you are not yet completely convinced of the truth of what you are saying. Start by telling yourself that you believe in God, that God is good, and therefore things must be good, even if you cannot yet see how. When you are facing obstacles, whether external or from within yourself, affirm your faith out loud: "God, I believe in You. God is good. God, help me find the good." Avoid talking negatively about situations and people, and, of course, about yourself. If you feel you can't find anything good to say, say nothing.

In the words of Rabbi Nachman: "When someone meets a friend, and the friend asks him how he is, and he replies, 'Not good,' God says: 'This you call not good? I'll show you what not good is' — and all kinds of bad experiences come his way. But when his friend meets him and asks how he is, and he replies cheerfully, 'Good, thank God,' even though in fact things are not good, God then says: 'This you call good? I'm going to show you what real good is!' " (*Siach Sarfei Kodesh* II:32).

Your Good Points

Those who study Torah literature on personal development and make a genuine effort to live up to Torah ideals are very likely to look at themselves and feel they are far away from where the Torah says they ought to be. Even after years of effort trying to improve oneself, one may scrutinize oneself and one's behavior carefully and feel that the Torah itself would condemn one.

It may well be that one has done, and continues to do, much that is wrong. One's behavior and personality may be far from what the Torah asks. Nevertheless, it will not help to get depressed about it. Instead of dwelling on one's bad points and failures, one should try to find good points and mitigating factors.

A person should not blame himself for having a Turkey side. God created him with it. If we did not have a baser side, our service of God would be worth nothing. If God had created us perfect, it would be as if God were serving Himself. Our service is worth something precisely because we are exposed to the full force of our lower instincts and desires yet we still try to fight against them and channel our energy into Torah and mitzvot.

The evil urge may lead people into sin, yet it was God's will to create us with it because of the preciousness of our efforts and sacrifices in trying to overcome it. Looking for the good in oneself does not mean pretending that the bad does not exist. The Torah teaches us very clearly what is good and what is bad. One cannot ignore the bad or perform some kind of intellectual trick and pretend it is good. The power of evil is very real, but this is, in fact, what gives value to the good we accomplish. The more people are pulled by their baser desires and involvements, the more precious their attempts to lift themselves up and come closer to God.

If one feels bad about oneself or some of the things one does, this in itself is an indication of an innate spiritual sensitivity. Instead of dwelling on the bad in oneself, one should train oneself to use this sensitivity to look for the good. One should remember the inner barriers one is fighting, and learn to appreciate the value of even a single good deed or mitzvah. Every act of charity and kindness, every word of Torah one studies, every prayer one offers, and every other mitzvah is a channel of connection with God's infinite goodness.

The world at large does not put much value on Torah and mitzvot — people are more impressed by luxury homes, flashy cars, expensive holidays and the like. Recognizing the preciousness of one's mitzvot means taking a bold step out of the value system of the surrounding culture. One can take pride in the fact that when one gets up each day, the first thing one does is to put on Tzitzit and Tefilin, bless God and pray for the world, rather than simply eating a big breakfast, going out to earn a lot of money, and trying to have fun.

The Music of Life

Rebbe Nachman teaches: "Search until you find a little bit of good in yourself. How could it be that you never did a single mitzvah or good deed in your whole life? You may start to examine this good deed, only to see that it is also full of flaws. Perhaps you feel the mitzvah or holy act was prompted by impure motives and you had improper thoughts and did not carry it out properly. Even so, how is it possible that this mitzvah or good deed doesn't contain the slightest good? Some good point *must* be there. You have to search until you find some modicum of good in yourself to revive yourself and make yourself happy.

"And in just the same way, you must carry on searching until you find yet another good point. Even if this good point is also mixed up with all kinds of bad, you must still extract some positive point from here as well. And so you must go on, searching and gathering together additional good points. *This is how music is made*" (*Likutey Moharan* I:282).

A tune consists of a succession of notes. A musical instrument is essentially a sound-box designed to amplify the vibrations caused when the player plucks or blows, etc., depending on the instrument. In order to play the tune properly, the musician has to play each note correctly. This means setting off the right vibrations instead of hitting the wrong notes.

Our personalities are like musical instruments, and the quality of our lives depends on the way we play ourselves. If we harp on the bad in us, it causes bad vibrations in ourselves and the world around us. Looking for our good points is like playing the right notes and setting off good vibrations. The art of living is to look for one good point after the other, turning life into a melody. This was how the Wise Man proceeded with his cure of the Prince. He put on one garment after another, one mitzvah after another — going from one good point to the next — until it became a rhythm.

"When a person refuses to let himself fall, but instead revives his spirits by searching out and finding his positive points, collecting them together and sifting them out from the impurities within him, this is how melodies are made. Then he can pray and sing and give thanks to God" (*ibid.*).

The more you get into the habit of concentrating on your good points and enjoying them, the happier you will be. You won't have to work to fight off lethargy and depression. They will go away by themselves, until eventually you will realize that you are free of them altogether.

In Hisbodidus

During your hisbodidus sessions, take time to look for your good points. One of the foremost components of hisbodidus is self-examination. You look into yourself and evaluate your personality and behavior in accordance with Torah criteria, in order to know where you need to change yourself.

People tend to judge themselves much of the time, feeling good when they do good and bad when they do things they know to be wrong. However, people's self-judgment is often very partial: there are many who blithely ignore their worst aspects while wallowing in self-recrimination over relatively minor matters.

Hisbodidus makes self-examination and self-judgment into a systematic discipline. In itself the word "judgment" does not carry either negative or positive overtones, yet many people in our culture find it a forbidding term. They assume that all judgment is bound to be condemnatory, and insist that everyone should always be non-judgmental about everything. Perhaps this is a reaction to the negative way many people tend to judge each other and themselves. But the solution is not to give up forming judgments — that would be tantamount to giving up any value system whatsoever. The solution is to learn to judge favorably, ourselves and others.

In hisbodidus you sit like a court in judgment on yourself. You review what you have been doing, things you have said, and your various thoughts and feelings. You must evaluate them truthfully and understand clearly where you acted correctly and where you went wrong. But when it comes to passing judgment on yourself, don't think you must be harsh. Don't simply condemn yourself for the wrong you have done. Judge yourself favorably. In a court, the accused pleads for understanding. Be your own advocate: look at yourself sympathetically, and try to probe the underlying factors that drive you to do the bad things you do.

Besides thinking about what's wrong in your life, make it a regular habit to review the good things as well. In fact, this is the best way to start a hisbodidus session. We have seen that "acknowledging God for what is past" is the first stage in hisbodidus (see above, pp. 132-4). Begin your sessions by enumerating all the good in your life — from your health and strength, the food you eat, your livelihood and other material benefits to the many mitzvot and good deeds God has enabled you to perform. Thank God for each one in turn. This is the best way to open up a channel of sincere communication with God. You should then find it much easier to speak to Him frankly and openly about things you have done wrong and feel contrition, and you will come away feeling cleansed and at peace.

It is a good idea to take a pencil and paper and literally make a list of your good points. Include things you may consider relatively minor, even good thoughts, such as ideas you may have had from time to time about things you would like to achieve even if as yet you are nowhere near achieving them. You may not be able to make a complete list of all your good points in one session of hisbodidus. Keep your list and add to it in later sessions. Look over it regularly and think about the great value of the mitzvot God enables you to do.

In All of Life

"It is a great mitzvah to be constantly happy."

Likutey Moharan II:24

Going from mitzvah to mitzvah and from one good point to the next is the pathway to enduring happiness. For some people the main joy in life is eating and drinking. For others it is their status and possessions, or their friends or families. But in the end only our mitzvot endure. As the Rabbis said: "A person has three friends in life: his possessions, his friends and family, and his Torah and good deeds. When he dies, he leaves all his physical possessions behind. His friends and family accompany him to the cemetery, but after the interment they too leave him. Only his Torah and good deeds stay with him for ever" (*Pirkey d'Rabbi Eliezer* 34).

If your happiness depends on something specific, you will only be happy when you have that thing. But when your happiness is from closeness to HaShem, you can always be happy. There is never a moment in the day or night that you cannot involve yourself in a mitzvah, thereby connecting yourself with God. Even when you are doing absolutely nothing, simply thinking of God is a mitzvah — faith — and "You are where your thoughts are" (*Likutey Moharan* I:21). Every single mitzvah is a connection with the living God.

If you want to make a lot of money, you must concentrate hard on the idea. Every day, all day, you must have one thought in your mind: am I gaining or losing, and how can I gain *more*? So it is with the mitzvot. Enjoy every mitzvah. Make it your goal to collect more and more. And constantly strive to improve and deepen the way you fulfill them.

Receiving the Torah and mitzvot at Mount Sinai was an event of pure joy. The key to the joy of the Torah path is to be found in the response of the Jewish People when God offered them the Torah. They answered that they would accept and fulfill it without first asking for an explanation of its deeper meaning. They agreed to carry out the practical teachings of the Torah in the faith that understanding would come later. "*Na'aseh ve-nishma* — We will do" — first — "and we will hear" — later (Exodus 24:7).

This means that each time one carries out a mitzvah, the practical action is followed by "hearing" — a deepening of one's understanding of the mitzvah itself and the Torah path in general. Every mitzvah we perform opens up new horizons of Torah and mitzvot — which in turn gives us new mitzvot to perform. Then, when we perform them, even greater horizons of Torah open up. Every mitzvah thus leads to further and deeper connection with God. *Na'aseh ve-nishma*, doing and then hearing, going from mitzvah to mitzvah, from good point to good point, from strength to strength, is the pathway of joy (*Likutey Moharan* I:22, 9).

Music

"The main way to attach ourselves to God from this lowly material world is through music and song."

Rebbe Nachman quoted in *Likutey Halachot, Nesi'at Kapayim* 5:6

Get into the habit of always singing a tune. This is something you can do at any time. It is one of the simplest and most enjoyable ways of serving God, and also one of the most powerful.

Sing the holy melodies that you personally like and find inspiring. You can do this at home, at work, in the car — literally wherever you happen to be. Even if you cannot sing well, you can still inspire yourself with a melody sung to the best of your ability. If you are embarrassed about singing aloud or feel it will disturb others, you can hum quietly to yourself (*Rabbi Nachman's Wisdom* #273).

If you do not know many songs, listen to tapes or records and learn some more. Hundreds and hundreds of recordings of religious music are available today with all kinds of melodies — joyous, devotional, etc. — from the various traditions, Chassidic, non-Chassidic, Oriental, etc.

When you listen to a recording, learn to distinguish between the *nigun* — the melody line — and the particular interpretation, style of orchestration, etc. of this recording. Although many contemporary recordings feature rich orchestration, most traditional melodies would originally have been sung with little or no instrumental accompaniment. Learn the nigun itself and sing it the way you most enjoy it. If you play a musical instrument, play holy nigunim for your own enjoyment and that of your family and friends.

In hisbodidus, experiment with different kinds of melodies — joyous and devotional. Choose the melody you sing according to the mood you wish to create. Sometimes when you first start singing you may feel uninspired, but if you carry on singing you will gradually find that instead of your carrying the melody, the melody will carry you and steadily lift you higher and higher.

Sing or hum a nigun before you begin to pray. Sing your prayers to a happy tune. Make a special point of singing *z'mirot* joyously at the table on Shabbat.

Dance

The heart yearns to rise toward God and rejoice, but the weight of our physical bodies tends to pull us down to earth! In dance, instead of letting the body pull it downward, the heart lifts up the entire body. The dancer jumps and skips and raises his arms and waves them about. Much of life revolves around serving the body: working to feed it, clothe it, and attend to our many other physical needs. In holy dance the tables are turned, and the entire body is employed in the service of the soul, to praise God.

This may help us to understand the statement of the Rabbis characterizing the blissful harmony that will reign in the future, when God's plan for the creation will be fulfilled and Godliness will be revealed on every level: "In time to come, the Holy One, blessed-be-He will make a *dance-circle* of the Tzaddikim" (*Ta'anit* 31a). In holy dance, the physical body is elevated and used for the glory God. A dance circle has no beginning or end, so no-one is first or last: everyone is equal. This symbolizes the harmony that will prevail in the future. No-one will have any reason to hate or be jealous of anyone else.

Holy dance is an art we must rediscover, brothers with brothers, fathers with their sons, sisters with sisters, mothers with their daughters. Joyous dance is one of the strongest weapons against depression and despair.

Chassidic dance requires no training at all. It is completely free-style. Why not put on a tape or record one day in the privacy of your own room and enjoy a dance for the love of God, expressing your gratitude for your life, your health, your body and everything else that is good. Move in whatever way comes most naturally to you and discover your own body-language.

Join the dancers on Simchat Torah, Purim and Lag Ba-Omer, at *chatunot* (weddings) and so on. Participate just as much or as little as you wish, and as vigorously or as gently as you want. Rebbe Nachman's followers, the Breslover Chassidim, have a custom of forming a circle and dancing to the tune of a joyous nigun after each of the daily prayer services. Suggest to a few friends that you try the same in your synagogue, especially after the Friday night *Kabbalat Shabbat* (Welcoming of the Shabbat) service, or at the end of your group study sessions.

Other Ways to Keep Happy

1. " First make yourself happy with worldly things. Do this to the best of your ability and you will eventually be able to attain genuine spiritual joy" (*Rabbi Nachman's Wisdom* #177).

2. "It may be impossible to achieve happiness without some measure of foolishness. One must resort to all sorts of foolish things if this is the only way to attain happiness" (*ibid.* #20). Well-timed joking and fooling can be life-savers, as long as you do not let innocent fun degenerate into laughing at others, licentiousness or scoffing.

3. "If you are disturbed and unhappy, you can at least put on a happy front. Deep down you may be depressed, but if you act happy, you will eventually be able to attain true joy. The same applies to every holy thing. If you have no enthusiasm, put on a front. Act enthusiastic and the feeling will eventually become genuine" (*ibid.* #74).

4. If you can't be happy yourself, try making someone else happy! "With happiness you can give a person life. A person might be in terrible agony and not be able to express what is in

his heart. There is no one to whom he can unburden his heart, so he remains deeply pained and worried. If you come to such a person with a happy face, you can cheer him and literally give him life" (*Rabbi Nachman's Wisdom* #43). *Smile at people!*

10

The Royal Food: Faith

Afterwards the Wise Man gave a sign, and they put down human food from the table. The Wise Man said to the Prince, "Do you think if you eat good food you can't be a turkey any more? You can eat this food and still be a turkey." They ate.

"Dwell in the land and feed off faith."

Psalms 37:3

Rebbe Nachman told a story about someone who was always searching for good. In fact, that was how he made his living. He was poor, and he used to dig clay and sell it. No doubt he was always on the look-out for a good find — some trinket someone had dropped or the like.

One day he was digging, and suddenly — what a find! Glinting through the clay was a diamond. And what a diamond! It must have been worth a fortune. The Clay-digger didn't know how much it was worth, so he went to a jeweller to value it. The jeweller told him it was so valuable that there was no-one in their country with enough money to buy it! Only in London would he be able to sell it. He would have to travel to England.

Imagine the mixed emotions of this Clay-digger. Here was good fortune beyond his wildest dreams, but he didn't have a penny to journey down to the port, let alone to pay the fare for the sea-voyage to London! Still, he was a plucky fellow. What did he have to lose? He decided to stake his entire life on this diamond. He sold everything he had, and he went from house to house, begging for help, until he had enough money to get down to the coast.

It sometimes happens that after all our years of searching, we finally discover something truly worthwhile, and we decide to devote our entire life to it. So it was with the Clay-digger. Here he was, setting off for a far-off country where he knew no-one and didn't even speak the language. Yet he was more than willing to take the risk, because he could see in his flashing diamond a future of abundant prosperity and happiness.

At the port, he found a boat that would shortly set sail for London. He had no money for the fare, but he went to the Captain — doubtless a burly, seasoned, old-time seaman — and showed him the diamond. The captain took one look at it and ushered the Clay-digger straight into the boat. "You're a sure bet!" said the Captain, showing him into a special first-class cabin affording the royalest of luxuries.

The Clay-digger's cabin had a window looking out over the sea, and as they sailed the ocean, rocking up and down, up and down, he would sit there enjoying himself immensely and rejoicing over the diamond, especially at mealtimes. Joy and good spirits are medically-proven aids to digestion! Riding the high seas of life is sheer pleasure when everything's going your way.

One time he sat down to eat, with the diamond placed on the table in front of him so that he could enjoy it. After his meal, he took a nap. While he was asleep, the cabin-boy came in to tidy up. He took the tablecloth to the window and shook out all the crumbs, together with the diamond, into the sea!

When the Clay-digger woke up, he quickly saw what had happened, and it did not take him long to realize that he was in big trouble. His entire fortune had gone out of the window, and with it his whole life. He almost went out of his mind wondering what to do. The captain was a pirate who would murder him for the price of the boat-ticket. There are times in life when you see the inescapable truth with chilling clarity. Your dearest dreams have been dashed to the ground, and death stares you in the face.

Imagine the cries and prayers that the Clay-digger poured out to God from the depths of his heart in those moments of complete honesty. Imagine his passionate entreaties for pity and mercy. What possible hope was there? "God of miracles! HELP ME!!!"

The Clay-digger now did the greatest thing he ever did in his whole life. At this supreme moment of trial, with nothing at all in his hands, and no hope whatsoever, he decided he would still *be happy*. He pretended to be happy, as if nothing at all was the matter.

Every day during the voyage, the Captain used to come in and talk to the Clay-digger for a couple of hours, and he did the same today. How trite their usual chat about adventures in exotic ports and the like must have seemed today as the Clay-digger sat facing the ultimate Truth. Nevertheless, he made such a show of being happy that the Captain didn't notice anything unusual at all.

The Captain said to him, "I know you're clever and honest. Now listen, I want to buy a large quantity of produce to sell in London — I can make a big profit. But my fear is that they'll accuse me of embezzling from the Crown. I'm suggesting that the purchase be made in *your* name, and I'll pay you for it handsomely." The Clay-digger felt it was a good idea, and he agreed.

Shortly after they arrived in London, the Captain died! Everything was left in the hands of the Clay-digger, and the produce was in fact worth many times more than the diamond!

Rebbe Nachman concluded the story by saying that the diamond did not belong to the Clay-digger, and the proof is that he lost it. The produce did belong to him, and the proof is that it stayed with him. "And he only came to his own because he held himself and kept happy."

(*Rabbi Nachman's Stories* #19)

How did the Clay-digger stay happy?

You may feel that the ending of the story seems a little rigged — but the truth is that nothing in the world stops God from doing whatever He wants. Salvation can come from anywhere, and help often appears from the most unexpected of places. A far more important and practical question is: How did the Clay-digger stay happy in that darkest moment? Life is like a voyage over the oceans: you go up and down, up and down. The main thing is to stay happy and keep going even when you're down and things are against you. But how?

When things are reasonably OK and just a little down, most of us can get by and keep our heads up. But when you're in a crisis as serious as that of the Clay-digger, what do you do then? As far as he knew at that moment, all possible hope had been dashed. He was most probably going to die a cruel death by drowning within a matter of hours. Even if he did somehow get to London alive, what was he going to do in a strange foreign city with no money, no friends, nowhere to go, and incapable of even speaking the language? *How did the Clay-digger keep happy?*

The Clay-digger was someone who had spent years making a living from looking for the good even amidst the slimy black mud. He knew that if you just keep searching, you'll always turn up something that will provide you with a bit of a living. He had then had occasion to see the most amazing, miraculous, totally unexpected *chesed*, the unstinting *generosity* of the Creator of the World, in the shape of his diamond. And then he suddenly saw the truth of life as he had never seen it before: "HaShem gave and HaShem took." "Naked I came out of my mother's womb, and naked I will return there. HaShem gave and HaShem took. Let the name of HaShem be blessed" (Job 1:21).

HaShem is everywhere. In the world. Beyond the world. In every situation. Whether we go up or down. Alive or dead. "If I go up to Heaven — there You are, and if I make my bed in Hell — You are there" (Psalms 139:8). Even in the worst possible situation, one must hold oneself and have faith that even there, one still has hope, because HaShem is present there too. (See *Likutey Moharan* I:6 end.)

HaShem is all good and His only intention is for good. "Since the ultimate goal is entirely good, in the end everything will turn out to have been for good. Even when bad things happen and you are beset with troubles and suffering, God forbid, if you look at the ultimate purpose, you will see that these things are not bad at all, they are actually a very great favor. All suffering is sent from God intentionally for your own ultimate good, whether to remind you to return to God, or to cleanse and scour you of your sins. If so, the suffering is really very beneficial, because God's intention is certainly only for good" (*ibid.* I:65,3, and see *Garden of the Souls*).

Even death is ultimately good. " 'And God saw all that He made, and it was *tov me'od* — *very* good' (Genesis 1:31) — 'very good' refers to death" (*Bereishit Rabbah ad loc.*). Death is the ultimate atonement for sin, and leads to final purification and eternal life. "Know that in this world a person has to cross a very narrow bridge. The main thing is not to be afraid" (*Likutey Moharan* II:48).

The Clay-digger had come face to face with the worst of all possibilities, and he was willing to accept it if necessary. He could do that because he knew God is good. Even if sometimes God does things that seem bad to us, ultimately everything is for our good. Without faith in God there would have been no basis for any positive hopes or feelings whatsoever. But the Clay-digger kept his concentration fixed upon God and upon the ultimate good he would eventually come to, and he was happy.

In fact, he was overjoyed, because he now understood that although, in the vicissitudes of life in this world, sometimes things are good and sometimes bad, eventually we will definitely receive the good that is *all good, total good*, our eternal heritage in the World to Come. Compared to this, the diamond was worth nothing. No matter what might happen, the Clay-digger saw that in the end he would only gain.

Through complete faith in God under all circumstances he could always be happy and confident — and his very confidence is what now saved the entire situation. He determinedly ignored the looming disaster completely, chatting happily with the Captain... until the Captain politely invited him to sign his name to what was to be the deed of possession of something far more valuable than a mere trinket or diamond: an entire shipload of expensive foreign produce.

Faith and Personal Growth

The produce symbolizes "the fruit of the land" (Numbers 13:26). "The land" is faith, the ground of our being, the ground that we walk on, that holds and supports us more surely than the earth under our feet. "Dwell in the *land* and feed off *faith*" (Psalms 37:3). The soul is like a tree planted in the land. Our task is to dwell in the land and cultivate the tree. If the soil is good — if our faith is strong — and we do our work, the tree will grow and bear fruits. The fruits are our mitzvot and good deeds, which we enjoy in This World and the World to Come.

Many people think positive thinking is a good thing but basically a matter of blind man's bluff. You have no idea where you are going, but as you grope around, you put on a mighty front that everything's just wonderful. This is certainly true of "positive thinking" that is not based upon faith in God: there are no real grounds for confidence at all. Without God, everything is a matter of chance, and experience seems to show that the worst disasters can overtake the best people — *lo olenu*, not on us! In the end, everyone dies, and who really knows what comes after death? What is there to be positive about?

"People with a secular outlook have no life, even in this world. As soon as things go against them, they are left with nothing. They depend completely on nature and have nowhere to turn. When trouble strikes, they are left without any source of inspiration.

"But someone who has faith in God has a very good life. Even in times of trouble, his faith still inspires him. He trusts in God and knows that everything will be for the best. Even if he has to go through suffering, he realizes it will atone for his sins. And if this is not necessary, these troubles will ultimately bring him a much greater benefit. No matter what happens, he realizes that God ultimately only does good. Someone with faith therefore always has a good life, both in this world and the next" (*Rabbi Nachman's Wisdom* #102).

Faith is the only sure foundation for real personal spiritual growth. If you want to change and develop, you are bound to encounter problems. Life is a succession of ups and downs. Sometimes we are confronted with enormous obstacles to what we want to achieve. The only way to conquer them is through faith in God.

If your goal is to grow spiritually through the Torah and the mitzvot, you *know* this is what God wants, because He tells us so in the Torah. The hurdles and difficulties you encounter in trying to lead the life of Torah, prayer and hisbodidus may be very discouraging, but you can be sure they are not a message to you to give up. God wants you to keep on trying. And if, after all your efforts, nothing comes of them, there is still no reason to despair. You must accept that it was the will of God that things should turn out this way, and God wants your ultimate good. Eventually, things will turn out better than you could ever dream.

Faith is the soil for growth. "When a grain of wheat is planted in good earth, it develops and grows beautifully and comes to no harm even in strong winds and storms. This is because the growth-force is working in it. That is why nothing harms it. But when a wheat-grain is planted in earth that is not good for planting, it rots in the ground, because it doesn't have the growth-force. Faith is the force generating our growth and development. When a person has faith — the growth-force — nothing hurts him and he is not afraid of anyone or anything... But when a person is lacking in faith, he doesn't have the growth-force, and then he literally rots, like the wheat-grain. He is depressed, lazy and heavy and literally rots" (*Likutey Moharan* I:155).

Faith is the essential vitality-giving nutrient that causes development and growth — faith that what you are doing is right and important, and that you should make every effort to keep on doing it; faith in yourself — faith that you are precious to God and your efforts are valuable in His eyes; and faith that behind all the veils and obstacles, God is present, watching, helping and supporting you.

Faith involves patience — the willingness to just wait and sit things out when times are difficult, the way the Clay-digger sat when the Captain of the ship came in for his daily visit. When there was nothing he could do, the Clay-digger didn't try to do anything. He just sat out the crisis, waiting for the winds to change.

"When you have faith and patience, you are not afraid of anything and you pay no attention to interruptions and obstacles to your efforts to learn, pray, keep the mitzvot and serve HaShem. You just keep on doing as much as you can do. This is patience — when nothing can distract you and you pay no attention to anything: you just keep on doing what *you* have to do to serve HaShem...

"When you have faith in God you just take a long patient breath, no matter what interruption or obstacle may come up as you try to pray and serve God. You simply take everything in your stride without getting upset or discouraged. You take a long, deep breath and pay no attention at all. You just carry on doing your work. This is the way to overcome everything, until eventually you will not even notice the obstacles and barriers.

"All this comes from faith, which is the vital growth-force. The more you grow and blossom successfully in the Torah path, the less likely that something will be able to throw you off or cast you into depression and laziness. You will do your part energetically and happily without paying attention to any of the obstacles" (*ibid.*).

Trust

While faith is the *general* belief that everything is in the hands of HaShem, trust in God is the confidence that He watches over the *specific details* of our lives. To have trust in HaShem means to have confidence that He is taking care of us in every aspect of our lives, major or minor, and will help us and provide us with whatever we need.

To have trust, you have to have faith, but not everyone who has faith has trust. "Faith is like a tree, and trust is the fruit of the tree... but there are trees which do not bear fruit" (Ramban, *Emunah u-Bitachon* 1). "There are people who have a general belief in HaShem. They believe that everything is in His hands.

Yet they do not put their trust in HaShem in every single thing they do. They may remember HaShem and pray for success at the outset of some major venture or a dangerous journey and the like, but not when it comes to doing something small or going somewhere nearby.

"Genuine trust means putting one's entire confidence only in God and remembering Him in every detail of one's activities, being aware that no matter what one may attempt, success depends not on what one does, but only on the will of God. Remember that you could get hurt even somewhere nearby if not for God's protection" (Rabbenu Bachaye, *Kad HaKemach, #Bitachon*).

"The test of faith comes not when a person observes the Covenant and the Torah and serves HaShem in the quiet and comfort of his palatial home, with everything going well... but when reverses, hard times, poverty and persecution strike and drive a person to breaking point, and even then he still maintains his purity... This is why the Psalmist says (Psalms 62:9) 'Trust in Him *at all times*' " (R. Yosef Albo, *Sefer Ha-Ikarim* 4:46).

"Hope in God should be like the confident anticipation a person has of something that he is certain is going to come, as surely as day follows night. Have complete trust that God will certainly satisfy your needs without any doubt at all, since He has the power and nothing can stop Him — not like someone who hopes for something but has doubts if it will or will not come. Perfect trust will strengthen your heart and give you joy" (*ibid.* 49).

Food for the Soul and Food for the Body

"HaShem is my shepherd, I will not lack. In lush meadows He lays me down, He leads me beside tranquil waters."

Psalms 23:1-2

"HaShem is my shepherd." The Shepherd is the *Ro'EH*, and it is written, "*Re'EH emunah* — feed off Emunah" (Psalms 37:3). The food is Emunah. Wherever the Shepherd leads his flock, they always find something to graze off whenever they want: a mitzvah, a word of prayer, a melody, even just a sigh.

But people say: Faith is fine — it may be all very well spending time praying and learning, but you need to *eat*! How does the money come? By going out to make a living, no? You can't sit and wait for your food to drop out of the skies.

Certainly, you have to earn a living — but how many prayers have been stunted, how many sessions of Torah study and hisbodidus neglected, because of the need to attend to business? How many mitzvot have fallen by the wayside in the rush to earn money. The need to make a living is the Turkey's biggest concern: "pulling at crumbs and bones."

It is true: we do have to *act* to initiate the flow of livelihood. The sun shines, the rains fall, the plants and trees grow, and all good bounty comes out of the earth. But ever since the sin of Adam — "with the sweat of your brow you will eat bread" (Genesis 3:19). God provides us with a world of basic materials and opportunities, but it is up to us to work in order to actualize the potential, whether through cultivating the land, taking raw materials to make things and use or sell them, providing a service, trading at some level, or even going out to ask for charity!

It is the very fact that we do have to do something to earn a living that makes it so difficult not to think that it is "*my* power and the strength of *my* hand" (Deuteronomy 8:17) that makes our bread. How much do we have to do in order to know we have done our part? As we go through the ugly jungle of economic life, day by day, we can be forgiven for wondering what we are going to eat, and how we can ensure we'll have everything we need. What does God want of us? How much should we do? How does *He* want us to earn a living?

Only you can decide what you think the right answer to these questions is for you now. Ask God to help you to understand what you should do, and to develop trust in Him. Say the special prayers for livelihood as printed in the Siddur etc. In your hisbodidus, speak to HaShem about your needs and feelings and express what is in your heart. To whatever extent you can at present, arrange as much or as little time as you think you can reasonably spare for your prayers, Torah study and hisbodidus. Make every effort not to miss your sessions. Then do your best to go about earning a living in accordance with the halachah, using your intelligence to make the very best of your situation and talents and any opportunities that may come up.

Although we may be Turkeys under the table in this world, this under-the-table world is in fact *inside the King's palace*, and all the food comes from the King. *Bereishit bara Elokim*, God created *BeReiShiYT* — God is the Source, the *RoSh BaYiT*, the Head of the House. To a great extent it is up to us how we eat. If we want to be Turkeys and pull at bits of bread and bones, we are free to do so. But the royal food is right in front of us. "You can eat good food" — the food of faith — "and still be a Turkey," living in the material world.

Can you get rich through Torah, prayer, hisbodidus? Yes. "What? Real wealth — clothes, cars, furniture, holidays. No kidding?" Wealth, yes, and *what* wealth: the wealth of the King, for "the wealth is from You" (I Chronicles 29:12). "Who is wealthy? Someone who is happy with their share" (*Avot* 4:1). Look around you. Look at your hands and legs, and think of the amazing things you can do with them. Think of your vision and hearing, your ability to speak and act, your digestion, your breathing, your co-ordination... You have something to eat, you have clothes and somewhere to live...

Instead of thinking about what you don't have, thank God for everything you *do* have and enjoy it. If you can learn to discipline yourself to take exactly what you need from this world, no less and no more — whether food, comforts, pleasures or anything else — you will come to be perfectly satisfied with everything you have. You will accept and enjoy your body, your food, your clothes and housing, your family, your work, your synagogue, your study sessions, Shabbat, the festivals, and your deepening connection with God... and you will come to see that the whole of this world is really yours — the free fresh air you breathe, the light of day, the stars of the heavens, the rains, the grass, the trees and plants, the fish, insects, birds, animals, and worlds upon worlds of variety, whether you open a book, talk to people, go out into the streets or the fields, look outside yourself or go within... "The whole world was created only for me" (*Sanhedrin* 37a).

Fundamentals of Faith

1. God Controls Everything:

The first principle of faith is to know and understand that everything in the entire universe is under God's control. This includes everything that happens to you personally, both spiritually and materially, including what you yourself do, whether deliberately or unwittingly, willfully or under compulsion: everything is from God.

Appearances may sometimes seem to suggest otherwise, yet faith is "blind" in the sense that the believer does not pay attention to the external appearance of this world but to the underlying reality. There may be many philosophical questions about faith, but most of them are unanswerable. If you are prepared to accept the Torah unconditionally, you will eventually see with your very own eyes the truth of what you believe in.

Following the Torah pathway sincerely enables us to experience a dimension of existence which is otherwise simply inaccessible. You may be surrounded by radio waves, but you need a receiver to convert them into something you can experience with your sense apparatus. Faith is the "receiver" through which you experience the Divine. The essence of faith is believing that the One God controls everything.

2. Freedom:

What we ourselves do is ultimately controlled by God, but this is concealed from us by our own egos, which give us the sensation of being independent and separate from God. It is inherent in our make-up to think that our thoughts and actions are our own, and that it is "*my* power and the strength of *my* hand" (Deuteronomy 8:17) that makes things happen in our lives.

God created us like this in order to give us free will. Our task is to turn to God of our own free will, in order to discover the truth for ourselves and see that, in actual fact, God controls everything, including our thoughts, feelings and actions. In this world, we are given the freedom to make our own choices. Then, depending on the choices we make, God either reveals Himself to us or conceals Himself even more, according to a system of strict justice.

3. Action:

Even though all things in both the spiritual and material realms are in God's hands, this does not mean that our role is passive, waiting for God to do everything. God arranged the Universe in such a way as to give us freedom of action, whether in regard to carrying out the mitzvot, earning a living, finding a marriage partner, etc. We have to act — but always with the understanding that our need to act in this world is a test, to see whether we will exercise our free will in accordance with the Torah or not.

Whether in carrying out the mitzvot or in acting in the material world to make a living and attend to our other needs, we have to understand that although it is up to us to take the initiative and act *as if* everything is up to us, ultimately everything depends on God. No matter what we feel we ought to do, whether in our spiritual or material lives, our first step should always be to ask God to guide us in what we do and to bless our efforts with success.

4. Reverses:

When things turn out badly for us, we have to accept that this is God's will and that whatever happens is for the best. Even when things go wrong because of something we ourselves may have thought, said or done, we have to accept that this was also brought about by God. While we should feel contrite about our sins and make every effort to do better in the future, it is pointless to live with regrets about the past, because ultimately whatever happened came about through the will of God. Even when you observe the mitzvot and pray but feel that God is not responding, you must have faith that God is paying attention to everything you do, and that "if you get no answer, this is also an answer."

Other people are also free agents, yet, paradoxical as it may seem, everything they do is ultimately controlled by God. Therefore you should understand that if someone insults you or harms you in some way, this has been sent to you from God. If you respond by getting upset and venting your anger, it is a sign that you do not have complete faith in God's control over every detail of the Creation. When people insult you, it is God's way of cleansing you of your sins. If you respond with anger, it is as if you are refusing to accept His reprimand.

If things go against you, be patient. Take a deep breath and accept this as God's will. If somebody hurts you in some way and you keep silent, accepting it as atonement for your sins, this causes the outer veil of concealment to be removed, and God's control over the entire Creation becomes manifest.

5. Personal Growth:

Your spiritual development is also under God's control. You may feel a desire to grow in a specific area and accomplish something holy, but as long as you are not ready to achieve what you want, things will be arranged in such a way as to hold you back — either by external obstacles or through some idea that becomes implanted in your own mind to prevent you from reaching it. This does not mean that God is rejecting you, but He knows that, in the long run, this will be the best way to bring you to the ultimate good. The purpose of holding you back is to prompt you to cry out to God to help you rise from your present level and bring you nearer your true goal.

Even when you experience a breakthrough in your spiritual growth, do not imagine that from now on you will always be able to maintain your new level. Anything you may have achieved until now came about only through the love and help of God, and the only way you will be able to stand up to future challenges is also through His help.

While you must always try to do your part to develop and deepen your observance of the mitzvot, the central focus of your efforts should be your prayers to God for *His* help. Prayer reveals that everything is in God's power and that "it is in His hand to cause all things to grow and become strong" (I Chronicles 29:2). Ask God that no matter what may happen to you, you should always remember that the main thing is to pray.

6. Revelation and Guidance:

Since God is everywhere and in all things, everything we experience is actually a communication from God. This includes our inner thoughts and feelings. Even negative thoughts and feelings — heaviness, lack of enthusiasm, depression and the like — are from God. Whatever you hear, see, or experience in life, whether from people you know or from complete strangers — everything is a call to you from God. Through these communications everything you need in order to grow and attain spiritual perfection is sent to you.

We often find ourselves faced with unclear or even contradictory messages. These are also sent to us with a purpose: to give us free will and thereby test us. The way to sort out which messages to follow and which to ignore is through evaluating everything in the light of Torah teaching. The more you familiarize yourself with the Torah outlook on life, and especially the Halachah, which gives clear guidance about what is right and what is wrong, the more you will be able to interpret the various messages.

7. The Wise Man-Tzaddik:

Faith in God includes faith in the Tzaddikim that God sends into the world to teach us how to transcend our lowly state and fulfill our spiritual destiny. It is not enough to accept that God gave the Torah to Moses on Sinai. The Torah tells us that in every generation we can only resolve our doubts and questions about what is the right path to choose by turning "to the judge who lives in those days" (Deuteronomy 17:9).

God sends Wise Men in every age to lift Jewish souls out of our exile. "You must do according to what they tell you... take care to act in accordance with everything they teach you... Do not turn aside from what they tell you either right or left" (*ibid.* 10-11).

(Adapted from R. Yitzchok Breiter, *Seven Pillars of Faith*)

Emunah: The Twenty-Four-Hour-a-Day Meditation

"Habakuk came and based everything on faith."
Maccot 24a

Meditation has been defined as "deciding exactly how one wishes to direct the mind for a period of time, and then doing it" (Rabbi Aryeh Kaplan, *Jewish Meditation* p.3). In this sense, Emunah — faith — could be called the twenty-four-hour-a-day, lifelong meditation. The Torah way of life involves turning oneself to God in every thought, word and deed. "Know Him in all your ways" (Proverbs 3:6).

The first act of the day, the moment you wake up in the morning, is to recite "*Modeh ani*" — "I thank You, living and enduring King, for restoring my soul with love..." This is an act of faith. You remind yourself of the fundamental fact that there is a God, and you thank Him for the spark of divinity within you, your higher self or soul. With your first words of the day, you orient yourself to the ultimate goal of life — the perfection of the soul and union with God in the World to Come.

The morning prayers then begin with a series of blessings that take us through the various details of our physical life and relate each one of them to God. Then in the *P'sukei de-Zimra*, the "verses of song" (selections from the Psalms, etc.) which form the next main part of the morning service, we survey the world around us and remind ourselves of the many manifestations of the Creator in nature and society. "You open Your hand and satisfy the desire of every living thing" (Psalms 145:16). The entire creation is sustained by God.

One of the main climaxes of both the morning and evening services is the recital of the Sh'ma. To live the life of Emunah, make these the most intense and vital moments of your day. Pause before you take on the yoke of God's kingship. Prepare yourself to affirm your total faith in God in a way that will illuminate everything else you think, say and do throughout the entire day. Put all your powers of concentration and feeling into the first verse of the Sh'ma.

With the word "*Sh'ma*" — "Listen" — call yourself to attention, addressing your innermost heart and soul: "*Yisrael.*" Then, as you recite each of the Divine names in turn, "*HaShem, Elokenu, HaShem,*" take the time to think how HaShem is the eternal Master of All, All Powerful, and that beyond all the masks and veils — the plurality of powers manifested in the world — there is only HaShem. As you say the word EChaD, affirm the perfect unity of HaShem (Aleph = 1) in the seven heavens and on earth (Chet = 8) and in all four directions (Dalet = 4). As you say Echad, have in mind that you surrender yourself to the service of HaShem and the obligations of the Torah completely, and that your belief in HaShem is so strong that you are willing to sacrifice your very life for Him.

The affirmation of faith in the Sh'ma is developed in the silent Amidah prayer, repeated in the morning, the afternoon and evening. In a life based on faith, the Amidah is a homing point we return to three times a day in order to keep ourselves aware of the essential truth of our existence — that we are standing before HaShem at all times, and that every aspect and detail of our lives, both as individuals and as social beings, depends upon His blessing.

The opening blessing of the Amidah should be said with intense concentration and awareness of the immediate presence and overwhelming majesty and greatness of HaShem. Then, in the intermediate weekday blessings, we focus on all the important areas of life in turn, invoking the blessing of HaShem and asking for our most basic needs — wisdom and understanding, repentance, forgiveness, redemption, health, livelihood, and so on. We pray not only for ourselves but for the entire Jewish People and the whole world. On Shabbat and festivals, the theme of the intermediate blessing is the unique spirit of the day itself, enabling us to focus on drawing this spirit into our souls and consciousness.

The Amidah prayer is the center of the prayer services and one of the most important ways of keeping focused on HaShem. Take your time. Where you have specific needs in any particular area, you can express and develop your faith in HaShem by introducing a private prayer into the appropriate blessing. In the blessing of *Sh'ma kolenu* — "Hear our voice" — it is permitted to introduce specific requests for any private or general need, in any language. The same applies in the concluding prayer of the Amidah, after "Let Your right hand save, and answer me," before the closing "Let the words of my mouth and the meditation of my heart be acceptable..." Pray about all the things that are uppermost in your mind today.

The fixed prayer services do not replace hisbodidus, which is a separate and indispensable element in the pathway of faith. Hisbodidus is the work-shop of faith. You examine every aspect of yourself and your life in relation to God. You confront the things that separate you from HaShem and struggle to bring your whole life and being into His service. Only through the intimacy, spontaneity and freedom of hisbodidus is it possible to draw your entire self into your relationship with HaShem and cultivate your own unique soul-powers to the full.

Hisbodidus is different every day because each day is different. How are you feeling today? What is on your mind? Do you need to just sit and relax, or breathe? Are there strong emotions welling up in you that you need to let forth and express? Is there a particular issue or problem you need to analyze and discuss? Are there particular people and situations you want to pray about? What's happening in the world? What's happening in *your* world? What do you have on your schedule today? What plans do you have? What would you like to achieve? What steps will you have to take to do what you want? In what order? Where will you start?

Hisbodidus without Torah-study is, as we have seen, impossible. Daily study of the Torah, the will of God, is another integral element in the pathway of faith. It is not enough to study Torah out of purely intellectual interest. The goal is to learn in order to fulfill. The holy words in which the mitzvot and their details are explained to us, both in the Written and Oral Torah, are themselves beacons of faith, radiating God's light to us day by day. The Torah is God's communication with us, calling on us to ask ourselves the same question that He asked the first man: "Where are you?" (Genesis 3:9). "And now, Israel, what does HaShem your God ask of you except to fear HaShem your God, to go in all His ways and to love Him and to serve HaShem your God with all your heart and with all your soul" (Deuteronomy 10:12).

The prayer services come to an end, hisbodidus is over. You have studied Torah and you have asked God to help you fulfill what you learned. After all the affirmations and good intentions, now you have to go out into the world and get on with the business of daily life. This is the real test of faith, because the world we live in here under the table is the world of concealment. How do we find God on a busy shopping street? Where is God?

If someone asks you that question, said the Rabbis, "tell them God is in the great city of Rome, as it is written: (Isaiah 21:11) 'He calls me from Se'ir' (= Esau, from whom the Romans were descended)" (*Yerushalmi Ta'anit* Ch. 1).

"Evidently this person who questions where God is," says Rebbe Nachman, "is someone who is sunk amidst the *kelipot*, the concealing husks, because he thinks that where he is, there is no God. Therefore you must say to him: Even where you are, sunk amidst the forces of darkness and concealment, you can also find God, because God gives life to everything — 'And you give life to them all' (Nehemiah 9:6). Even from there you can attach yourself to God and return to God completely, for 'it is not far from you' (Deuteronomy 30:11) — it's just that in the place where you are, the veils are very many" (*Likutey Moharan* I:33,2).

"Every day brings its own thoughts, words and actions, and the Holy One, blessed-be-He contracts His Godliness from His infinite, endless heights down to the central point of the material world over which He stands, sending each person thoughts, words and deeds according to the day, the person and the place, clothing in these thoughts, words and deeds all kinds of hints and messages in order to draw him close to His service" (*ibid.* 54,2).

Faith is to know that God is everywhere and in everything — whether we are at work, driving on the highway, shopping in the supermarket, or anywhere else. Everything around us is a revelation of HaShem, though we should not expect to be able to understand all the Divine messages they contain. Our minds are too small to grasp the infinite flow of Godliness. It is enough if we strive to think carefully about the purpose of our lives and ascertain what God wants of us through studying the Torah. Then, if we find that people or circumstances are giving us strong messages that are in accordance with the Torah, we can be confident that this is a Divine communication.

To understand the constant revelation of HaShem all around us is a very exalted spiritual service, involving deep wisdom and perception. The way to walk through the sea of this world on dry land is by following the path of the mitzvot. Set out to be an observant Jew, simply and without sophistication. Believe in God, put on Tallit and Tefilin, say the blessings and prayers, set regular times for Torah study and hisbodidus, eat kosher, do business honestly, give charity, love your friends and family, keep Shabbat and the festivals, rejoice in God, and allow yourself to grow through the mitzvot, especially those you feel the most strongly drawn to.

"All your mitzvot are faith" (Psalms 119:86). If you want to find and connect with God, always look for the mitzvot. At every juncture in life there are mitzvot that relate to what you are doing. Each mitzvah is a way to reveal the Godliness present in the areas of life with which it is bound up. As you go through your day, keep the mitzvot in mind. Remember Shabbat — think of each day of the week as *Yom Rishon*, day one to Shabbat, *Yom Sheni*, day two to Shabbat, etc. Arrange your schedule around your morning, afternoon and evening prayers, your fixed Torah study sessions and your hisbodidus. And then, as you go about your other activities, use your growing Torah knowledge to be aware of which mitzvot are involved in what you are doing at any time.

"There is nothing in the realm of human life, whether on the level of action, speech or thought, seeing or hearing, that does not involve either a positive mitzvah or a prohibition" (*Yesod ve-Shoresh Ha-Avodah* I:9). Whether you are at work, around the house, with family or friends, travelling, meeting people, eating, at leisure... at every moment one or more of the mitzvot are relevant.

Nevertheless, we are human — Turkeys as well as Princes. We get tired, impatient, distracted, negative, depressed... or just so involved in what we are doing that we simply lose our sense of connection with HaShem. But no matter where you are or how you feel, your simplest, most powerful instrument of connection with God always goes with you: your mouth. Use whispers, words, phrases, songs, cries, sighs, groans, laughter, thanks... any form of expression that appeals to you, in order to direct yourself to God. "Ribono shel Olam! Ribono shel Olam!" Even if you are in the middle of doing something completely secular and suddenly a Godly thought comes into your mind, pause for a moment and express your thought in a few words of prayer. "Bring me closer" (*Avanehah Barzel* p.67).

Sometimes things may be very bad. No matter what you try, you feel you cannot connect with God. What do you do when nothing works? Rebbe Nachman said: "When things are very bad, make yourself into nothing... Close your mouth and eyes — and you are like nothing. Sometimes you may feel overwhelmed by the Evil Urge. You are confused by evil thoughts and very disturbed, finding it impossible to overcome them. You must then make yourself like nothing. You no longer exist, your eyes and mouth are closed. Every thought is banished. Your mind ceases to exist. You have nullified yourself completely before God" (*ibid.* #279).

...At last the day comes to an end. You are tired. You have said your evening prayers and studied a bit. You need to go to sleep. Sleep is also service of HaShem. "There are times when the way to keep the Torah is by taking a break" (*Menachot* 99b) — in order to come back with renewed strength and vigor.

"*Be-yad'cha afkid ruchi* — In Your hand I entrust my spirit" (Psalms 31:6, recited in the bed-time prayer). Sleep is the greatest act of faith. You give up conscious control and hand yourself back to HaShem. As you sleep, your soul rises to higher worlds and is permitted to travel in accordance with your thoughts and deeds of the day. Amidst the strange images of dreams, your soul transmits to you some hints of what she sees (*Zohar* II:195, *Sha'ar HaKavanot, Drushei HaLaylah*, and see *Likutey Halachot, Netilat Yadayim Shacharit* 4:2). At times, God speaks to us through our dreams, and through the thoughts, understandings and intuitions we have as we lie in bed at night, half asleep, half awake.

As you lie in bed waiting to go to sleep, speak to HaShem simply and intimately. Tell Him about anything you may have on your mind, tell Him what you need, and ask Him to help you. If you have particular questions or problems, express them to

HaShem directly and be assured that HaShem is definitely going to help. Settle your mind and entrust your limbs and your soul to HaShem. "In His hand I will entrust my soul at the time I sleep. I will awaken! And with my spirit, my body. HaShem is with me, I shall not fear" (*Adon Olam*, closing words of the bed-time prayer).

"You can eat good food and still be a Turkey"

Maybe you have questions about God or doubts about faith. It is only natural, living as we do in this under-the-table world. We are all exposed to the media and, whether we like it or not, we tend to absorb something of current thinking among scientists, philosophers, artists, popular writers and journalists, etc. The prevalent tone of most of the world is secular — even though every honest scientist will admit that all scientific theories rest on axioms that can no more be proven than religious doctrines, and that ultimately this world is a mystery. Nevertheless, amidst the popular ferment, it's hard to avoid confusion, lay to rest all our doubts and questions, and accept Emunah wholeheartedly.

Even so, as the Wise Man said to the Prince: "You can eat this food and still be a Turkey." You may have nagging doubts and questions, or even atheistic thoughts, but you can still believe in God.

"There are many searching questions about God. But it is only fitting and proper that this should be so. Indeed, such questions enhance the greatness of God and show His exaltedness. God is so great and exalted that He is beyond our ability to understand Him. It is obvious that with our limited human intelligence, it is impossible for us to understand His ways. It is inevitable that there should be things that baffle us, and it is only fitting that it should be so" (*Likutey Moharan* II,52).

"You can eat this food and still be a Turkey." Even if you have doubts about your faith, you can still *say*, "I believe that God is One — first, last and always." Even if you don't have much faith in prayer, you can still pray. Even if you feel God is not listening, you can still talk to Him. Call out, and ask: "Where are You?"

11

Up to the Table: The Personal Connection

Then the Wise Man said to the Prince, "Do you think a turkey has to sit *under* the table? You can be a turkey and sit up at the table."

The Baal Shem Tov related: "A certain king had a treasure-house, which he surrounded with what appeared to be a series of walls and barriers, though in fact they were merely optical illusions. People would come to these walls and think they were real. Some turned back immediately. Others succeeded in breaking through one barrier, but when they came to the second, they couldn't break it. A few managed to penetrate further barriers, but then they reached one they could not overcome.

"Eventually the king's son came. He said: 'I know that all these barriers are nothing but optical illusions. In actual fact there are no barriers at all.' The Prince went forward confidently and overcame everything" (*Likutey Moharan* II:46).

This world was created in such a way as to make it appear as an independent realm (see Chapter 2). Godliness is concealed behind a veil of *kelipot* — husks that make our universe seem like an arena governed by a plurality of conflicting forces rather than the unitary system it really is. The world may seem to be as much under the sway of natural law and chance as anything else, and we sometimes wonder if there is any justice.

Not only can the kelipot deceive us about the true nature of the outer world. There are kelipot of the inner self that may hide our Godly essence from our very selves. These are the Turkey thoughts, desires, mental states and personal identities that govern so much of people's lives.

At times the power of the kelipot may seem overwhelming, yet ultimately they are nothing but illusions. The fundamental truth is that everything in the entire universe is under the constant supervision of God. The kelipot themselves were made by God for a purpose. Godliness was concealed in order to create the conditions in which man would have free will. This gives him the opportunity of turning to God of his own volition, lifting himself spiritually through his own efforts. In this way he is able to earn God's goodness for himself. Everything in the world was created to serve this purpose.

"God gave over the earth to mankind" (Psalms 115:16). The whole world lies open before us: within certain limits, we are free to do whatever we want. We are provided with everything we need to accomplish our Godly mission — both the outer opportunities and the inner resources. Innumerable alternative options are also available. From all directions we are plied with invitations to invest our lives and energies in all sorts of activities and involvements. We are promised every kind of gratification and satisfaction in return. Some of the things offered are permissible, others sinful. We are free to choose whatever we want.

"God gave over the earth to mankind" — yes. But nothing can change the underlying truth, that "The earth and its fullness are God's" (*ibid.* 24:1). Everything in the world was created by God, including the kelipot. Everything is under God's constant supervision. Therefore, no matter which direction we choose to go in, regardless of what we do in life, we are always eating from God's bounty. In fact, the whole world is God's table.

The question is: are we aware of it? Do we sit *up* at the table, and receive from God directly. Are we aware that everything we are given in this world is from God, and do we act accordingly? Or do we remain *under* the table, in a Turkey world, feeling separate and alienated from God, just wanting to get on with our "own" lives, taking whatever comes our way and seems good to us, without thinking where it comes from and why?

Yes, the whole world is God's table. Deciding to sit *up* at the table does not involve a change in the world or our place in it. It requires only a shift in our orientation and perception. To sit at the table means to accustom ourselves to viewing the world as a Godly creation and making every effort to act accordingly.

In the Baal Shem Tov's parable, as in the story of the Turkey-Prince, the king's son is the Godly soul in us. The "treasure" is the true goodness: connection with God. It is called a "treasure" because it is the most valuable thing in the entire world, and in order to enjoy it, the first essential is *Yir'at HaShem*. "*Yir'at HaShem* is His treasure" (Isaiah 33:6).

Yir'at HaShem is often translated as "the fear of God," but *yir'ah* does not signify fear in the sense of a nervous response in the face of danger. Rather, it has the connotations of awe and reverence. These are emotions which arise out of our *awareness* of God as the supreme Source and Ruler of the entire universe. Awareness of and reverence for God are the foundation for enjoying His goodness. Yir'at HaShem is intimately bound up with Emunah, the absolute faith in God that should permeate every level of one's being.

The "barriers" surrounding the treasure are the kelipot — the multitude of temptations and distractions that hold people back from this awareness and keep them from developing their connection with God. In our mundane, Turkey states of consciousness, these barriers may seem very compelling. "People would come to these walls and think they were real." But the Prince, the Godly Soul, views everything in the light of Torah truth, with the eyes of faith, and sees through the surface appearance of the world to the underlying truth. The kelipot may appear to be independent forces, but ultimately this is an "optical illusion." God created everything, and God is present even within the things that separate us from Him.

The Prince is a believer. He ignores the superficial appearance of this world. He closes his eyes to it, as we do when we affirm our faith: "Sh'ma Yisrael... HaShem is One!" The Prince makes a leap of faith to the underlying reality. With this leap, he overcomes all the barriers. Through Emunah it is possible to know and see the truth even in this world of concealment, and thus come to the "treasure." The Hebrew word *YiR'AH*, awe and awareness of God, is thus made up of the same letters as the word *Re'iYAH*, meaning vision. With faith and reverence, one *sees* the underlying truth of the world with the inner eye of spiritual awareness.

Eating at the table is symbolic of being directly connected with God, rather than receiving from Him indirectly. Getting *up to* the table is a matter of reaching out to God and trying to *make* the connection. In fact, the endeavors we make to arouse ourselves and turn to God on our own initiative — the "arousal from below" — must ultimately originate in an "arousal from above" initiated by God. Thus Rebbe Nachman points out that the letters of the Hebrew word for table, *ShULChaN** have the numerical value of 394.* This is the same as the value of the letters in the phrase *YKVK YeKaRVeNU*, "May HaShem draw us *close*" (*Tzaddik* #476).

---

*Shin 300 + Vav 6 + Lamed 30 + Chet 8 + 50 = 394.

What does it mean to be "close" to HaShem? What is it to be "connected" with God? Does one have constant visions and religious experiences? Does one have one's own "hot line"? Does God talk back, and if so, how?

It is impossible to generalize and say what connection with God is like for everyone. "God calls each one according to the person he is. To some He calls with a hint, to others literally with a cry; in some cases the person resists, and He strikes them: this is their call. The Torah cries out: 'How long will you be gullible and love foolishness?' (Proverbs 1:22). The Torah is God Himself, calling people and asking them to come back to Him"(*Likutey Moharan* I:206).

Since God calls each person individually, people's experience of God differs. And so too, each one has his or her own unique way of connecting with God. In general terms, being connected with God means being aware of His existence and His presence in our lives, His love and care for us, and His intimate involvement in every aspect and detail of all we do. This gives a sense of meaning and purpose to life, especially to our prayers and Torah study, our mitzvot and good deeds.

The foundation of connection through prayer is the belief that our prayers are important to God because they are channels for the flow of His goodness into ourselves and the world as a whole. The essence of connection in prayer is to speak to God simply and directly, praising Him and asking for His blessing. Connection through Torah study means being aware that the Torah is God's direct message to us. The purpose of study is to search out and verify exactly what God wants of us, both in general and in all the specifics of the various mitzvot. The greater our understanding of the mitzvot and their significance, the more our various mitzvot and even our mundane activities become acts of outreach and attachment to God.

Life in all its different aspects then becomes a unitary search for God. For the Turkey, life may be a matter of "crumbs and bones" — a multiplicity of mundane involvements which do not necessarily have much to do with one another. But the lover of HaShem searches for the one God in all the different areas of life. "Know him in all your ways" (Proverbs 3:6). Each person has his own unique life-situation, and his own mitzvot and good deeds, and thus each one has his own unique way to "put HaShem before me all the time" (Psalms 16:8).

Avodat HaShem: Service of God

In the story of the Turkey-Prince, getting up to the table is the last stage in the Prince's cure that Rebbe Nachman tells us about in any detail. The cure is still not complete, but getting up to the table is a climactic step. If sitting at the table symbolizes a personal connection with God, we may well ask if in real life there is a specific moment when one "gets up to the table." Does one have some kind of glorious reunion with God, after which one enjoys a permanent state of intimate connection and lives happily ever after? Some people have a notion that spiritual enlightenment is a once-and-for-all experience which they imagine to be followed by a state of constant grace, illumination and pleasure. Is this correct?

Certainly people sometimes have intense religious experiences that may cause their entire perception of themselves and their lives to shift rapidly. It is often experiences such as these that initiate the process of Teshuvah, the return to God. Then, as one follows the path of Emunah, there may be times of intense awareness of God, when the spiritual seeker has a sense of profound closeness. Prayer, hisbodidus, Torah study, Shabbat and practice of the other mitzvot can all lead to joyous moments of *hitorerut* — arousal, *hitlahavut* — fervor, *hasagah* — perception, and *he'arah* — illumination. The mental states involved are termed *mochin de-gadlut*, literally "mentalities of greatness" — enhanced spiritual awareness and vision, as opposed to everyday states, which are called *mochin de-katnut*, "mentalities of smallness." Each person experiences these states of mind in his or her own unique way.

However, as we have seen (above pp. 162-4), moments of self-transcendence and intimate closeness with God — "running" — can only be temporary in this life. God's will is that as long as we remain in this world, these moments of merging with God should be followed by a "return" to ourselves and our more mundane states of mind. This applies even to the greatest Tzaddikim. Rabbi Nathan thus tells us that Rebbe Nachman would at times reach amazing spiritual heights and reveal extraordinary teachings, but then soon afterwards he would feel spiritually darkened and dissatisfied. He now had to start pushing forward all over again in order to rise even higher. (See *Tefilin* pp. 26ff.)

Many of the most outstanding Tzaddikim of all times had lives marked with obstacles and difficulties. The Rabbis tell us that after Jacob's struggles with Laban and Esau, it was precisely when he finally sought to settle calmly in the Land of Israel and lead a life of tranquillity that the tempest of Joseph's disappearance broke out. "When the Tzaddikim want to settle down and lead a calm life, the Holy One says: Isn't it enough for them that they are going to enjoy what is in store for them in the World to Come? Do they want tranquillity in this world as well?" (Rashi on Genesis 37:2). Jacob had experienced the most exalted visions and closeness to God, such as in the dream of the ladder. Even so, the Divine Presence now left him for twenty-two years.

In this world, there is no such thing as final, absolute illumination, and the reason is simple. God is infinite. How could any created being attain final knowledge of God? The greater one's perception, the more one recognizes one's own smallness and yearns to advance ever further. No matter how much one knows, there is always more to know. "The goal of all knowledge of God is to know that one is truly ignorant" (*Chovot HaLevavot* 1:10, and see *Rabbi Nachman's Wisdom* #3). With every day and every moment, one must strive to add to one's holiness and strengthen one's connection with God (*Likutey Moharan* I:6,3, 22,9 and 60,3 etc.).

At moments of special intimacy with God, one's awareness of His presence may be so intense that one may feel quite certain that nothing will ever again separate one from God or dampen one's enthusiasm. The feeling may last for an hour, a day, two days, a week, or even longer, but then mundane activities once again demand attention, Turkey thoughts and feelings begin to rear their heads... and before one knows it, prayer, Torah study, hisbodidus and practice of the mitzvot are again an uphill struggle. Those on the path of Teshuvah know how initial euphoria often gives way to periods of spiritual dryness. It may take a fair amount of work before rising to a new level of connection.

It is clear from our story that even when the Prince gets up to the table, his Turkey side is still a force in his life. The Wise Man has to tell him that "you can be a turkey *and* sit up at the table." Still, there is an important difference between being *under* the table and sitting *up* at the table. Under the table, the Turkey is the dominant force: one tends to identify oneself primarily with the mundane aspects of the self and not be even faintly aware of the spiritual dimension of life most of the time. For the Turkey, spirituality may be acceptable, but only until the going gets difficult.

Sitting *up* at the table means that although one's Turkey outlook, interests and involvements may still have a considerable influence over one's life, the Turkey side does not overshadow all of one's spiritual awareness. Because of the continuing influence of the Turkey, the intensity of this awareness may frequently fluctuate. At times it may be very strong, while at others it may become weaker. There may even be periods when it goes underground completely. Nevertheless, one generally puts more of one's energies into trying to lead the life of the Prince, even when one's spiritual awareness is weaker. With growing experience, one learns to recognize when one's spiritual level has fallen, and one begins to understand how to motivate oneself to climb up again.

At court, those who sit at the royal table enjoy the finest foods and wines. The conversation flows from subject to subject, encompassing statecraft, government, and the various arts and sciences. Those at the table have the ear of the king and can directly influence the administration of the kingdom. Yet all these privileges can be enjoyed only when one submits to the code of royal conduct in all its details. Sometimes the requirements may be onerous, yet one observes them even when one does not feel like it. While life at court has its moments of glory, the defining feature is not glamor but *service*: noblesse oblige.

The same applies to the life of Emunah and the search for connection with God. The code of Torah life is itself called the *Shulchan Aruch*, the "set *table*," teaching us how to conduct ourselves at every turn in life. The royal foods are the finest: "Happy is he who is worthy of eating many chapters of Mishnah and drinking many Psalms" (*Rabbi Nachman's Wisdom* #23). The desserts are exquisite and amazing: "The cycles of the stars and planets and numerology... these are the desserts of the feast of wisdom" (*Avot* 3:18).

There is no area of knowledge and enquiry that the Torah does not broach — the meaning of the human form, the powers of precious stones and plants, healing, astrology, the significance of dreams, altered states of mind, prophecy... to name but a few. "In the future all the wisdoms will be laid out like a *set table*, as it is written, 'The earth will be full of the knowledge of God' (Isaiah 11:9)" (*Likutey Moharan* I:7,5).

There is no greater privilege than to sit at God's table and enjoy the feast. But to do so takes commitment — the willingness to *serve* and to *work* for the connection, even at times when you don't particularly feel like it. To "be a turkey *and* sit at the table" means that you accept that there may be periods when serving God seems very dry and unrewarding, but you are still willing to continue trying.

Yir'ah and *Ahavah*

The ideal of service of God, Avodat HaShem, is very exalted. It has two fundamental aspects. The first is *Yir'ah*, awe and reverence. The second is *Ahavah*: love. *Yir'ah* means approaching God's service with a humility and shyness that stem from one's awareness of one's own smallness and shortcomings. The root of *Yir'ah* is awe at the exaltedness of God. Each time one prays or carries out a mitzvah, one has to remember that one is doing so before the King of kings, who is exalted beyond all imaginable blessing, praise and perfection.

It is not enough merely to practice the mitzvot: one must honor them, carrying them out with scrupulous attention to detail, and in as fine a manner as possible. " 'This is my God and I will beautify Him' (Exodus 15:2) — Beautify yourself before Him with mitzvot — with a beautiful Succah, a beautiful Lulav, a beautiful Shofar, beautiful Tzitzit, a beautiful Sefer Torah..." (*Shabbat* 133b). One should think: How would I act if I wanted to offer a gift to a most important personage. Such is the honor one must give to the mitzvot, to the Torah and to those who study it.

Ahavah, love, "means that one should long and yearn for closeness to God, and seek out holiness the way one pursues something of the utmost preciousness, until the very mention of

His blessed Name, speaking His praises and studying His Torah are sheer pleasure and delight, like the love one has for the beloved wife of one's youth or for an only son — a love so strong that even speaking of them gives pleasure and delight... Certainly someone who loves his Creator with true love will not falter in His service for any reason in the world unless something physically prevents him. He will need no incentive to serve God: his own heart will lift him and he will enter into God's service willingly..." (*Mesilat Yesharim* Ch. 19).

Love includes *devekut*, attachment. One's attachment to God should be so strong that nothing else has the power to distract one, especially during one's prayers, study sessions and other acts of service. Another integral part of love is *simchah*, joy: "Serve HaShem with joy, come before Him with rejoicing" (Psalms 100:2). "The Divine Presence dwells not where there is depression, lethargy, wildness, lightheadedness, chatter and idleness, but through the joy that comes from engaging in a mitzvah" (*Shabbat* 30b). True joy is the sense of uplift that comes from serving the One God and occupying oneself with Torah and mitzvot, which are the source of eternal joy and perfection.

Love also involves *kin'ah*, zeal, for the honor of God's holy Name and a passionate longing that His service should be done and His glory revealed to all the world. Obviously, someone who has a dear friend cannot bear to see him being hit or abused, and will certainly come to help him. So too, one who loves God's blessed Name cannot bear to see it profaned or His commandments transgressed. (See *Mesilat Yesharim* ch. 19.)

The concept of the Prince is that of one who combines both *Ahavah* and *Yir'ah* in his service. As a son, the Prince is drawn to his Father by love. But his Father is the King, and must be approached with due reverence and awe. In the service of God, "one aspect is being the son who searches in the treasuries of the King, while another aspect is being a servant of the King. A servant must only do the work that is assigned to him, without asking for reasons and explanations. But then there is a son who loves his Father so much that his very love for Him impels him to take on the work of a simple servant. The son leaps straight into the thick of the battle and goes down into the trenches. He is willing to undertake the most menial labors for the sole purpose of giving pleasure to his Father. And then, when his Father sees the strength of his love and his willingness to throw himself into complete servitude because of it, He reveals to him secrets that would not normally be entrusted to a son.

"There are areas in the King's treasuries where even the King's son is not normally permitted. That is, there are levels of spiritual perception which even the son cannot attain. But when the son casts aside his sophistication and is willing to throw himself into service, his Father is filled with love for him and reveals to him secrets that are normally not even divulged to a son — the mysteries of God's providence, such as why the righteous suffer while the wicked prosper" (*Likutey Moharan* II:5,15).

Ups and Downs

> *"Serving God requires great obstinacy. Understand this well, because anyone who wants to enter God's service must inevitably undergo an endless series of ups and downs and endure all kinds of rejection. There are times when a person is deliberately thrown down from serving God. It takes unremitting firmness to stand up to it. At times you may find that the only way you can strengthen yourself is through sheer obstinacy. Remember this, because you will need it many times."*
>
> *Likutey Moharan* II:48

"Getting up to the table" in the sense of throwing oneself into Avodat HaShem — concentrating intensely on one's prayers and Torah study, pouring out one's heart in hisbodidus, and putting effort into one's mitzvot — can be a very heady experience. At times you may develop such a momentum that you may think you have finally mastered the Turkey side of yourself and transformed yourself into a spiritual being, and now God will surely sweep aside the veils of concealment and reveal His glory.

Then you pause and look around — and everything seems exactly the same as it always was. It's the same old world with the same streets and buildings. The same old problems are all there: at work, in the home... and in your own self. All the old tensions and worries are back, and with them your doubts. You question whether your prayers are having any effect, if you've made any progress in your studies, and if all your spiritual efforts are really worthwhile. Turkey thoughts and desires assert themselves as strongly as ever. You may feel even further from God than before, and experience a bitter sense of rejection and alienation.

Deepening spiritual connection can itself sometimes engender feelings that tend to increase one's sense of alienation. Growing awareness of God's greatness and glory, His love, compassion and patience, may cause one to feel deeply ashamed of one's Turkey traits and involvements. One may feel pain and regret over past behavior and fear of God's all-encompassing judgment. Within limits, such feelings may well be in place during hisbodidus, but one has to balance them with positive thinking and faith in God's abundant love and forgiveness. Otherwise they can leave one with a sense of personal inadequacy that may easily lead to depression.

At times Avodat HaShem can seem very daunting, particularly as one becomes increasingly aware of the supreme importance of the Torah and mitzvot. All too often we may have a strong sense of what we *ought* to be doing, yet find it almost impossible to get ourselves to actually do it. Sometimes there seems to be so much to do that we simply do not know where to begin, and may end up doing nothing. When depressed, we may be well aware of the solutions we *should* be applying in order to elevate ourselves — relaxing, breathing, eating properly, exercising, meditating, learning, praying, searching for good points, faith, etc. — yet find it incredibly difficult to practice any of them.

There are many different ways one can fall spiritually. People often go through many ups and downs in one and the same day. At times it may seem as if everything is conspiring to throw us down and prevent us from achieving our spiritual goals. During moments of frustration and defeat, old Turkey instincts are very likely to rear their heads again. One may have worked for months or even years to steer clear of a bad trait or habit, only to find oneself pushed into a situation that causes one to fall right back into it. Naturally, this is a devastating experience. One may think that all one's work has been undone, and one will never be able to change.

Even a single small lapse can sometimes throw a person into a chronic spiritual morass — a state of demoralization and stagnation that may last for days, weeks, months or even longer. There are times when it seems impossible to get up. One feels inescapably locked into all of one's old ways, and falls deeper and deeper into depression and despair. Each one of us knows in our own heart the way we are in our worst moments.

It is vitally important to understand that regressing is an integral part of the spiritual path. Everyone has to go through it. It is impossible to move forward in any way without first slipping backward and experiencing some kind of relapse. At that moment, everything may seem hopeless, but in reality the purpose of the regression is to prepare the way for an advance. "All this climbing and falling and turbulence are a necessary preliminary to entering the gates of holiness. All the Tzaddikim have endured all this" (*Likutey Moharan* II:48).

In order to give man free will, Godliness had to be concealed in this world. This means that any new level of connection with God you may aspire to is always "covered over" by a kelipah of its own. The new level is the "fruit." Before you get to it, the first thing you must encounter is the husk. As you begin to emerge from your present level and rise up to the next, you must first experience the kelipot of the new level. They may appear in various guises — in the form of external obstacles and distractions, or in attacks of inner turbulence and confusion, morbid thoughts, doubts, fears, anxiety, depression, material lusts and desires, and so on.

Here you are, trying to come closer to God, and you feel further away than ever. "There are many serious spiritual seekers who become very discouraged when they find themselves suddenly confronted by all these obstacles and temptations. They begin to think they must have fallen from their previous level, because for some time now they had not experienced such severe problems. However, it is important that they should understand that what they are experiencing is not the collapse of everything they have worked for. On the contrary, the time has come for them to advance from one level to the next. This is the reason why these obstacles and temptations have reared their heads again" (*Likutey Moharan* I:25).

In order to lift yourself up and move forward, you must first understand that all the different obstacles, external or internal, are being sent as a test. "When God appears to reject us, His purpose is really to draw us closer. A person who wants to draw closer to God often finds that all kinds of hardship, suffering and other obstacles descend upon him, at times with tremendous force. He may start thinking that he is deliberately being rejected. But really these experiences are very beneficial, and they serve to draw him closer" (*Likutey Moharan* I:74).

"No matter how you may fall, never let yourself become discouraged. Remain firm and resolute, and pay no attention to what has happened. In the end, the fall will be transformed into a great advance. This is its whole purpose. This applies to all the different ways one can fall. There is much that could be said on this subject, because each person always thinks that his own situation is so bad that none of this applies to him. People think it applies only to those on very high levels who are continually advancing from level to level. But you should realize that it holds true even for people on the lowest of levels. For 'God is good to all' " (*Likutey Moharan* I:22).

"When a person falls from his level, he should understand that this is something sent to him from Heaven with the sole purpose of drawing him closer. The intention is to encourage him to make new efforts to bring himself nearer. The thing to do is to make a completely fresh beginning. Start serving God as if you had never started in your whole life. This is one of the basic principles of serving God. We must literally begin all over again every day" (*Likutey Moharan* I:261).

The way we rise to the new level is through our efforts to search for God in the actual situation we are in: "It may seem impossible to find God in such situations, but the very act of searching for God from there, asking, 'Where is the place of His glory?' is what brings growth and healing. The more you see how far you are from God's glory, the more intently you should search, and ask: 'Where is the place of His glory?' Your cries, your questions, your anguish and yearning for God's glory will themselves lift you up. The essence of repentance is to search at all times: '*Where* is the place of His glory?' Then the fall will be transformed into a very great advance. Understand this well" (*Likutey Moharan* II:12).

Daring

The opening words of Rebbe Nachman's story of the Turkey-Prince, translated literally, are: "Once the king's son *fell* into madness." The Prince's thinking that he was a Turkey and going to sit under the table was the archetypal spiritual "fall." His lower, Turkey side pushed itself boldly to the forefront of his conscious mind and engulfed him completely through sheer assertiveness. And likewise, through boldness and daring, the Prince returned to himself.

We see evidence of this quality of daring at every step in the Prince's cure. The Wise Man never *forced* him to do anything. When he wanted the Prince to put on his shirt, the Wise Man put his own shirt on, and then suggested to the Prince that he could do the same. The Prince was perfectly free *not* to do so. Yet he did. Something in him pushed him to take up the Wise Man's challenge and try something new: the shirt, the trousers, the royal food, and now, getting up and sitting at the table. This, in spite of the fact that at every stage the Prince still felt very much a Turkey, as we have seen.

This Princely quality of boldness and daring is the essential counter to the brazen assertiveness of the Turkey, the Yetzer HaRa, which is constantly pushing its way into our minds with Turkey thoughts and impulses. Through holy boldness and assertiveness we climb out of all our spiritual falls.

The Wise Man tells the Prince: "You can be a turkey *and* sit up at the table." This means that even when you feel distanced from God or rejected by Him, you can still push yourself forward and say, "But I *want* to connect with You! After all, I'm your child. Help me!"

Rebbe Nachman teaches: "God calls us His children, as it is written (Deuteronomy 14:1): 'You are children to the Lord your God.' You may think that you have done so much wrong that you are no longer one of God's children. But remember that

God still calls you His child. We are taught that 'for good or for evil, you are always called His children' (*Kiddushin* 36a). Let us assume that God has dismissed you and told you that you are no longer His child. Still you must say, 'Let Him do as He wills. *I must do my part and still act like His child*' " (*Rabbi Nachman's Wisdom* #7).

What does a little child do when his father pushes him away? He comes back regardless, and *protests*. This is a child's prerogative. "It is good to express your thoughts and troubles to God like a child complaining and pestering his father" (*ibid.*). In essence, this is the same idea as that of searching for God and asking "Where is the place of His glory?"

What does it mean to "search for God"? God is invisible! The force of the searcher's question, "Where is the place of His glory?" is this: you feel yourself thwarted and frustrated, rejected by God, in a totally *unspiritual* situation. Nevertheless, you are still prepared to believe that this situation does have some Godly purpose. You cannot see or understand it, but you call out to God for help. "Where *are* You in all this? What do you want of me? Help me!"

It is this very act of faith that redeems the whole situation. Falling spiritually means that God becomes concealed in some way, but by asking "Where is God?" one strengthens one's faith that God *is* present, and thereby peels off the kelipah of surface appearances in order to penetrate to the reality beneath.

Obviously "searching for God" in one's life in general includes studying Torah teachings about God's relationship to the creation, reflecting on where God comes into one's own life, and striving to deepen one's connection with Him through Torah study, prayer, hisbodidus and observance of the mitzvot. At moments of crisis and difficulty, however, the way to "search" is by *talking to God directly*: "Where are You? Help me! Draw me closer!"

Opening your mouth and reaching out to God with words, cries, groans, screams, sighs, songs and melodies is the most powerful means of spiritual searching. This is holy daring. (See *Likutey Moharan* I:22,4.) The hardest spiritual work is easier than the easiest physical labor. Even the least strenuous physical labor involves effort of some kind — lifting, pushing, shifting, etc. The hardest spiritual labor is even easier: all you have to do is move your lips and speak to God, even in a whisper (Rabbi Eliahu Chaim Rosen). You may feel heavy and demoralized. You may feel ashamed to speak to God. Even so, you can still force yourself to say a *few* words: "Ribono shel Olam! Help me!" Express what you really feel, truthfully and sincerely.

When you feel closed in by problems and oppressed by negative thoughts and desires, anxiety, tension, doubts and the like, tell God what you are going through. Talk about your feelings of distance, and ask God to help you. Even a single word of prayer has the power to transform the whole situation.

There is a part of you that wants to connect with God, but if you fail to express it out loud, it remains *potential*: it stays on the level of thought and impulse, and has little or no effect on your actual situation. But as soon as you bring out this part of yourself, whether in words, a cry, a sigh or some other way, you *actualize* it and bring it forth into this world, giving it power.

"Speech is the vessel with which we receive the flow of blessings. According to the words, so is the blessing. One who attains perfection in the way he speaks receives abundant blessings through the vessels formed by his words. This is why when we pray, we must actually pronounce the words with our lips" (*Likutey Moharan* I 34:3).

You can talk to God even when your heart is not in the words you are saying. "Speech has a great power to arouse a person even when he feels he has no heart... Sometimes merely by speaking persistently, even if you do so without any heart whatsoever, you can eventually come to tremendous fervor and spiritual arousal" (*Likutey Moharan* II:98).

Wherever you go, your mouth goes with you. Learn to use it to lead yourself, your thoughts and feelings, in the direction in which you wish to go.

"Speech is 'a mother of children' (Psalms 113:9). Just as a mother always stays with her child and never forgets him even if he goes to the filthiest of places, so the power of speech never leaves a person even if he finds himself in the worst situation. Even one who has sunk to the lowest of levels can always remind himself of God's presence by speaking holy words of Torah and prayer. Regardless of your situation, make every effort to speak to God... This way you will always be able to remind yourself of God's presence, no matter how far you may feel from God... Understand the tremendous power of speech. This idea can save you from destruction" (*Likutey Moharan* I:78).

The Table — Speech

"And he spoke to me, 'This is the table that is before God'."

Ezekiel 41:22

"Sitting at the table" is symbolic of the connection we form with God by talking to Him directly. Speech is man's defining faculty. (See above, Chapter 6, pp. 105-13.) When the Turkey is sitting on top of the Prince and riding high, the way to turn the tables and put the Prince back in his rightful place is through talk.

"Woe to the children who are in exile from their Father's table" (*Berachot* 3a). The Prince's being under the table is a symbol of exile. To be in exile, whether personal or national, means to be banished from one's proper place. Spiritual exile means being distanced from one's own authentic self, the Godly Soul — the Prince or Princess, whose rightful place is "at the table," having the intimate connection with God that is forged through our single most powerful spiritual faculty: speech.

For this reason, the Hebrew name for Egypt — the archetype of all Jewish exiles — is *MiTZ'Rayim*. The Hebrew word *MeTZaR* means a narrowly constricted passage. Spiritual exile is the exile of speech. Instead of coming forth from the mouth and bringing Godly blessing into the world, the words remain caught in the narrow passage at the back of the throat. One thinks, one wants, one yearns — but one does not actualize the thoughts and yearnings by expressing them out loud. Redemption is the redemption of speech. For this reason, the festival celebrating the redemption from Egypt is called Pesach: *Peh Sach* — "the mouth speaks" (see *Likutey Moharan* I:62,5).

There is an old custom of turning the tables upside down on Shabbat HaGadol, the "Great Shabbat," which comes just before Pesach. Rebbe Nachman's explanation of this custom (*Rabbi Nachman's Wisdom* #88) is one of the main keys to the symbolism of the table in the story of the Turkey-Prince.

Rebbe Nachman brings his proof that the table symbolizes speech from a verse in Ezekiel (41:22). A heavenly angel shows the prophet the Temple altar: "And he spoke to me, 'This is the Table that is before God'." Every word in the verse is significant. The angel *speaks*. His message is about the *table* — an allusion to food and sustenance. All one's food and sustenance in life, material and spiritual, are drawn through *speech*, as we learn from the verse in Deuteronomy (8:3): "On all that emanates from God's *mouth* man will live."

On Shabbat HaGadol, prior to Pesach, the time of redemption, speech is still in exile. This is why the tables are turned upside down. When speech is not in exile, then the Table is turned towards us the right way up, "face to face." "And he spoke to me, this is the Table that is *before* God." "Before" is *lif'ney* — literally, "to the face of." When "he *spoke*," then the

Table is *facing*. This is a symbol of direct, face-to-face communication.

Speech remains in exile until Pesach. Speech is in Egypt, *MiTZ'Rayim*, until the Exodus. On Shabbat HaGadol, therefore, the tables are turned upside down, showing that speech is not yet "face to face." As yet there is no direct connection with God. But with Pesach comes redemption. Speech emerges from exile. Peh Sach. The mouth speaks. And then the tables are turned the right way up (see *Rabbi Nachman's Wisdom #88)*.

We may be in exile under the dominion of the Turkey, but as soon as we open our mouths and speak to God, the tables are turned on the Turkey. Speech comes out of its exile, and the Prince comes back to the table.

Thus Rebbe Nachman points out (*Tzaddik* #476) that the numerical value of the letters of *SHuLChaN*, table — 388* — is the same as that of the letters in the words in the expression *KeLIPaH NiDCheH PIHah* — "As for the kelipah, its mouth is cast aside." When you "sit at the table" — when you boldly express the Prince or Princess in you and speak to God, then the Turkey, the kelipah of the self, is silenced. The value of the letters of *ShuLChaN* — 388 — is the same as that of the letters of the phrase *TzU ReFU'AH*, "For healing" (*ibid.*). Speaking to God brings healing of the soul.

---

*Shin 300 + Lamed 30 + Chet 8 + Nun 50 = 388. In this calculation, the word Shulchan is spelled without the letter Vav.

The Divine Conversation

> *"God may give you food and clothing and everything else you need even though you do not ask for them. But then you are like an animal. God gives every animal its food even without being asked. He can also give it to you this way. But if you do not draw your life through prayer, then your life is like that of a beast. A man must draw all the necessities of life from God through prayer."*
>
> *Rabbi Nachman's Wisdom* #233

The way to become the Prince — a spiritual achiever — is by using the power of your mouth. One may have spiritual yearnings, but the only way to fulfill them is by articulating them in words. Rebbe Nachman says: "Know: It is not sufficient to have spiritual yearnings in your heart. You must express your longing out loud. Yearning in the heart creates the *potential* soul. It is only when you express your yearning in words that the soul becomes *actualized*. The main place where the soul comes forth is from the mouth. 'My soul came forth through *speaking*' (Song of Songs 5:6)" (*Likutey Moharan* I:31,7).

The spoken word has the central role in the spiritual pathway of Emunah — Torah study, prayer and practice of the mitzvot. When studying Torah, we enunciate the words of God's Wisdom out loud, thereby hearing them and making them a part of ourselves, drawing the light of God's revelation into our selves and the world. The Torah is God's teaching about Himself and how to connect with Him — through the mitzvot.

Out of all the different mitzvot, it is prayer that fosters the most intimate connection with God. Prayer is a matter of words. Through them, we channel Godly blessing. Just as lovers take pleasure in repeating the name of their beloved, so we express our yearnings to connect with God through repeating the many Holy Names, the praises, the requests and supplications which make up the daily blessings and prayer services.

Words also play a part in fulfilling most of the other mitzvot, even in cases where the essence of the mitzvah is a physical action, such as binding oneself with Tefilin, sitting in the Succah, eating Matzah on the first night of Pesach, etc. An all-important concomitant of the physical action is the blessing. Saying it helps to focus and channel the spiritual energy that comes into us through performing the mitzvah. Reciting a *kavanah* prior to carrying out the different mitzvot is another verbal means of enhancing the connection they create.

The traditional Siddur, the prayerbook, contains the classic Hebrew formulas for approaching God through the set prayers and blessings, and the *kavanot* before various mitzvot, etc. However, "It is hard for us to express everything we feel in Hebrew. In addition, our hearts are not drawn after the words. This is because we are not accustomed to the language" (*Likutey Moharan* II:25).

Rebbe Nachman was saying this to his own circle of followers two hundred years ago. The majority of them were deeply learned, and they had certainly been familiar with the Hebrew language since their early childhood. Even so, he urged them to supplement the set prayers by speaking to God in their own words, in the language they spoke every day. How much more does this apply to us today!

The way to inject our practice of the Torah and mitzvot with vitality and make it into a personal spiritual pathway is by weaving our own words, whispers, cries, sighs, songs and prayers in and around the classic forms. When studying a Torah text in Hebrew, besides singing the words, we should translate them into our own language and concepts, formulating to ourselves any problems we have in understanding the meaning, asking God to enlighten us, and requesting that He help us to fulfill the teaching.

When the time comes to pray, we can talk our way into the service in our own words: "God: I am here to pray before You. Let me remember that I'm standing before You. Help me to put all my energy into saying the words of the prayers and concentrating on what they mean. Let me start this day by thanking You for all Your goodness. Let me begin right now. *Baruch Atah...*" And so on. We should introduce our own private requests at the appropriate points in the service. What we cannot put into words, we should express with sighs, cries, songs...

We can likewise talk and whisper our way into all of our different mitzvot. "It's Shabbat! Let me forget about work! Let me enjoy the peace and the joy of Shabbat." "I want to take the Lulav and Etrog. What do I know about Lulav and Etrog? God, let me manifest Your Kingship over the world through this mitzvah!" "This person is asking me for a donation. He/she probably needs it. God, let me take some of the money You have given to me and use it to open the gates by giving charity for Your sake." "I'm bursting to tell *X* about what *Y* did, but that would be malicious gossip. God, help me not to say anything at all about this. Let me speak only good." And so on.

This applies to the whole of life. "God, let me get up in time ... do my exercises ... eat like a holy Jew ... be organized and do my work efficiently ..." and so on, and so on. If you are in the middle of your daily business and some thought or impulse to reach out to God comes into your mind, stop right there and then, and *articulate* the thought. Put it in words. Make it into a prayer. Then carry on with what you're doing. "When a thought of repentance comes to you, stop for a moment in the very place where you are — even if you're in the middle of the marketplace! — and offer a prayer to God. If you wait till you get to the synagogue, the thought will have gone!" (*Avanehah Barzel* p.67 #43).

Words are the simplest, most accessible, most portable way of connecting yourself with God at any time, in any place, in any mood and any situation. When you think of God, you may think of the endless expanses of the Universe and feel overawed by His greatness. Yet the Rabbis taught that the true measure of God's greatness is His humility (*Megilah* 31a). God lovingly supervises every detail of the entire creation, down to the smallest and lowliest. At your own table, in the living room, kitchen, bedroom, car, office... the King is present at your calling, and you can bring yourself into His presence simply by saying one word: God.

The key element in developing a true, deep connection with God is setting aside time for hisbodidus. How good it would be if we could regularly discuss everything we need to talk to God about in an ordered way — thanking Him for His many blessings and for all the good in our lives, regretting the bad we have done, working on ourselves, resolving our problems, examining what our true purpose is, asking how we can achieve it, and requesting help to take the practical steps needed to do so, in order to come to the ultimate good (see Chapter 6).

There are times when hisbodidus flows. For those who are assiduous in their practice, hisbodidus can bring one to find and develop the Godly Soul to perfection, each in his or her own way. Hisbodidus is the foundation of a close, intimate, reverential yet loving relationship with God that provides inner strength, peace, confidence, conviction, a sense of purpose, vigor and joy for a lifetime.

For those who are interested in following the classic path of Jewish spiritual devotion, the literature of Mussar, Chassidut and Kabbalah teaches us the way to work on our character traits and to cultivate love and fear of God. There are works which depict the highest and most radiant spiritual levels. The Code of Jewish Law itself — which applies to everyone — *begins* with the devotion of "I place HaShem before me constantly" (*Orach Chaim* 1:1). Keeping God's presence in mind at all times and seeing His name before one's eyes are most exalted forms of devotion, not to speak of the inner intentions of the prayers and mitzvot, Kabbalistic meditations, and so on.

However, it is impossible for anyone to achieve any of these levels or to practice any of these devotions truthfully and meaningfully without hisbodidus. "From the smallest to the greatest, it is impossible to be a truly good Jew except through hisbodidus" (*Likutey Moharan* II:100). Rebbe Nachman named numerous famous Tzaddikim and stated that in all cases they attained their levels only by means of hisbodidus.

How good it would be if we could make the time for hisbodidus and discuss all the things we need to talk to God about in an ordered way! But there's a Turkey that doesn't always let us! In real life, just making time for hisbodidus can be quite an effort, let alone talking.

Sometimes hisbodidus works. Sometimes it may not. Even so: "You can be a turkey *and* sit up at the table." When you can, talk to God about everything you want, in whatever way you want. And when you can't, try to say a little, even if it's just: "God, it's hard to talk to You." Or simply repeat the one word: "God." If you find you can't talk, simply sit for a while. If nothing works, leave it for now and try again later. If you are willing to make an effort, you will eventually succeed.

Through hisbodidus, the Jew becomes a partner with the Holy One in the work of creation. God says to the Jewish People: "I will put My word in your mouth and I will cover you with the shadow of My hand, to stretch out the heavens and to establish the earth and to say to Zion, '*Ami atah*, You are My people' " (Isaiah 51:16). The Holy Zohar comments: "Do not read the words as 'Ami atah' — You are My people — but '*Imi atah*' — You are *with* Me: You are partners with Me. Just as I created the Heavens and Earth with My word — 'Through the word of HaShem the heavens were made' (Psalms 33:6) — so you too become a creative partner with God through words" (*Zohar, Introduction* 5a).

Through hisbodidus, you enter a partnership with God in the unfolding of your self, your life and the creation as a whole. What is your goal? What do you want to achieve? How can you get to it. What will you have to do? What steps must you take? What step are you going to take right now? Ask for God's help and now do it!

There is no end to God's amazing miracles. There are growing numbers of people who are making an effort to practice hisbodidus sincerely. They can testify that they have proof of these miracles in their daily lives and their own selves. God is able to do things for you that you would not believe possible. God loves you more than the most loving father. He wants you to succeed. Just try to talk to Him.

The Dangers of Subjectivity

> *"Someone who is in fetters cannot release himself from prison by himself."*
>
> *Berachot* 5b

The literal meaning of hisbodidus is "making oneself alone." The spiritual path of Emunah, of which hisbodidus is an integral part, ideally involves social life with family, friends, community and the wider world on the foundation of "love your neighbor as yourself" (Leviticus 19:18). However, hisbodidus itself is unquestionably and necessarily a solitary and individualistic pursuit.

If you are alone, how can you know whether you are really on the right track or not? How do you know if you are doing hisbodidus correctly? How do you know if you are going about your spiritual development in the right way? Everyone has his blind-spots about himself. As we've already discussed, spiritual life can sometimes be very heady and tempestuous. Could it not be dangerous to go about it all by oneself? Spirituality and religion are matters of life and death: to look for God is to look for the ultimate goodness in this world and the next. Going wrong could be very costly, to say the least.

The Turkey is the notorious trickster who plays with the mind. "The Prince had gone mad. He *thought* he was a Turkey." The Prince thought something that was simply not true, yet he was totally under the spell of the illusion. He really believed he was a Turkey. He knew it. How can we be sure we are not under illusions of a similar nature in our own spiritual lives? There are kelipot on every level of the creation. The Yetzer HaRa is active in all areas of life, including our spiritual lives. Spiritual deceptions can be the most powerful of all.

Religion deals with powerful moral categories: Right and Wrong. It is thus very prone to abuse. History shows no lack of cases where individuals, groups and whole societies have used "religious principles" to sanction the most cruel, destructive acts of wanton greed and folly. Even if we do not consciously *want* to deceive ourselves or anyone else, is there not a danger that natural human weakness may induce us to unconsciously misinterpret spiritual and religious teachings in order to provide rationalizations for our own unhealthy attitudes and behavior? As Rebbe Nachman says: "The way the Yetzer HaRa deceives a person is by first dressing itself up in mitzvot, persuading him that the thing he is tempted to do is really a mitzvah" (*Likutey Moharan* I:1). And even with no ulterior motives at all, one can sometimes simply get things wrong.

The Torah itself gives objective guidance over the whole of life, but it is impossible to learn the Torah all by oneself. The Written Torah is inseparable from the Oral Torah, and neither can be understood except from live teachers. Since the time of

Rabbi Yehudah the Prince in the second century of the common era, more and more of the Oral Torah has been put into writing in the form of the Mishnah, Talmud, Midrashim, Responsa, Codes, Kabbalah, and so on. Even so, it is impossible to grasp the true spirit, nuances and implications of the Oral Torah without learning from an experienced teacher.

For this reason, a Torah scholar is called not a Chacham, a Wise Man, but a *Talmid* Chacham, the *pupil* of a Wise Man. The first step in becoming wise is to have the humility to admit that one can be wrong without even realizing it, and to seek responsible outside guidance.

"The main cause of all madness is failure to listen to the words of those with wisdom and intelligence. If a madman were to listen to what others with intelligence tell him, he would certainly not be mad at all. In his crazed state it might seem clear and self-evident that he has to act in the crazy way he does. Even so, someone greater than himself is telling him that it is unnecessary for him to act this way. If he were to put aside his own ideas and accept the opinion of this other person, who is wiser than himself, his whole madness would certainly go away" (*Rabbi Nachman's Wisdom* #67).

The Prince who thought he was a Turkey was the ideal madman! He had the good sense to follow all the Wise Man's suggestions — and he was cured! Most of our discussion about this story has been concerned with the allusions it contains to various aspects of the spiritual path of the individual. We have tended to look at the different characters as personifications of different parts of the soul, notably the Godly Soul, the Yetzer HaTov, and the Animal Soul, the Yetzer HaRa. Nevertheless, taking the story at face value, it tells us about a relationship between two separate people — one who needed help badly, and another who helped him in the most remarkable and compassionate way.

If the Prince had been left to himself, it is doubtful whether he would ever have recovered. He would have had no way of knowing that his Turkey illusions were false, destructive and against his own best interests. It took someone else from the world above the table to come down and lift him up. Not just anyone was able to do it. The other doctors tried whatever they could, but they failed. It was only the kind, simple, humble Wise Man, willing as he was to take himself right down there next to the Prince, who was able to teach him the priceless art of getting things done a little at a time.

Although an amazing figure, the Wise Man had no pride whatsoever. He didn't hold himself to be anything. He did not look down on the Prince in any way. In fact, he equated himself with him. He pulled at crumbs and bones and said, "I'm also a turkey." Not only is the Wise Man a symbol of the ideal teacher, he is also a symbol of the ideal friend. Two of the greatest practical lessons coming out of our story are: "Get yourself a teacher and acquire a friend" (*Avot* 1:6).

Finding a Teacher

"Seek out the greatest possible Tzaddik. When you seek a teacher, choose only the greatest Tzaddik."

Rabbi Nachman's Wisdom #51

"Each one should search for the right guide. It takes a very great teacher to explain Godly wisdom in terms that are comprehensible to people on a lower spiritual level. The lower a person is and the further away from God, the greater the teacher he needs. Thus when the Jews were on the lowest level, in exile in Egypt, they needed the greatest, most awesome leader and teacher — namely Moshe Rabbenu. The sicker the patient, the greater the doctor he needs. Each person knows in his own heart how lowly he is and how far from HaShem. The more one realizes this, the more one needs to find the greatest possible doctor for one's soul" (*Likutey Moharan* I:30).

Spiritual life is bound up with issues of life and death and ultimate destiny. Who wouldn't want a personal Wise Man like the Prince had, a true spiritual guide who could see to the very roots of one's soul and understand one's deepest needs, and who could lead one to perfect fulfillment and happiness in the sweetest, easiest way! If you are one who has found the right teacher for yourself, I bless you that you should joyously walk the path of Torah at all times, and let HaShem be with you for ever!

For those who have not yet found their teacher, it can be a long, frustrating search, with many disappointments. As always, the first practical step to take in finding the right teachers is to pray to HaShem. "HaShem, nothing is more important to our whole being as Jews than finding our true guide in life. Please help us and send us our righteous Mashiach quickly, that he should take each one of us by the hand, speak sweetly to our hearts, and lift us out of our exile. Help us to find good teachers for everything that we need to learn..."

Make the search for reliable, sympathetic teachers into a project that you will accomplish step by step. What is in your own ultimate best interests? What are you looking for? Be as honest with yourself as you can. What do you need? Who do you know, or know about, that might be able to help you? What practical steps will you have to take to get what you need?

There are all kinds of false and unscrupulous "Rabbis," teachers, professors, instructors, psychologists, therapists, gurus, friendly advisors, etc. who might offer your their services. Such people are often extremely talented, sophisticated and impressive: it may be hard to discern what they really are and where they might lead you. It is your prerogative to make careful inquiries from whomever you can about any teacher, leader,

Rabbi, doctor, therapist, etc. to whom you may decide to entrust your life and spiritual destiny, or any part of them. Think carefully about what God wants of you, as set forth in the Torah, and ask yourself honestly if this person can help you.

If a particular teacher makes you feel uncomfortable, ask yourself: in what way? Our Sages said, "When there's a Rabbi whom people like, it's not because he's so good but because he does not reprove them about serving HaShem" (*Ketuvot* 105b). "People hate the one who gives reproof" (*Likutey Moharan* I:10,4). If you feel uncomfortable because your teacher makes you aware of urgent personal business that you need to take care of, that is good. But this does not mean that you have to submit to teachers with attitudes that make you feel irredeemably crooked. Steer away from teachers who make you feel negative about yourself and your spiritual aspirations. Oh to find the teacher who tells you the real truth and makes you feel good about it!

Do not expect to find the ideal spiritual mentor, teacher, counsellor, helper, etc. all rolled into one. Be ready to learn what you can from everyone, including those from whom you learn how not to behave! Everyone has his strengths and weaknesses. You may need a variety of teachers in different areas — Halachah, Hashkafah (faith and outlook), Chassidut, inner growth, prayer, Gemara, nutrition, fitness and anything else you are interested in. For some purposes regular sessions may be necessary, for others periodic consultations may be sufficient.

As regards the way you relate to your teachers: "Be bold, even with the Rav himself, and have the courage to talk with him just as much as you need to. Don't be shy! The fact that one person may be closer to the teacher than another is only because he is more determined and adventurous and therefore speaks to him more" (*Likutey Moharan* I:271). Work out your needs and questions, and ask freely. Press for private time if necessary.

Where personal access is not possible, try writing letters explaining clearly what you need.

Good teachers are rightly jealous of their time — time is life. One reason they may not pay much attention to you could be that they want to test you to see if you are really serious. If you pester them persistently enough, you may be able to persuade them to give you the time you need.

For those interested in using hisbodidus to work on deep personal problems and effect far-reaching changes in their lives, it is desirable to find a reliable, knowledgeable, understanding and sympathetic counsellor/friend, if at all possible. Everyone has blocks, resistances and blind-spots about themselves that cannot be overcome without outside assistance. When you need help, don't be too proud to ask for it!

Quite often the help we need is not available, but "Which great nation is there that God is close to like HaShem our God whenever we call to Him?" (Deuteronomy 4:7). Cry out to God for whatever you need. Be persistent. Nag. And be patient.

By this point in the book, the true identity of the Wise Man should be perfectly clear. He has been quoted on practically every single page. What is Rebbe Nachman really saying to you? Read his books, in Hebrew if you can, or in translation. Read *everything* he has to say, even if you disagree. Watch for the way he carefully qualifies much of what he says. Details can be important. Take time to think about his message.

True, the Rebbe himself stated clearly: "There is no comparison between hearing from the Tzaddik's own mouth and studying what he has to say in a book" (*Likutey Moharan* I:19,1). Rebbe Nachman ascended to the higher life in 1810. His body is under the ground. How can you know for certain which way to interpret what he says? He tells us to "speak to the Tzaddik" (*Likutey Moharan* I:34,8). How can you speak to Rebbe Nachman and get answers?

Studying Rebbe Nachman's teachings from a book may seem far less personal than hearing Torah from a living Tzaddik. Somewhat less remote is hearing his teachings from the students of his followers, who heard them direct. Among Rebbe Nachman's present-day adherents, the Breslover Chassidim, there are reliable teachers who received the tradition from a line of five generations of outstanding Torah leaders going back to Rabbi Nathan, Rebbe Nachman's closest follower, and other disciples. Search out Breslover Chassidim who strike you as being responsible and genuine in their efforts to practice Rebbe Nachman's teachings, and discuss hisbodidus and other aspects of spiritual growth with them.

Can't you talk to Rebbe Nachman? Yes you can! It is an ancient Jewish custom to visit the graves of the Tzaddikim, to pray to God and ask the Tzaddikim to intercede on our behalf. Rebbe Nachman invited people to come to his gravesite, give charity, and recite Ten Psalms which he called "The Complete Remedy." (The Psalms are 16, 32, 41, 42, 59, 77, 90, 105, 137 and 150. See *Rabbi Nachman's Tikkun.*) Rebbe Nachman's burial site is in the town of Uman in the Ukraine, U.S.S.R, and can be visited today. One does not pray to the Tzaddik, God forbid, but one can talk to the Tzaddik in just the same way as one might pour out one's heart to a live person sitting opposite.

Rebbe Nachman had an interesting way of communicating with Tzaddikim whose graves he could not visit in person. After moving from his birth-place in Medziboz, where his great-grandfather, the Baal Shem Tov, was buried, there were times when he wanted to speak to him. Rebbe Nachman would then visit the grave of a renowned Tzaddik who was buried nearby and he would ask this Tzaddik to transmit his message to the Baal Shem Tov, telling him what he needed (*Rabbi Nachman's Wisdom* p.22).

In Eretz Yisrael there are many holy burial sites of outstanding Tzaddikim where one is free to pray and talk out all one's needs. There are also graves of celebrated Tzaddikim in the Diaspora. "The Tzaddikim are greater after their death than in their lifetime" (*Chulin* 7b).

Friendship

> *"Two are better than one... for if they fall, the one will lift up his fellow... And a threefold cord is not quickly broken."*
>
> Ecclesiastes 4:9-12

Not only must we try to find ourselves a teacher. We must also try to acquire a *chaver*, a true friend. In the Rabbinic teaching to "acquire a friend" (*Avot* 1:6), the Hebrew word for "acquire," *k'ney*, literally means buy — "*buy* yourself a friend." It is well worth paying a good price in terms of effort and devotion in order to develop genuine friendships based on spiritual love and support.

One of the reasons why hisbodidus has to be a solitary pursuit is that the social environment most of us live in confronts us with endless distractions and negative influences. It is necessary to set definite times to separate oneself from them in order to re-establish our personal connection with God. "Other people can be great detractors. If you were alone, without the influence of others, you would always direct yourself toward the path of life. You might be confronted with every type of confusion, worry and frustration, but you would eventually end up on the right path. It becomes much more difficult when others confuse you" (*Rabbi Nachman's Wisdom* #81).

On the other hand, the goal of hisbodidus is not to turn oneself into a hermit. It is to develop inner strength in order to lead the Torah life in this world in the best way possible. Life necessarily involves other people. Interpersonal relations are an integral part of the spiritual journey. "Love your neighbor"

(Leviticus 19:18) is the foundation of numerous daily mitzvot. Interacting with real live human beings can be very difficult at times, and it is precisely through the practice of honesty, kindness, acts of giving and other mitzvot, *despite* the difficulties, that we develop Godly qualities in ourselves. In addition, God reveals Himself to us through other people in all kinds of ways: both through our casual interactions with strangers and our longer-term relationships with family, friends, work associates, etc.

Each person is God's unique creation, having a spark of Godliness in him that is quite unlike anyone else's. The Torah commands us to "judge your fellow man fairly" (Leviticus 19:15) — to search for the good in others and judge them favorably (see *Azamra*). Nevertheless, "love your neighbor" does not mean you have to become intimate friends with everyone. Each person has good in him or her somewhere, but it is not necessarily the good that you need for your development right now. The concept of acquiring a spiritual "chaver" means choosing one or more friends that you get on well with in order to give each other support and to search for God together, whether through joint study, deep and intimate discussion, or work on projects, etc.

Choose your *chaverim* carefully. Look for individuals who are truthful. One of the best ways of judging whether a friendship is good for you is by evaluating the time you spend together and how you feel afterwards. Is the time well-spent or wasted? Are the things you do together constructive or not? Do you come away feeling spiritually re-energized, uplifted and positive, or drained, frustrated, irritable, depressed, pessimistic and the like?

There are many different kinds of chaver-relationships. Sometimes it is enough that you have a regular appointment with someone in order to study or practice hisbodidus, etc. even though you then study separately or go aside to meditate individually. These can be difficult disciplines to adhere to alone: having the fixed appointment with a friend can be highly supportive. Joint study sessions can be of mutual benefit even when the two partners are at different levels and one tends to be more the giver while the other receives.

Nothing is more precious than a chaver you can talk to on your own level easily and frankly — someone loving and honest with whom you can discuss the deepest spiritual issues and who will tell you what you most need to hear. "Everyone should discuss the spiritual journey with a friend in order to receive inspiration from his unique Godly spark. Just as the angels on high 'receive one from the other,' so human beings should receive from one another" (*Likutey Moharan* I:34,8).

A good basis for such a relationship can be regular sessions focused around study of a text that is of mutual interest (e.g. Chassidut, Mussar) out of which your discussions can then develop. The main thing is to search for the truth. Do not insist on winning arguments or having your viewpoint accepted. "The need to win makes a person intolerant of the truth" (*Likutey Moharan* I:122). Hear, and try to understand, what your friend is saying, even if you do not agree. Evaluate everything according to Torah teaching. "Sometimes your friend may not be able to grasp your words, but you can still gain from the conversation... You can be motivated by your own words. Your words literally bounce off your friend and are reflected back to you.... The same words may have had no effect, had you spoken them to yourself" (*Rabbi Nachman's Wisdom* #99).

"It is good to tell your teacher or a reliable friend about all your negative thoughts and feelings — those which go contrary to the Torah — whose source is in the Yetzer HaRa. You may have many such thoughts and feelings when you are studying and praying, when lying in bed or in the middle of the day. Don't hide things because of shame: through articulating what is in your mind and heart you break the power of the Yetzer HaRa, which is then unable to overwhelm you to the same degree again. This is in addition to the good spiritual advice you can receive from your friend" (R. Elimelech, *Tzetel Katan* #13).

It can be very beneficial to talk over deep problems in this way, but be cautious. You may sometimes feel a strong urge to pour out your heart to another, but it is not wise to entrust the intimate details of your inner life to just anyone. Being honest does not mean you have to be open to everyone about everything. Some people are unable to keep secrets, even after promising faithfully not to divulge information. Even the best-intentioned friend may unwittingly abuse your confidence. You should also understand that although a close friend may have many fine qualities, there may be aspects of your inner life that your friend does not have the strength to deal with. It may be best to speak about deep issues in your life to an experienced and responsible counsellor.

"*Buy* a friend." The best way to develop a successful chaver-relationship is to concern yourself not so much with what you can get out of it as what you can give. Greet your friend with a warm smile! "With happiness you can give a person life. A person might be in terrible agony and not be able to express what is in his heart. If there is no-one to whom he can unburden his heart, he remains deeply pained and worried. If you come to such a person with a happy face, you can cheer him up and literally give him life" (*Rabbi Nachman's Wisdom* #43).

Empathize with your friend. Put yourself in his shoes and try to understand the way he feels and sees things. "You should be able to feel another's troubles in your own heart. This is especially true when many are suffering. It is possible to clearly realize another's anguish and still not feel it in your heart. When an entire community is in distress, you should surely feel their agony in your heart. If you do not feel it, you should strike your head against the wall — i.e. the walls of your heart. You must bring the realization from your mind to your heart" (*ibid.* 39).

Even if you see much that you find negative in your friend, remember that "you should not judge your friend until you come to his place" (*Avot* 2:5). Only God understands the tests and trials each one is put through. Always try to focus on looking for your friend's good points. If you feel an obligation to offer criticism, do so as sensitively and constructively as possible. It is good to discuss the purpose of life with people. We all benefit from gentle reminders that human life is very fleeting and that in the end we have to give a full account.

Give your friend every kind of encouragement in his search for God. Want the best for your friend. Rebbe Nachman said: "I would like nothing better than for all my friends to be great Tzaddikim. This would be my greatest expression of love and friendship. This is how you must love your fellow man. You should want him to attain his true goal in life as ordained by God's goodness. This is true Jewish love" (*Rabbi Nachman's Wisdom* #119). Pray for your friend's welfare and success.

The Torah was given at Chorev. The letters of ChoReV are the same as those of ChaVeR, friend. And just as "two are better than one," so, "a threefold cord is not quickly broken" (Ecclesiastes 4:9-12). Extend your group of spiritual friends, one by one.

"Sometimes a circle of people are happy and dancing, and they pull in someone who was standing outside, miserable and depressed. They make him join the dance, and eventually he becomes happy too" (*Likutey Moharan* II:23). Talk to people about the purpose of this world and the joy of serving HaShem. The more we do to influence the people we have contact with, the closer the day when all flesh will call on God's name and He will make the dance-circle of the righteous that will be the antidote to all grief and suffering (*Ta'anit* 31a and *Likutey Moharan* II:24).

12

The Last Laugh

This was how the Wise Man dealt with the Prince, until in the end he cured him completely.

"Dressed in strength and splendor, she will laugh to the last day."

Proverbs 31:25

In the story of the Turkey-Prince, as in a number of his other stories, Rebbe Nachman relates the ending only in the most general terms, without giving any details. The story ends happily: eventually the Prince was cured completely. But what occurred along the way, how long it took, and what happened to the Prince afterwards, we are never told.

We are left wondering. Somehow we are still in the middle of the story. And in fact that is exactly where we are: in the middle. We are all in the middle of the story of our own lives, struggling to lift ourselves up to the spiritual plane and be the Princes and Princesses we yearn to be. We want more than a mere assurance that in the end everything is going to turn out right. *How*?

The fact is, we have already heard how — in the main body of the story. The way to succeed in life is by thinking positively, looking at the good in ourselves and our lives; by being ambitious, but knowing that great goals are accomplished through taking small steps; by being patient, especially with ourselves, and accepting that "you can be both... and...."

The simple idea that "you can be a Turkey and still take the next challenging, daring step in your life" is the recipe for personal transformation and growth, and the key to success in everything you do. There is only so much that Rebbe Nachman can share with us. The rest is up to us. We have to be wise for ourselves and live these teachings in practice. The greatest wisdom is to do everything simply, like the Wise Man.

There is no end to the levels that can be attained in *Avodat HaShem*, both along the inner pathway of self-mastery, refinement of character, Torah-study, prayer and devotion, and along the outer path of practical mitzvah-observance, love, kindness and service to others. The goal is nothing less than perfecting the way we live in God's amazing world and achieving complete happiness.

However the only way to achieve any goal is by making a plan and following it patiently, step by step. The word for this is *seder*, order. You have to put your affairs in order and keep them that way. Order is what eating at the table and living the life of the Prince is all about. Not a regime that stifles, but a self-discipline that enables you to *live* and enjoy the Torah life to the fullest.

That is why the prayer-book is called the *Siddur*: the daily prayers and mitzvot are arranged in the necessary order, because this is the only way they work. All successful people are *mesudar* — organized. Some of the great teachers of Mussar composed a *Seder HaYom*, "Order of the Day" — listing the spiritual practices one should try to follow each day in order to serve HaShem. (See Rabbi Yitzchok Breiter, *A Day in the Life of a Breslover Chassid*, and similar works in this genre.) Each person has to develop his own *Seder HaYom*.

No matter what your goals, you have to establish your priorities and then develop a realistic, viable plan of how you will try to attain them. You must make a general timetable, and then plan out what you are going to do *today*. Your timetable must be practical. It must suit your personal situation and all your needs and foibles. If you find your plan unworkable in practice, you must think again. Having developed a reasonable plan, now try to follow it step by step.

If what you want is very precious, it is more than likely that problems will arise, whether from the world outside or from within yourself. Still, don't despair. Heave a sigh. Revise your plan. Say a prayer. Now concentrate on taking the next step!

*

"Are not my words like fire, says God, and like a hammer smashing a rock?" (Jeremiah 23:29) — "Just as the sparks fly from the hammer, so a single verse may have many implications" (*Sanhedrin* 34a). The same could be said of the teachings of Rebbe Nachman, who stated that his fire will burn until the coming of Mashiach. His teachings have a unique generality. They apply to a multitude of individuals and situations. At one and the same time they pertain to the greatest spiritual masters, to average people, and to the very humblest and lowliest.

This entire book has at best reflected only a tiny fraction of the wisdom in the story of the Turkey-Prince. The main angle here has been to look for hints as to how we should deal with ourselves in order to attain our spiritual goals. Obviously the lessons of the story could be applied to any project in life.

A second major dimension of the story — one mostly neglected in this work for reasons of space — is its insights into the factors contributing to success in interpersonal relationships. Another whole book could be written on this subject alone. The Wise Man surely won the Prince's eternal friendship, and he certainly influenced him!

The Wise Man's approach to the Prince should be a model for us all in our relationships with others. The Wise Man was friendly without being imposing. He empathized. He was non-judgmental, positive, patient, and infinitely loving and caring. There are lessons here for parents dealing with their children, teachers with their pupils, counsellors, people in everyday domestic and work situations, doctors, psychologists, social workers, and a host of others. How much tragic loss of human talent could be avoided if the Wise Man's approach were to be taken with the handicapped, problem-cases, the emotionally disturbed, juvenile delinquents, and so on.

The story has many other dimensions as well. The stark image of the naked Turkey-Prince is not only a personal symbol. It is an incisive historical and social comment on the exile of the Jewish People as a whole, which has left so many of our brothers and sisters with distorted identities, like the Jews of Egypt — "naked and uncovered" (Ezekiel 16:7): naked of mitzvot. Who is going to take each one by the hand and lovingly bring them back? Where is the Mashiach?

On yet another level, this simple story has cosmic significance. It concerns a father and a son, and one who reconciled them. The Creator is "Father." The creation is "son" (*Zohar* II:178b). The Tzaddik brings them back together. So does every one of us with the mitzvot we do. With each mitzvah, we connect ourselves and the world with God, making unity.

In fact, the ramifications of the story are practically endless. It could be used to throw light on many different aspects of Torah, on the prayers, and on various mitzvot. One example would be Shabbat, with the Turkey racing after crumbs and bones symbolizing our weekday activities and outlook, while the Prince sitting up at the table symbolizes Shabbat and the "Extra Soul" with which it clothes us. The story also relates to profound Kabbalistic concepts, such as those of "Tzimtzum," the "Breaking of the Vessels," the "clothing" of the Divine Light in Vessels, and the Tikkun through which the Partzufim are brought face to face, etc. (See *Tzaddik* #476 for some of the Kabbalistic allusions in the concept of Table.)

Rebbe Nachman encouraged us to try to find ourselves in his teachings. Each one of us is entitled to draw a personal message from the story and use it as an aid to spiritual growth in our own individual way.

*

People ask about the ending of the story. They question whether the Prince was ever really cured completely. The original definition of his madness was that "he thought he was a Turkey." At every step of the cure, the Wise Man told the Prince that he could still be a Turkey *and* take that step. This was how the Wise Man induced him to get up to the table.

The question is: did the Prince ever finally stop thinking he was a Turkey? It may be that by the end of the story he is "dressed in strength and glory," wearing all his royal garments, eating the royal food, and sitting at the table with his father. But does he *laugh*? Does he really cherish being the Prince and enjoy it? Or does he still think he's a bit of a Turkey, even if only very slightly. Do we ever rid ourselves of our Turkey side once and for all?

One answer is that the "Prince" finally becomes himself when the Godly Soul is revealed in all its glory in the World to Come. Life in this world is a test. Up until the very last day there are continuing problems and challenges, both from the outside environment and from within ourselves. Throughout its journey in this under-the-table world, the Godly Soul is always accompanied by its outer kelipah, the Animal Soul — the "Turkey" — which animates our bodies. No matter how high a spiritual level one reaches, in this world the Godly Soul is always somewhat darkened by the Animal Soul and cannot shine in its true radiance.

However, when the Neshamah leaves the body after death, it is cleansed of any remaining stains and can then radiate in the celestial "clothing" of mitzvot prepared in the course of our lives in this world. This is the same idea as in Rabbi Nathan's parable of the king who told his subjects to prepare beautiful garments and avoid getting themselves dirty in order that they should be able to attend the king's banquet and receive precious gifts. (See above pp. 23-4) The banquet and gifts symbolize the reward of the life of the World to Come. "This World is like an ante-chamber before the World to Come: prepare yourself in the ante-chamber so that you can come into the banqueting hall" (*Avot* 4:21).

"In the World to Come there is no death and no sin and no transgression, but each one rejoices in his wisdom and understanding" (*Tanna deVey Eliahu Rabba* 2). In the World to Come, the Prince is completely cured and enjoys bliss. But as long as we are in this world, our lives must always be a matter of "running and returning" — having moments of elevation, enthusiasm, Godly inspiration and insight, but then returning to lower, more mundane levels from which we must constantly strive to rise even higher. The Wise Man in our story represents a Tzaddik on the highest of levels. Yet the Wise Man himself says, "I'm also a Turkey." Even the Tzaddik himself has a Yetzer HaRa.

Once a funeral procession was passing in front of Rebbe Nachman's window. The people in the procession were crying and wailing, but the Rebbe commented, "Presumably the dead man is laughing in his heart. When someone dies, people cry over him as if to say: How good if you had lived in this world even longer and suffered even more trials and torments, and then you would have had even more bitterness. At least this will be the end of his pain and suffering, because once he has gone through anything he might have to go through in Gehenom, he will enjoy the reward for the good he did in this world" (*Tzaddik* #446).

*

"The dead man is laughing." Good for him! But what about us in this world? We want to *live*, not die. The suggestion that the Prince is only finally cured in the World to Come is not entirely satisfying. We want to know if there is a complete cure in *this* life.

Death is an uncomfortable topic for many people, but coming to terms with the fact of our own mortality is one of the most liberating steps we can take in life. Death is a great mystery. The prospect is awesome, especially when we think about the strange, painful end some endure, and the possibility of punishment after death.

Rebbe Nachman himself said that when he was young he had a terror of death, yet he forced himself to think and pray about it, until eventually he overcame it completely (*Rabbi Nachman's Wisdom* #57). Periodically, it can have a very salutary effect to contemplate the inevitability of one's death. It helps one to appreciate the preciousness of this life, and to put one's mundane desires and worries into their proper perspective.

"People have all kinds of fears about other people or objects that in fact cannot harm them at all. The only time a person can think clearly is when he is dead. When he is lying on the ground with his feet to the door [as the corpse is customarily placed immediately after death], he will finally see the truth. He will then realize that all his fears and apprehensions were mere foolishness. They were about nothing. What could a mere mortal do to him? The same is true of his desires and temptations. Lying there dead he will realize that he wasted his days in vain. He will know that his most overwhelming desires were mere foolishness and silliness. For who really forced him?" (*Rabbi Nachman's Wisdom* #83).

Thinking about death from time to time is a way of shaking ourselves out of our sleep. We tend to put off doing what we know we ought to do. But in fact, conquering our own personal Turkeys and living our lives the way we should is not really so very hard. The Wise Man has shown us how to make it easy. "One grain of intelligence can overcome the world and all its temptations" (*ibid.* #51). "If you will learn to understand yourself, you can rid yourself of all worldly fears and desires. *You must only realize that something else within you is responsible for them.* Understand this and you can overcome everything. You have free will. You can easily train your mind to avoid the thing inside you that is responsible for your fears and desires" (*ibid.*).

It may be unpleasant to contemplate worldly suffering and the possibility of punishment after death, but "the only way to begin serving God is through fear of retribution. Without it, it is impossible to even take the first step. Even the righteous must have such a fear, for few can devote themselves to God merely because they love Him deeply.

"One can also serve God out of a sense of awe, because He is so great and powerful. This is a higher level of fear, but it is difficult to attain. For most people, the path to devotion is the simple fear of punishment... It is man's nature to be drawn to worldly temptations, and this can only be overcome through the fear of punishment. Only then can one begin serving God" (*Rabbi Nachman's Wisdom* #5). In other words, we should learn to *use* our fears of suffering, death and punishment as a stimulus to work on ourselves and achieve higher levels of Godly awareness and service.

The truth is that God has no desire to punish us. God is a loving Father who wants His children to enjoy the greatest good. If God threatens and punishes, it is "as a man chastises his son" (Deuteronomy 8:5). No loving father wants his child to suffer needlessly. "Do I want the death of the wicked person? No, but that he should return from his ways and live" (Ezekiel 18:23). All we have to do is to try to serve God to the best of our ability. "Teshuvah and good deeds are a shield against punishments." (*Avot* 4:11).

Rebbe Nachman teaches: "A person who wants to taste the Hidden Light, the secrets of the Torah which will be revealed in the future, must elevate his fear to its root. This is achieved by judgment — secluding oneself in hisbodidus and conversing with God, expressing one's whole heart to God and judging oneself in all the details of one's life. By doing this, one removes all one's mundane fears and elevates one's awe of Heaven."

The Rebbe explains: "When a person neglects to examine and judge himself, he is examined and brought to judgment from on high. God has many ways of executing His judgments. He has the power to clothe them in anything in the world, because all things are His messengers, and He can use whatever means He chooses to execute His judgments. We can actually see this in the world around us. When something bad happens to a person, the particular cause which precipitates the problem is often quite insignificant. One would never have expected a small thing like this to bring on such a train of consequences — illness, suffering and the like. The explanation is that the Divine decree passed against him has been clothed within these mundane circumstances in order to give him his deserts.

"But when a person examines and judges himself of his own accord, the decree above is removed. There is no need for him to be afraid of anything. Worldly objects and events will no longer be used as a veil and a cloak for executing the decree of

God. By bringing himself to a reckoning, he has removed the judgment from above. He is already sufficiently aroused and spiritually awake without needing things of this world to shake him. This is what is meant by elevating fear to its root. He is afraid of nothing except God. Because of this he will be worthy of the Hidden Light" (*Likutey Moharan* I:15).

Rebbe Nachman conquered his own terror of death by repeatedly praying to God and telling Him he was willing to die to sanctify His Name. Every Jew is required to "love HaShem your God... with your whole soul" (Deuteronomy 6:5). To love God with your whole soul means to love Him "even if He takes your soul" (*Berachot* 54a). One's life is the most precious thing one has. Offering it for God is the greatest act of faith there is. It is an act of faith in God as the Giver of life, who has the power to reward one with eternal life. A person who is willing to die for God is certainly willing to *live* for Him. And once you are not afraid of death, you are not afraid of anything.

In 1943 there was a man in Russia who was worrying about death. He was a Breslover Chassid from Poland, who was now being held in a Stalinist labor camp in northern Siberia. His crime? Being Jewish.

The prison camp was so far from any human habitation that it did not need to have walls around it. No escaping prisoner had a chance of getting anywhere. The ice-cold conditions would certainly kill a would-be fugitive long before he could reach safety. In fact, the prisoners had to guard *themselves*. Wolves were liable to steal into the prisoners' huts at night and snatch people while they were sleeping. For this reason, each night one of the prisoners had to stay awake to keep watch.

Tonight it was this Breslover Chassid's turn. As he sat outside in the freezing cold, shattered by yet another long day of hard labor, it was a desperate struggle to keep awake. He begged God not to let him go to sleep, because if he went to sleep the wolves would probably kill him, and then he would not have a Jewish burial. "At least let me die like a Jew. Please."

He prayed and prayed, and then, totally exhausted, he drifted off to sleep... He dreamed that he was back in his native Poland before the war. He was looking into the sweet, smiling face of the teacher who had introduced him to Breslov Chassidut. "Is that how we taught you to pray?" asked his teacher. " 'To *die* like a Jew'? Pray to *live* like a Jew!" And, indeed, this Chassid lived to tell the tale many years afterwards.

The purpose of thinking about death is to fire ourselves to live life to the full. Living like a Jew is to "love HaShem your God with all your heart" (Deuteronomy 6:5). "With all your heart" means "with your two Yetzers, the Yetzer HaTov and the Yetzer HaRa" (*Berachot* 54a). At the beginning of the spiritual journey, when a person first begins to wake up and see the Turkey side of himself for what it is, the Yetzer HaRa can be experienced as a tough obstacle to God's service. One takes an honest look at oneself and sees how one's sins have distanced one from God, and how one's desires and other traits continue to keep one far away.

But by steadily following the path of Teshuvah through its ups and downs, we are able to elevate evil and transform it into good. We do this through acknowledging our mistakes and changing our way of life. By admitting our sins to God and regretting them, not only do we neutralize their power over us; the sins themselves become the spur to our inner transformation, and thus "the transgressions are turned into virtues" (*Yoma* 86b). The Yetzer HaRa then ceases to be an obstacle. The Baal Teshuvah may continue to be subjected to Turkey thoughts and impulses, but now his response to them is different: he sees them as a challenge that motivates him to higher and higher spiritual achievement.

The key to Teshuvah is to be completely open and honest with God about all of one's conflicting thoughts, feelings, actions, hopes and aspirations. The Hebrew word for this openness is *Vidui*. This is often translated as "confession," a word which for some may have confusing connotations. In fact, *Vidui* is a fundamental Jewish practice. It is the essence of Teshuvah. (Leviticus 26:40 and see *Mishneh Torah, Hilchot Teshuvah* 1:1.) *Vidui* means owning up to God over any wrong one has done, and regretting it.

Vidui is thus one aspect of a far greater service to God: acknowledging Him for everything — for one's life, for all the various things one goes through, positive and negative, for one's own actions, good or bad, and for all the different aspects of oneself, holy and unholy. "You shall love God... with all your *might*" (Deuteronomy 6:5). Loving God "with all your might" means: "whatever way God deals with you, acknowledge Him" (*Berachot* 54a). Through acknowledging God, one recognizes His presence in one's life, and thus becomes connected with Him.

Vidui is therefore related to the Hebrew root meaning to acknowledge, from which the word *Hodu*, "give thanks," derives. The Turkey side of us, the Yetzer HaRa, may cause us to do bad, but we can come to serve God with it by means of *Vidui* and Teshuvah, through which even the worst sins can be turned into merits. Our story touches on this: "Who are you and what are you doing here?" — "I'm a Turkey." — "So am I!" Honest confession. Through acknowledgement, the Turkey side can be transformed into pure good in the end. *Hodu.* Acknowledge and give thanks. *Hodu la-Shem ki tov* — "Give thanks to God, for He is good, for His lovingkindness is for ever" (Psalms 118:1). Acknowledge and give thanks even for bad, because ultimately it is for good.

The Hebrew word for Turkey is *Tarnegol Hodu* — the *Hodu* Bird. Through Teshuvah and acknowledgement, the Turkey itself turns into *Hodu*: thank you. "Thank You, God." Eventually the Prince can be completely cured in *this* world — through acknowledging and thanking God for everything. This is the future mode — "...to thank and praise His great and blessed Name and to recognize Him. Through this we are attached to Him and near Him. The more you know and recognize God, the closer you are to him" (*Likutey Moharan* II:2).

The letters of *Hodu* have the numerical value of 21. This is the same as the Divine Name *EKYH*, the Holy Name associated with Redemption and Teshuvah, and with the Sefirah of Keter, the Crown — the source of the entire Creation. Through acknowledgement and thanks to God, the Hodu-Bird rises up to Keter and merits the royal Crown. The Prince is cured completely.

The tribe of turkeys have come in for much abuse in the course of this book. But if there's one thing turkeys are good at, it is *pecking*. Life goes very quickly. The art is to take whatever good thing is available at each passing moment — a prayer, some words of Torah, a mitzvah here, a kind deed there, a little charity, some words of thanks to God... And one final gem of wisdom every turkey knows: it doesn't pay to bite off more than you can chew. Do things bit by bit.

*

Sources and Further Reading

This appendix of sources, works cited in the text, and suggestions for further reading, is divided into the following sections:

1. The Parable of the Turkey-Prince
2. Under the Table
3. Relaxation, Diet, Breathing and Exercise
4. Works of Rebbe Nachman cited in the text
5. Other works cited
6. Suggestions for further reading

1. The Parable of the Turkey-Prince

The original version of the parable of the Turkey-Prince appears on pp. 26-7 of a Hebrew work entitled *Sipurim Nifla'im* — "Amazing Stories" — a collection of stories and sayings of Rebbe Nachman, and anecdotes about him. We are given no information about when Rebbe Nachman told this parable or to whom. We do not even know who wrote it down. All we are told is that it was one of several parables by the Rebbe found in a bundle of papers in the possession of Rabbi Naftali, a life-long friend of Rabbi Nathan and, after him, Rebbe Nachman's second closest follower.

It was R. Nathan who wrote down most of Rebbe Nachman's teachings. However this parable could have been recorded by another follower. The bundle of papers in which it was contained, together with the rest of the material making up *Sipurim Nifla'im*, was passed down among the Breslover Chassidim for a hundred and twenty-five years after Rebbe Nachman's passing. Unlike other collections of Rebbe Nachman's teachings, which had been printed much earlier, *Sipurim Nifla'im* was not published until 1935, when Rabbi Shmuel Horowitz, one of the leading Breslover Chassidim in Jerusalem, brought it to the press. Nevertheless, the story of the Turkey-Prince had long before found its way into Chassidic folklore, and has been told and retold way beyond the circles of the Breslover Chassidim.

In the printed text in *Sipurim Nifla'im*, almost all of the story is given in Hebrew, except for two sentences, which are given in Yiddish. Rebbe Nachman would have told the story in Yiddish, but apart from his longer stories, almost all his teachings were transcribed and printed in Hebrew, the standard language of Jewish religious literature. In translating the story for this book, I have tried to stay as close as possible to the original except where an over-literal translation of the phrasing would have made for unidiomatic English. Rebbe Nachman's followers were particular about recording what he said accurately, and nuances in the phrasing may be important for the interpretation of the story.

The main key to its interpretation is found in a few brief words printed directly after the text of the story in *Sipurim Nifla'im*. (There is no indication whether these words are a quotation from Rebbe Nachman or a comment by the Editor of *Sipurim Nifla'im*.) "When a person wants to draw nearer to the service of the Creator, blessed be He, he is a Turkey — he is garbed in materialism etc. But in this way one can little by little draw oneself closer to the service of the Creator until one enters it completely. In the same way one can also draw others closer." Besides these few words of comment, there is no further discussion of the story in existing Breslov literature.

It is clear from these comments that the Prince's Turkey identity and activities symbolize a materialistic outlook and interests, and that the purpose of the story is to offer guidance as to how one can rise above them and come to Avodat HaShem, service of God. This guidance applies to two separate categories of people: individuals who are trying to work on themselves, and spiritual guides or teachers who are trying to help others. The main focus of this book has been to elaborate the implications of the story for those in the first category.

2. Under the Table

The general view of the creation and its purpose that underlies this book is expressed most clearly and succinctly in *Derech HaShem — The Way of God* by Rabbi Moshe Chayim Luzzatto, translated by Rabbi Aryeh Kaplan (Feldheim 1988). For the concept of the two souls of the Jew — the Divine and Animal Souls — see there pp. 177-181 and the notes on pp. 346f.

It is obvious to all students of Aggadah, Rabbinic lore, that the king in the story of the Turkey-Prince symbolizes God, while the king's son is the individual Jew, or, on another level, the Jewish People as a whole. ("God calls us His children, as it is written (Deuteronomy 14:1) 'You are children to the Lord your God' " — *Rabbi Nachman's Wisdom* #7.) Ceasing to eat at one's father's table as a symbol of exile is found in the Gemara ("Woe to the children who have gone into exile from their father's table" —*Berachot* 3a.) A discussion by Rebbe Nachman of the concept of the tables being turned over as one of the exile of speech is brought in *Rabbi Nachman's Wisdom* #88.

During the period of exile, the Jewish People are described as being "naked and uncovered" (Ezekiel 16:7) — "naked of mitzvot" (Rashi *ad loc.*) The idea of the Torah and mitzvot as clothing is mentioned by Rebbe Nachman in many places — see especially *Rabbi Nachman's Wisdom* #23 on the naked souls. See also Rabbi Nathan's parable in *Likutey Halachot, Choshen Mishpat, Matanot* 4.

As mentioned above, the Editor of *Sipurim Nifla'im* himself tells us that the idea of the Turkey is that of excessive materialism. Rebbe Nachman teaches that one of the most important realizations a person has to come to is that "it is not the person who desires, but something else within him" (*Rabbi Nachman's Wisdom* #83). We can infer that prior to this realization, a person is under the illusion that this thing within him that desires *is* himself. "He thought he was a Turkey."

For the idea that the real madman is the evil urge see *Likutey Moharan* I:1. The idea that repeated sinning causes the sinful nature of his actions to be concealed from the sinner is discussed in *Likutey Moharan* I:56,3. For the idea of the true doctor as the Sage and Tzaddik, the doctor of the soul, see *Likutey Moharan* I:30.

3. Relaxation, Diet, Breathing and Exercise

A. Relaxation:

It is obvious that a relaxed physical state and suitable posturing of the body are preconditions for successful spiritual work. The literature of Torah spirituality contains many references to various postures for prayer and meditation. Some of the sources are brought in this work in Chapters 4 and 6. The concept of *hityashvut* — settling oneself in preparation for clear thinking and spiritual work etc. — is frequently found in Torah literature.

Nevertheless, we do not find in Torah literature a detailed description of specific relaxation techniques of the kind given in Chapter 4. One might conjecture that prior to the contemporary technological era, which has brought so many new stresses and strains into our lives, there was less need for a specific relaxation technique. Moreover, while deep physical relaxation is clearly involved in intense meditation (see *Sha'arey Kedushah* — "The Gates of Holiness" — by R. Chayim Vital, Part 3, Section 8:5, for example), it is not surprising that in Torah sources we do not find more than fleeting references to techniques for achieving this.

Kabbalah Meditation skills were highly guarded secrets, and practical details were communicated directly from master to pupil.

The relaxation technique described in Chapter 4 is devoid of any religious or philosophical overtones. It is based on the standard technique of neuromuscular relaxation pioneered by Dr. Edmund Jacobson in the 1920's and now used and advocated by recognized medical organizations, such as the Mind/Body Medical Institute under the auspices of the Harvard Medical School, etc.

B. Breathing:

The relationship between the way we breathe and our physical and spiritual states was recognized by the Rabbis (see *Hanhagat Ha-Bri'ut* 4:2 and *Likutey Moharan* I:8, 60,3, 109, II:5 and *Tzaddik* #163 etc.). Breathing techniques play an important role in advanced Kabbalah meditations (see R. Aryeh Kaplan, *Meditation and Kabbalah*, Weiser 1982, especially pp. 87-106). However, as discussed in Chapter 5, a deep knowledge of Kabbalah is required even to begin to understand these methods, let alone to practice them. In Rebbe Nachman's teachings, where breathing is a recurrent theme, the emphasis is on the long breath.

As in the case of relaxation, we do not find any detailed description of the physiological process of breathing in Torah literature. Nevertheless, there is nothing mysterious about the process of breathing. The description of the phases of respiration given in Chapter 5 is founded on basic physiology, and with a little experimentation can be verified empirically by anyone.

C. Diet and Exercise:

Most of the practical suggestions regarding diet and exercise contained in Chapter 5 are based upon the teachings of Rabbi Moshe Ben Maimon, the "Rambam" (1135-1204). Besides being one of the outstanding Torah giants of all times, the Rambam was also one of the greatest healers in the history of medicine, and had a profound and subtle understanding of the workings of the human body.

The most accessible source of the Rambam's teachings on basic health care is to be found in the *Mishneh Torah, Hilchot De'ot* — "Laws Concerning Attitudes and Personal Behavior" — Chapter 4. The simple and concise recommendations given there are elaborated in the Rambam's *Hanhagot Ha-Bri'ut* ("Guidelines for Health"), a short work which he wrote at the request of the then Islamic Sultan in Egypt, whose personal physician the Rambam was. *Hanhagot Ha-Bri'ut* is not available in English.

The Rambam's teachings form the basis of much of the guidance about diet and health care found in later Rabbinic literature, such as in the *Kitzur Shulchan Aruch* — "Concise Code of Jewish Law" — of R. Shlomo Ganzfried, Chapter 32 — "Natural Care of the Body". Another work which contains a wealth of additional teachings from the Talmud and other Rabbinic sources is the *Tav Yehoshua* — "Joshua's Note" — by R. Yehoshua Briskin (Eshkol, Jerusalem, 1978). The author was Rabbi of Odessa in the latter part of the 19th Century.

There are some who question the relevance of the Rambam's advice on healthy living today, given the drastic changes in living conditions since his time. In order to discuss this issue meaningfully, it is necessary to distinguish a number of different areas. The Rambam's practical guidance as to when and how to eat, his emphasis on the importance of exercise, and many of his other health-care recommendations, would seem to be fully endorsed by contemporary thinking among the majority of health practitioners.

The main area where the question of relevance comes up is in the Rambam's detailed recommendations about *what* to eat. Technology has revolutionized the way we feed ourselves. Modern methods of food production, preservation and transportation have made a vastly wider range of foods available today than was available to even our grandparents and great-grandparents. On the other hand, science and technology have caused new problems which were unknown in previous generations. Many of the foods we eat, and even the water we drink, have additives of one kind or another, many of which are now thought to be hazardous to health.

Owing to the complexity of this issue, detailed nutritional guidance has been omitted from this work, and those interested in healthy nutrition are advised to follow the *Kitzur Shulchan Aruch* (32:7) and consult with nutritional experts in order to find which foods are best suited to their own personal constitution and lifestyle.

4. Works of Rebbe Nachman cited in the text

A. Works in English published by the Breslov Research Institute, Jerusalem:

Note: In many of the quotations from Rebbe Nachman's writings in the course of this book, I have given my own translation rather than rely upon existing English translations. I did this especially when I felt a need to bring out an important nuance in the Hebrew text more strongly than it came across in the existing translation. The same applies to translations of Biblical verses.

Advice translated by Avraham Greenbaum. A compendium of practical spiritual guidance arranged by subject, based on *Likutey Moharan* and other works of Rebbe Nachman.

Ayeh — "Where?" Translation and commentary on *Likutey Moharan* II:12 on the theme of searching for God and overcoming spiritual darkness and despair.

Azamra — "I will sing!" Translation and commentary on *Likutey Moharan* I:282. Rebbe Nachman's pathway to happiness through finding the good points.

A Day in the Life of a Breslover Chassid Translation of *Seder HaYom* (lit. Order of the Day) by R. Yitzchok Breiter (1886-1943).

Garden of the Souls edited by Avraham Greenbaum. Translation and commentary on *Likutey Moharan* I:65 on the theme of pain and suffering.

Likutey Moharan Vols. I-IV On-going project to translate Rebbe Nachman's major work together with a full commentary. To date, lessons 1-32 of *Likutey Moharan* Part I have been translated.

Rabbi Nachman's Stories translated by Rabbi Aryeh Kaplan. Contains Rebbe Nachman's thirteen major stories and his shorter parables, together with a full commentary.

Rabbi Nachman's Tikkun translated by Avraham Greenbaum. The Ten Psalms in Hebrew with English transliteration and translation, and extensive commentary material.

Rabbi Nachman's Wisdom translated by Rabbi Aryeh Kaplan. Rebbe Nachman's conversations on faith, joy, meditation and many other subjects. One of the best introductions to his teachings.

Restore My Soul translated by Avraham Greenbaum. Teachings on how to fight depression and despair.

Seven Pillars of Faith by R. Yitzchok Breiter. A summary of the fundamentals of faith. Printed with "A Day in the Life of a Breslover Chassid".

Tefilin translated by Avraham Greenbaum. Translation of Rabbi Nathan's discourse on Tefilin in *Likutey Halachot, Hilchot Tefilin* 5, discussing the deeper meaning of practically every aspect of the mitzvah of Tefilin.

The Aleph-Bet Book translated by Moshe Mykoff. Rebbe Nachman's aphorisms.

Tsohar — "Light!" Translation and commentary on *Likutey Moharan* I:112 on the theme of truth as the key to devotion in prayer and hisbodidus.

Tzaddik translated by Avraham Greenbaum. Rabbi Nathan's intimate biography of Rebbe Nachman, and our single most important source for his life. Includes a wealth of anecdotes, sayings, dreams and conversations.

B. Works currently available only in Hebrew

Avanehah Barzel Stories and teachings of Rebbe Nachman and his disciples, collected by Rabbi Shmuel Horowitz (1903-73).

Kochvey Or Stories and teachings of Rebbe Nachman and his disciples, collected by Rabbi Avraham ben Nachman of Tulchin (1849-1917).

Likutey Halachot by Rabbi Nathan. Monumental 8-volume work on Breslover thought and Kabbalah, following the order of the Shulchan Aruch and taking the form of extensive discourses on its laws.

Likutey Moharan by Rebbe Nachman. His primary work containing all of his major Torah discourses. First printed in Ostrog in 1808 and subsequently published in more than 50 editions.

Shir Na'im — "Pleasant Song". An acrostic poem by Rebbe Nachman expressing the fundamentals of Torah faith. Printed at the beginning of the Hebrew edition of *Likutey Moharan*.

Siach Sarfei Kodesh published by Agudat Meshech HaNachal, Jerusalem, 1988. A collection of sayings and anecdotes of Rebbe Nachman and his followers, many of them hitherto unpublished.

Sipurim Nifla'im Anecdotes about Rebbe Nachman, together with previously unpublished teachings and stories, collected by R. Shmuel Horowitz.

5. Other works cited in the text:

A. Works available in English

Chovot HaLevavot — "Duties of the Heart" by Rabbenu Bachya Ibn Paquda (d.1161), translated by Moses Hyamson (Feldheim). Classic Mussar work

Derech HaShem — "The Way of God" by Rabbi Moshe Chayim Luzzatto (1707-46) translated by Rabbi Aryeh Kaplan (Feldheim). Classic exposition of the fundamentals of Torah faith and outlook.

Gateway to Happiness by Rabbi Zelig Pliskin (Aish HaTorah Publications 1983). A practical guide to attaining peace of mind culled from Torah literature.

Kitzur Shulchan Aruch — "The Code of Jewish Law" by Rabbi Shlomo Ganzfried (1804-1886). Classic compilation of the basic laws of Jewish life. Available in several translations. See below 6(b).

Likutey Amarim (Tanya) by Rabbi Shneur Zalman of Liadi (1745-1812). Bi-lingual edition (Kehot, New York 1973). A guide to devotion and battling the evil inclination. Basis of Chabad Chassidism.

Mishneh Torah by Rabbi Moshe Ben Maimon (the Rambam — 1135-1204). Classic codification of Torah law covering all the mitzvot. Translations of some sections of the Mishneh Torah are now available, including Hilchot De'ot, "Laws Concerning Attitudes and Personal Behavior" (Moznaim Publishing Corporation, New York.)

Strive for Truth by R. Eliyahu Eliezer Dessler (1891-1954), translated by Aryeh Carmell, Vols 1-3 (Feldheim). Important modern Mussar work.

B. Works in Hebrew

Chayey Adam by R. Avraham Danziger (1748-1820). Code of laws applicable in daily life.

Hanhagat Ha-Bri'ut — "Guidelines for Healthcare" by Rabbi Moshe Ben Maimon (the Rambam — 1135-1204). (Rabinovitz, Israel). Covers diet, personal hygiene, exercise and preventative medicine.

Iggeret HaRamban by Rabbi Moshe ben Nachman (Nachmanides — 1194-1270). The Ramban's letter to his son, giving a concise and powerful statement of the fundamentals of devotion. Published in many larger Siddurim.

Kad HaKemach by Rabbenu Bachya (d. 1340). Mussar work.

Orchot Tzaddikim — "The Ways of the Righteous" Author unknown. Classic Mussar work.

Sefer HaIkarim by R. Yoseph Albo (1380-1444).

Sha'arey Kedushah — "The Gates of Holiness" by Rabbi Chaim Vital (1543-1620). (Eshkol). Contains Mussar and guidance for self-purification and preparation for ru'ach hakodesh.

Shevachey HaBa'al Shem Tov — "Praises of the Ba'al Shem Tov" compiled by R. Dov Ber (beReb Shmuel) Shubb of Linetz (Machon Zecher Naftali, Jerusalem 1990). Collected stories of the Baal Shem Tov and his closest followers.

T'nuat Ha-Mussar R. Dov Katz, (Baitan Hasefer, Tel Aviv 1952, 1963).

Tzetel Katan by R. Elimelech of Lyzhensk (1717-1787). Brief guide to the fundamentals of devotion. Printed in many larger Siddurim.

Yesod ve-Shoresh Ha-Avodah — "The Foundation and Essence of Service" by R. Alexander Zisskind (d. 1794). (Rozenfeld, Jerusalem 1987). Guide to devotion, explaining kavanot of all the prayers and daily mitzvot, Shabbat and the festivals.

6. Suggestions for further reading:

A. General:

Handbook of Jewish Thought by Rabbi Aryeh Kaplan (Moznaim). Invaluable collection of basic information about Jewish belief, development of the religion etc.

Mystical Concepts in Chassidism by Rabbi Jacob Immanuel Schochet (Kehot Publication Society). Systematic explanation of the fundamental concepts of the Kabbalah.

Innerspace by Rabbi Aryeh Kaplan (Moznaim). Introduction to the Kabbalah view of the world.

B. Observance:

The Mitzvot: The Commandments and their Rationale by Abraham Chill (Keter).

To Be A Jew: A Guide to Jewish Observance in Contemporary Life by R. Hayim Halevy Donin (Basic Books, New York). Introduction to the basics of Jewish practice.

The Metsuda Kitzur Shulchan Aruch A new linear translation of the classic guide to Jewish Law (Vols. 1 & 2) by Rabbi Avrohom Davis (Metsuda, distributed by Israel Book Shop Inc. 410 Harvard St. Brookline MA).

The Concise Code of Jewish Law by Rabbi Gersson Appel. Vols I & II (Ktav/Yeshiva UP). Updated version of the Kitzur Shulchan Aruch taking account of contemporary conditions of life.

The Sabbath by Dayan I. Grunfeld (Feldheim).

A Practical Guide to Kashrut: the Dietary Laws by Rabbi S. Wagschal (Feldheim).

Taharas Am Yisroel: A Guide to the Laws of Family Purity by Rabbi S. Wagschal (Feldheim).

The Sanctity of Speech: A Compendium of the Laws of Loshon Hora [=Bad Talk], by Rabbi Y.K. Krohn & Rabbi Y.M. Shain translated by Rabbi Hillel Danziger (Chevras Shmiras Haloshon).

The Book of Our Heritage by Eliahu Kitov translated by Rabbi Nachman Bulman. 3 volumes. (Feldheim). The Jewish Year, including the Festivals — background and practice

C. Bible:

The Living Torah Translated by Rabbi Aryeh Kaplan (Moznaim). Clear modern translation of Five Books of Moses.

D. Prayer:

Siddur Etz Chaim — The Complete Artscroll Siddur (Nusach Sefard, i.e. the Chassidic version — published by Artscroll/Mesorah). Clear translation of the prayers, detailed guide to all the services, and a full commentary. (Other Nus'cha'ot are also available in the Artscroll format.)

My Prayer by Nissan Mindel (Kehot Publication Society) — Chassidic insights on Prayer.

The World of Prayer by Rabbi Dr. Elie Munk. 2 vols. (Feldheim) — Detailed explanations of the meaning of the prayers in the Siddur.

E. Meditation and Hisbodidus:

Outpourings of the Soul translated by Rabbi Aryeh Kaplan (Breslov Research Institute). Selected teachings of Rebbe Nachman on hisbodidus.

Jewish Meditation by Rabbi Aryeh Kaplan (Schocken Books). A straightforward basic survey of some of the main techniques.

Jewish Spiritual Practices by Yitzchak Buxbaum (Jason Aronson Inc.) Compilation of Chassidic teachings on devotion from a wide variety of sources.

Meditation and the Kabbalah by Rabbi Aryeh Kaplan (Samuel Weiser

Books). A scholarly survey of advanced Kabbalah meditation techniques, including translations of many sources.

F. Learning Hebrew:

Introduction to Hebrew by Moshe Greenberg (Prentice Hall) — straightforward introduction to Biblical Hebrew, including grammar.

Prayerbook Hebrew the Easy Way by Anderson, Motzkin, Rubenstein & Wiseman (EKS Publishing Co. POB 11133 Oakland CA 94611).

The First Hebrew Primer for Adults by Simon et al. (EKS Publishing Co.)

Breathing p. 83
Hisbodedus p 104 f
Sitting p 65 f

Torah study
- What to study pp 150 f

→ pocket קיצור
clear משנה ברורה
electronic - מילון
or
pocket
clear Halachic texts in English → cf Artscroll and Feldheim

"The Torah way of life involves turning oneself to G-d in every thought, word and deed. "Know Him in all your ways" (משלי ג׳) " pg 222

R. Aryeh Kaplan
- Outpourings of the Soul
- Jewish Meditation
] cf bibliograp

"אבנה ברגל" p255

Gloria

→ lower offer

Rabbi Nachman's Wisdom →
cited throughout the book
(is it on the list in the
back end-cover of the
other Azamra book?)

זכרון נצח
לעילוי נשמת

מרת **רייזא** בת ר׳ **בנימין הריס** ע״ה
נפ׳ ד׳ אלול תשנ״ז

ת.נ.צ.ב.ה.